THE SECULAR MAGI

THE
SECULAR MAGI

Marx, Freud, and Nietzsche on Religion

WILLIAM LLOYD NEWELL

**UNIVERSITY
PRESS OF
AMERICA**

Lanham • New York • London

Copyright © 1995 by
University Press of America,® Inc.
4720 Boston Way
Lanham, Maryland 20706

3 Henrietta Street
London WC2E 8LU England

©1986 The Pilgrim Press

The biblical quotations in this publication are from the *Revised
Standard Version of the Bible*, copyright 1946, 1952 and © 1971,
1973 by the Division of Christian Education, National Council of
Churches, and are used by permission.

Library of Congress Cataloging-in-Publication Data
Newell, William Lloyd.
The secular magi : Marx, Freud, and Nietzsche on religion /
William Lloyd Newell.
p.   cm.
Includes bibliographical references.
1. Marx, Karl, 1816–1883—Religion.   2. Freud, Sigmund,
1856–1939—Religion.   3. Nietzsche, Friedrich Wilhelm,
1844–1900—Religion.   4. Religion—Controversial literature—
History and criticism.   I. Title.
BL2759.N49   1994   200'.92'2—dc20   94–33064 CIP

ISBN 0–8191–9588–X (pbk. : alk. paper)

 The paper used in this publication meets the minimum requirements of
American National Standard for Information Sciences—Permanence
of Paper for Printed Library Materials, ANSI Z39.48–1984.

For my wife,
Lois Mathieu

Contents

Prologue

People die hard, gods even harder. But both died in the past few generations, because they had become inhumane. Intellectuals all across Europe had brought God to the bar of justice and God had failed the test. The religious rich got richer by just being good according to their religion's lights; and their bourgeois goodness caused the evils that made the poor wretched. Something had to give. If God's religion underwrote the evils of the rich, then the poor and those who gave voice to their sufferings would have to do something about it.

God was no longer the theological caulk for the gaps of human impotency. We had made too many scientific discoveries to retain that deity. Was God still Mighty God then? No. Was God Counselor and Prince of Peace? Hardly. The advice of religion kept the intelligent mediocre; and the truly mediocre pretty much ran things in religion. Those with sense and intellect found little meaning and less consolation in religion.

God's titles were falling like autumn leaves. The last to go was Father. The world searched for a new paternity. Both the poor and the powerful slipped away from God, some with a shout, some with an essay, most in anguished silence.

If religion and its God were making rich and immature and perpetuating proletarian misery, then another reform was needed, much like the bone-rattling one of the Reformation. Someone had to mount the pulpit and shout, *"Pecca fortiter"* with the panache of a Luther and make it stick. Three unbelievers mounted that pulpit and dethroned the godlings of their day so that new men and women, and a new God, could be born in the ensuing vacuum. The names that Marx, Freud, and Nietzsche threw out were Injustice, Immaturity, and Mediocrity. The monstrance of supernaturality contained no more host. God was to be found in the streets, in one's heart, and in one's talent.

Marx, Freud, and Nietzsche would insinuate themselves so deeply into the center of our radically unwilling, complacent religion that they endowed it with a new spirit. Just as the infidel king Cyrus was seen as a messianic instrument of Yahweh, so we Christians have come to see these three nonbelievers as the fathers of a renewed Christian church. God changed because we changed.

Marx engendered in us a new feeling for the poor and the ripe knowledge that in large part it was we religious people who either caused or perpetuated their penury by the muscularities of our bourgeois wealth. By his critique of not only our religion, but also its very roots in middle-class democracy with Luther and Calvin he allowed us to see that fused with the freedom of the Spirit was the spirit of capitalism, an essentially egoistic economic system that would ultimately edge the ignorant poor toward the despairs he saw in nineteenth-century Europe. By changing our hearts from vapid, selfish, religious ones into human ones he allowed the birth of the social gospel. Marx found community again, when the dust of rugged individualism cleared from the battle scene.

And if God's name changed, so did ours. By standing God and the supernatural on their heads, he allowed us to rediscover our own humanity within that of the natural, human Jesus: little, vulnerable, poor, and a brother to us all. Marx's fatherhood is not of a ruggedly insular Christian, but a brotherhood of the simple. The worker saw through the cultured patina that had put God out of reach as a Man who cared because he was one of them. God's new name was Little and Just; and ours was Unjust, as sinner, and Brother and Sister, as penitent.

Freud's find was in the chancy stuff of ambivalence, in disabusing us of automatic religion, replete with absolutes and easy solutions. He stood us on our feet without the neurotic guilts that locked us in our illusions of religion and freed us to live adult lives, peaceful in the knowledge that doing the good or being mature always left us with the naked feeling that we could be wrong and probably were, at least in part. Freud saw what Paul saw when he said that we are merely earthen vessels. What he fathered in religion was that the sacrament of God was held in human mud, no better, no worse. And he left us happy in the freedom to take our new names: Angry, Frightened, Lustful, Hateful . . . knowing full well that at our core we were God-good because Jesus was there as redeemer, gently allowing us to know those names only after we knew Jesus was our Lover. In doing away with the false God of unremitting, sick guilt, Freud helped to endow us with theological guilt, the kind that always points through our evils to our deeper goodness and God's forgiveness. God's new name was Healer and ours was Mature. Freud invented conscience and responsibility that we could live with: the ability to withstand the *chiaroscuro* of our nature.

Nietzsche's gripe was that our religion had taken away our joyous naturalness and replaced it with a mediocre supernaturalism. He told us that our hidden dark necessities could be the very place in which we would find God. And that if we couldn't do better, then we should will those necessities and get on with our lives because they weren't about to go away and weren't that meaningful and certainly weren't terribly perfidious anyway. God's new name was The-Good-of-the-Is. And ours became An-inner-joy. Nietzsche reinvented the natural by ridding us of the otiose category of the supernatural.

We didn't accept their inventions without a struggle—a struggle that still goes on. But in speaking to social justice, humanism, healing, and morality as they did, new names have attached themselves to us ever since. No one names oneself, and certainly no one names God. God has broken through a hidebound religion and baptized us with new names, ugly at first and now comfortable with use. These three men allowed us to become human so that God could be God again, free, undivided, Father to us all, universal Brother, Sister, and as loving and insistent Spirit, Mother.

They invented men and women again so that god could become God; Advent was celebrated in the cave of human invention. When these Secular Magi, the Wise Men from the West, came to the darkened cave, the star of humaneness guided them. The gold of justice (Marx), the frankincense of human brilliance (Nietzsche), and the myrrh for healing (Freud) brought gifts befitting the child. If they brought Jesus something, he brought them even more. There would have been no Epiphany without the Magi, nor could there have been one without the Child.

And religion has slowly patented the new God, conceived in the fertile humanity that these three great men helped to engender by allowing its shepherds, humbler in gifts than the brilliant unbelievers, to come and see the wonder wrought in the new Bethlehem. To see in a secular babe a God and allowing God to reinvent a new transcendent Epiphany for these three Secular Magi. Critical unbelief created vision enough to find a man-God. And the belief engendered by the renewed vision is fathering their invention, allowing us to sing once again, Glory to God on High, and on earth, peace because of your good will. Epiphany began in gifted unbelief and ended with religion.

Introduction

In South America there are the Base Ecclesial Communities. In the United States there are Network, Sojourners, Eastern Mennonite College's Washington Study-Service Year, Community Creativity Incorporated, the Church of the Saviour, and the Friends Committee on National Legislation, to name but a few. In Cincinnati there is the New Jerusalem Community, and in Baltimore, The Julie Community Center. What all these groups, Protestant and Catholic, have in common is that they are doing theological reflection, shaped around the praxis of their group or community, looking for God in their personal and collective experience. What makes this unique is that, in some way or another, the way they go about their Christian life is heavily influenced by derivatives of Marxist social analysis.

Pastors in all communions and Jesuit novice-masters find it most useful to drop the normal labels used by traditional theology when dealing with the necessities imposed by the fragilities of their charges. They seek for the Spirit beyond, in a sense, good and evil, finding it better to look for life—the Spirit's gifts—rather than categories, no matter how time-tested the latter. Freudian techniques have freed spiritual directors and pastors to look to the natural to find God. Nietzsche's "will the necessary" has permitted a joy in what were the sad, dark corners of our lives.

The churches, both Protestant and Roman Catholic, have been engaged with these three men for generations, at first heaping condemnation on them without stint and then hesitantly reading them in context, liking part and rejecting the rest, doing theses on them in the universities, doctoring their most intelligent in how to combat their "enemies." It was these intellectuals who, slowly but surely, sent messages into the parishes— through either book or former students—that we needed to listen to these three men; that we stood in need of reform; that we were losing some of our flocks because they could not live decent, intelligent lives in the contemporary world. Ultimately, the story is too well known to need much detail; young pastors absorbed what they saw as good in Marx's social justice program and his thesis that church vision was not only faulty but illusory, in Freud's healing technique and trenchant critique of Christian infantilism, and in Nietzsche's soaring faith in the goodness of all creation and its epitome: men and women.

I have chosen these three men to explain, especially to the somewhat advanced student and the uninitiated in seminary and university, just how they influenced not only the shape of our theology, but also, and especially, how we perceive ourselves and God. Theology and church life are, in large part, reactive; something happens, someone speaks or writes something telling and we respond, frequently badly and inadequately at first, and then slowly—by absorption—we take on the best of the critical vision offered by genius.

Modernity, the secular child of Protestantism, was making it increasingly difficult to find God. It held no brief with transcendence. Truth and reality were jettisoned as medieval ambitions beyond the ken of the empirical. All one could know was what one knew and could validate under laboratory conditions. If it could be quantified, it was scientific; if not, it wasn't. And God is not scientific; there is no love in a number, nor is there any person in a test tube. Science demanded more modest goals than categories like God, person, soul, good, and evil. Even the science of the person, psychology, could deal with humanity only in its parts. Order and control are more important in modernity than person. Reason can discern that order and assume command over creation through its knowledge. Empirical science demands that human fulfillment consist in knowing and following the laws of nature that it discovers.[1] This desire for control makes modernity's epistemologies empirical and mechanistic, even in theology. Thus, all things are to be judged by one's personal experience, by what one can see and measure. This demands that the explanation of human beings and things be impersonal, i.e., mechanistic. (H. Smith, 77) In ontology we moderns must be naturalistic in the sense that the real is the material component of a thing or person; whatever is not material does not exist or does not count. Our ethics are to be humanistic, making us the measure of the good. The efficient cause of all is evolution and its final cause is progress. (H. Smith, 110) Religion had not caught up to this mentality when Marx, Freud, and Nietzsche went beyond it to help create what some call postmodernity. It is a mind-set, first, based on the sovereign assumption that the world may not be ordered, or if so, it may well be beyond our comprehension. Second, whatever reality is, it is certain that it is not personal. (H. Smith, 77)

Marx, Freud, and Nietzsche began with what they wanted and advocated that we follow their example. The thrust of their thought deals with motivation or desire, therefore. This in turn creates epistemologies: truth is what we want or takes us where we want to go. Epistemologies create ontologies; that is, if one can know, then one can say what the real is. These ontologies say that matter (Nature) is real. Finally, ontologies generate anthropologies: a human being is part of nature. Hence, Nature, not God or the transcendence, makes one meaningful. (H. Smith, 134) Moderns have been wary of the transcendent for centuries; Marx, Freud, Nietzsche, and their postmodern colleagues accepted this as normative. An epistemology so relentless in its quest for control rules out the very possibility of transcendence. (Ibid.) If modernity had weakened belief as a religious category, postmodernity all but crushed it. Wilfred Cantwell Smith says that the conceptual links between belief and truth had become so tenuous that it was something alien to one's religious life.[2] Belief itself actually became an attack on religious life, subverting it not only from without, but also from within. W. C. Smith says that Protestant churches especially found no stomach to fight the encroachments into its realm because many had lost their liking for "belief" and had begun to think in secularist terms. (Ibid.) He does not find that all bad, since the foundations of religious faith are isomorphic with secularistic faith. He defines faith as an openness to a vision of truth, beauty, and goodness, allowing one to both symbolize it (belief is just such a symbolization) and live a rich life in accordance with this transcendent dimension. (Faith, 141)

Marx, Freud, and Nietzsche were secularizers par excellence. What they did was to clarify our vision of the linguistic obscurantisms and affective obstacles that had prevented us from living mature and effective lives. They are primarily anthropologists, therefore. Their concept of man and woman is their courageous and noble attempt to push not only beyond the limits of dated and somewhat illegitimate language, but also beyond modernity itself. Modernity had become a code word for bourgeois Protestantism—and the Jew, half-Jew, and rebelling Protestant wanted none of it. Liberalism was Christianity's darling, but it was sheer egotism for the first two and déclassé egalitarianism for the latter. Hegel had secularized Luther, but that was not enough for Marx. Feuerbach had secularized

Hegel; it was still insufficient. Marx wanted to stand "man" on his own two feet; Hegel and Feuerbach had merely reconstituted Christianity in secular dress. Marx carried it to its limit. Men and women would live in a world ordered simply by historically determined dialectical clashes. Freud pushed beyond this utopianism, which he considered a naive dream. Men and women would live in a world not necessarily ordered, but they would live in their loneliness as mature and good people. Nietzsche would rediscover the imago dei (image of God) in us by ridding us of the category, if not the person, of the deity. His was not a tragic world, even though the end of each of us was tragic—death. He found the joy in our necessities, allowing us to return to our natural, noble state to overcome the mediocrity necessarily imposed by massive institutional religion.

These three men carried us out of the modern paradigm to a new and as yet unnamed (postmodernity is at best an interim, and somewhat barbaric, neologism) era. The assumptions of the old, modern paradigm gathered a community of scholars and laity around them who knew who they were. They had a common language, allowing them to identify their fellow moderns as well as allowing them intellectual commerce. Thomas S. Kuhn's now classic work on scientific revolutions and the paradigm shifts that allow them to happen has been proved wrong. When we shifted from modernity to "postmodernity" we should have been able to identify our friends and know who we are. The new secular paradigm leaves us not knowing whether there is order, and we are alone to fend for ourselves. Marx, Freud, and Nietzsche created a world in which our radical alienation (in religious language, Original Sin) from God, self, and neighbor was not taken away, rather, it deepened it by finishing the process of community disintegration begun by modernity. Freed individuals, replete with maturity and civil rights, ruggedly individual and well educated, were utterly devoid of community and the knowledge of where they were going. They were impoverished by the very riches with which they had endowed us. Religion would have to criticize the critics after it had heard them and begun its necessary reform. A new man and woman would be necessary to re-form the Christian community. Modernity had proved insufficient to the task, pushing religion's head ever deeper under the waves. If it were to survive, it would have to show modernity, as had Marx, Freud, and Nietzsche, that modernity itself lacked what people really wanted beyond the empirical norms: the More of transcendence. But before it could do so it had to descend into the hell of its own impoverishment, a poverty largely created by its adherence to the categories of the past—more a

Roman Catholic sin than a Protestant one—and a vapid understanding of its own involvement in modernity—the besetting Protestant sin. The one was lost in another time; the other was lost in its own time. Both dreamed the illusions of weak religion: that they were truly at home in the world and helping their fellows. They had lost their homes and were helping few. The knowledge of this was the hell imposed by Marx, Freud, and Nietzsche. The howls of outrage that greeted their brilliant critiques of religion proved by the decibel level that they struck where religious people were most vulnerable: they were peddling specifics for diseases that had disappeared years before; they were offering illusions instead of Christ's risen reality.

The overriding problem dealt with by all three was the problem of evil. Their theodicies proved to them that God, brought to the bar of judgment, was not worth the trouble that religion put them to. With evil went the problem of guilt. How each handled it will be seen in the essays that follow. For now, suffice it to say that Freud took the Hebraic view of the genesis and texture of our evil and changed it into a Greek tragedy: the Oedipus myth. The root of evil, ours and his, was, for Freud, rooted in a primal patricide the desire for which we all carried in our hearts. Freud rid us of sin and neurotic guilt, but he admitted to evil by outlining our libidinous cravings for patricide, cannibalism, and incest. The mob needed the lid that religion capped on their desires; only the elite could attain full maturity.

Marx's view of humanity was one of an evolutionary cleansing, in which we are "baptised" of our egotism—he hated rugged individualism and its parent, liberal democracy—on the way to a communitarian innocence. Both he and Friedrich Engels, his friend and collaborator, rid the world of evil by not only a deterministic history, but also—more immediately—by the reconciliation of opposites. Evil would become good, and the putative good of the bourgeois Christians would be shown up for the evils they were. Their view was one of innocence and their "sacramental rite" was one of conversion and inversion, in which values were turned upside down at first and then converted into humanistic and naturalistic terms. Marx knew that capitalism orchestrated evil—the avaricious lusts of the eye— to put them to good use for the companies and nations that it served. A U.S. ambassador told me just that in his residence in South America: "You liberals are soft on evil; we conservatives use greed to serve American interests. It's the best deal we can make in a dirty world." Freud dealt with the lusts of the bedroom, Marx with those of the boardroom.

Marx knew that Christian capitalism and its offshoot, Jewish capitalism, could not produce the selfless person of politics that he knew we were at heart. Instead, capitalist politics was greed annexed by civility in the service of necessity. But the prophet of necessity was Nietzsche, not the historicist Marx.

Nietzsche was the most honest and realistic of the three; not that his elitism was realistic; it wasn't. He took people as he found them and mapped out strategies by which they could live. Like the other two, he rid us of the troublesome God of our fathers. But unlike the others, he took the troubles to their sources: necessity was overlooked by the fragile, who accounted their imperious and inescapable concupiscences as "sins," rather than as the weaknesses they so frequently were, because theology demanded that the acts and actors be named. They were sinners because they followed instincts. Nietzsche said that people were to find a joy in the midst of their necessities by willing them and getting on with life and love. Too much time was spent on naming one's instincts and hating one's neighbor. He dealt with evil by admitting that it had a tragic term: our deaths. But on the way we were to live joyously in the face of our darknesses because we did not create the necessities; they created us. His was not a systematics, making each person a principle—although some existentialists would make it so. Rather, it was a tactic, allowing one to live decently playing out the hand that had been dealt by parents and culture. Neither Marx nor Freud had come so close to a viable solution to the problem of evil. If Nietzsche did not solve it, his tactics proved a solvent to many a sufferer who felt locked into sin when all it was was fragility wearing the mask of sin.

Freud and Marx were Jews; Marx had been baptized because his father could not practice his profession of law unless he converted. No Jew could fully trust the gentile. The dominant, at their best, were oppressors. The culture and tradition demanded that the Jew be alien. His testament was "Old"; ours was "New." He was backward and clumsy in learning gentile polities. And both secular and nonsecular Christians had made polities into pieties for centuries. Whatever was "nice" was Godly or goodly. They had to pay a high price for assimilation into gentile society: their disappearance as Jewish persons. In their place there would be bland and bourgeois goyim. It was a case of the bland leading the bland, and both took routes around what they considered liberal assassination: to be killed by liberal republicanism left one just as dead as to be killed by medieval conservative monarchists. Neither they nor Nietzsche had any love for things modern. They either killed Jews as such or they took the heart out of Christians. This book is an assay of their critique of religion and an essay on the impact it had on us in the Christian churches. I believe it to be concise and accurate, as well as sympathetic. On the way I offer insights and conclusions that I hope will challenge the reader to push further than a simple "what x said about y approach." At the end the reader should have a solid and incisive grasp of these Secular Magi.

Part I

❧

MARX'S CRITIQUE OF RELIGION

CHAPTER 1
Religion as Unreality

The criticism of religion is the premise of all criticism.

—Karl Marx

Karl Marx was born in Trier, Germany, in 1818. He died in London, England, in 1883. His father, Herschel Ha-Levi Marx, was preceded by two generations of pious rabbis. He was a practicing lawyer who had tried to assimilate himself into the dominant Christian culture by joining with them in their common belief in rationalism, humanitarianism, and God. The elder Marx could practice law in Germany only because the Napoleonic Code had given the Jews enfranchisement, thus opening up new worlds to the hitherto ghettoed Jews of the *Galut* (Dispersion). He was enjoying some professional success when disaster struck. In 1816 the new king of Prussia enacted laws making it illegal for any Jew to practice law in his domain. This imposed on Marx the necessity of either finding an alternative—and far less appetizing—way of earning a living or making the classic Jewish move: convert to Christianity to make life bearable for him and his family. Because he was not actively attached to any synagogue and was something of a deist religiously, dogma was no deterrent. Further, the Lutheranism of his day was agreeably liberal and enlightened. So he converted to Christianity in 1817, changing his name to Heinrich Marx. He converted neither out of affection for Lutheranism nor for Christianity, but in the hope that he could cut his losses best by joining a community that upheld his humanistic ideals. Karl, his eldest son, was born a year later.

A significant number of Jews assimilated themselves in the same way as did Karl's father, but unlike him, many became somewhat fanatical in

3

their practice of Christianity. Others fell into an equally fanatical repudiation of all religion as the oppressor of their forebears in the past and an obscurantist force in the present. Karl ultimately would become rather vehement against Jews, Christians, and all religion.[1]

Karl was an unusual and somewhat difficult child; he was sharp and lucid of mind and stubborn and domineering of temper. He was truculent in seeking his independence. Emotionally, he was restrained to an exceptional degree, but he had a voracious and insatiable appetite for things of the intellect. In letters to Karl, his timorous and good father begged the fractious boy to be more compromising and civil, to adapt himself to his surroundings and not so to antagonize his benefactors. (Berlin, 26f.)

Karl's humanist father accepted the belief of Condorcet in the innate goodness and rationality of man and woman; that the removal of the obstacles, the last citadels of which were the reactionary Catholic Church and the feudal nobility, would open the way to the inexorable march to progress through reason. Priests and rulers had created social, political, religious, and racial barriers to thwart progress; both classes were obstacles to a liberal future, in his view. Their removal would allow all people to be equal both in law and in their personal lives. He looked to a new day of emancipation for his children, who would be free born in a just and liberal state. He was a true son of the Enlightenment, placing his trust in the force of reason to change things for the better. Karl, on the contrary, did not believe that rational argumentation could change the real situation; but he was, nonetheless, something of a rationalist in believing in human perfectibility in the sense that social progress was a wholly intelligible evolutionary process in which each stage is nearer the rational ideal than the preceding one because each stage develops to a higher plane than its predecessor. So, society is inevitably progressive. Karl detested any emotionalism, and he could not abide any belief in supernatural causes as an explanation for things. This latter conceit led him systematically to underestimate the solidarity and power inherent not only in religion, but in all metarational forces, such as nationalism. His formation by his father was in rational, lucid argumentation, which preserved him from the metaphysics of the romantic movement. But if his approach was rational, it was also empirical. This enabled him to take the philosophy of the day—Hegelianism—and alter it to his positivist purposes. (Berlin, 29–31 passim)

In high school his essays on moral and religious topics won high praise for their elevated ethical tone. By the time he entered university, however, he was a convinced atheist. His socialism would come later. He knew mathematics and theology well but really loved art and literature best. His father and father-in-law, Ludwig von Westphalen, had great influence on the young Karl—the one for his ideas on human nature and the other for both those ideas as well as his great love of literature. When he started his own family, Karl would sit each night with his children and read Shake-speare to them. The positive influence of both his father and father-in-law had so affirmed him that he emerged a man whole and psychologically sound, which was to give him strength during a life lived in poverty and personal illness and fraught with struggles. (Berlin, 31–33 passim)

So much of modern theology is based on finding the revealing God in one's heart. In our feelings we can both know and appropriate the Self in the motions of the affects, which is both a cognitive and feeling function. In this sense, all knowledge is self-knowledge, and it is precisely in the discernment of the Self that God reveals the Godself. Marx thought that this kind of reasoning was pure rubbish, since all philosophy and theology can change is one's mind, not the real world of politics and economics. Both philosophy and theology, therefore, were "plugged into" wall sockets that went nowhere. They were illusions, and the greater of the two illusions was theology. The categories that they engendered caused one to lose oneself, to become reified. Religion and philosophy had turned people into things, and Marx knew that no one had the right or privilege of doing that, even if the thing were supernaturalized—*especially* if it was supernatural. This whole line of thinking would turn both disciplines on their heads. Hard-headed Marxist positivism forced its practitioners to look for the realities, and people were the realities that they sought. (At least this was so with the young, humanist Marx of the 1840s.) Later, those in religion who sought to begin their search with man and woman rather than with God would arrive at conclusions that would warm the heart of Marx in following his methodology, if only they would refrain from apply-ing them.

This was so since Marx despised liberals of any stripe: political, philosophical, and the future social gospelers, whom he would see as merest do-gooders more in it for their own purposes—like salvation—than out of love for the poor. In Marx's view the liberals of his day appealed to illusion in their reforming schemes, since dogma was only what they *wanted* to believe, what Freud and Nietzsche would later call projection, that served them as pediments for their reform edifices, not as a grounding for truth. For Marx, truth was then to be found in the inexorable laws of history. Liberals and the young Hegelians of Marx's day had locked themselves away from the facts of the world in their scholasticisms, which a wag of the day said were merely answers in search of questions to fit them. Marx felt that values viewed without facts would be worse than useless; they were pernicious because they were based on benign illusions, affording their possessors the warm feeling of knowing and doing "good" for people, when the reality was that they were doing good for themselves or their institutions. Marx said that one must see the historical laws governing the universe and then one would know what had to be done in life irrespective of the moral laws that one held in the abstract. So changing one's heart—doing penance in religion and converting to another paradigm in philosophy—would be tantamount to changing one illusion for another. Unlike his liberal peers, Marx appealed not to feeling and a compassionate heart—he despised emotionalism, even though he was a warm family man—but to the intellect, the practical intelligence, as the sole organ of change. He felt that all one had to know in order to change from the chaos of his day to the cosmos of historical utopia was to know the *actual conditions* in which one lived. Later, Freud would hold similar views about achieving mental health by knowing one's real conditions as a precondition *for* and cause *of* changing those realities.

Hence, unlike the democratic liberals of his day, Marx did not see the exploiter of the poor as necessarily wicked or as the problem to be worked on. Rather, it was the laws of history that determined that one class would exploit another. One's duty, one's program, was to know those laws of history that were the engine running human destiny; and those laws demanded war between the classes, not because war was a value in itself, but because all things and people ran dialectically into one another, notwithstanding violence, on their way to progress in an ultimate synthesis. (Berlin, 6–8 passim) Moral arguments were, moreover, irrelevant when one knew the facts about things; these facts would solve the problems of the poor. The workers are the exploited class, and in the eyes of Marx, they were the rising, progressive class. So Marx hitched his wagon to their star because they were the fact of history and both morality and philosophy were *perhaps* facts about history, at best, and illusions, at worst. Religion was about the symptoms of history: pain. And the pain itself would work for its own assuagement without any help from armchair philosophers and liberal, socialist church leaders. He had cast Hegel's philosophical body away in shedding the latter's idealism, but he kept his mentor's heart in retaining the dialectical view of history. So the question

6

of exploitation was solved by knowing the facts and doing something about them. Moral arguments, human rights, and questions about the freedom of one's conscience are irrelevant because they are illusory. Socialism points out the facts of human existence and makes demands because of them, so there was no need to make appeals. History will make all things right; so why talk of human rights? Justice is coming inexorably, so aid it! The experiences that the liberals base their moral arguments on are conditioned experiences limited by their culture and their time.

Marx rejected the notion of the Liberals, Utilitarians, and Utopian Socialists, who thought that all people wanted the same things and that they knew what those desires were. (Berlin, 9) He fought them because these interests were particular—what he would call egoistic. These interests, in turn, were incompatible with Marx's view of "species man," type who was aware of being a member of a class, of a species, that one's interests were those of the class, not of one's own personal needs. Liberal and religious people were what Marx would call "civil men"; i.e., parochially inclined to self-fulfillment, not to filling out the laws of history, which laws should have allowed one to find oneself in not alienating labor and its fruits from oneself. Hegel saw a transcendental symbol in labor; Marx saw no such thing. Where Hegel saw self-renunciation as a universal desire, Marx saw it as alienation and inverted it to recover the self. To Marx, a laborer is his or her labor; it is not extrinsic (*Kapital* i, 6). Hegel said that one appropriates the self through one's labor by making it an object intrinsic to the substance of that labor. Marx said that his objectification alienated the self from the self.[2] Marx broke away from Hegel for the same reason that he broke away from the liberal elements in society: he could not stand their emotionalism or their romanticism. All humanitarianism was bourgeois illusion for him. He wanted to appeal to no idealistic feelings and certainly not to the "brooding joy" of German Romanticism. He broke from the healthy positive secularism of his day, which believed in moral progress, eternal justice, and human equality; in the rights of individuals and nations; in liberty of conscience; and in the fight for civilization. Such ideas were mere cant in Marx's estimation. They could change nothing. For him progress and progressive society were to be found in developing along the lines that history inexorably took. Reaction and reactionary societies were to be found among those groups that were actually headed for chaos and collapse because the firmly established laws of history demanded it.

For Marx, the universe was built on a rational plan according to which it creates and according to which it sweeps away detritus. Humans can aid the plan by knowing it and living in accordance with it. He felt that philanthropy so often harbored a horror for the reality of history and tried to forestall it by goodness; but benignity was illusory before the revolutionary and dialectical discontinuities—and their attendant pain—which the "good" tried to avoid by their very goodness. Marx saw his work as one of dealing in the coinage of truth by "doing" justice in the truth of history. (Berlin, 10–13 passim)

Communism was not new with Marx. Mably, Babeuf and his followers, or German variants of these French Communists were possibly the sources for Marx's theories. Further, historical materialism was not new with Marx either; Holbach treated it fully a hundred years earlier, and even this was rooted in Spinoza's work and largely restated by Feuerbach. The concept of class warfare was well stated by both Linguet and Saint-Simon and adopted by Marx's French contemporaries Thierry and Mignet. The idea of the cyclical regularity of economic crises was first scientifically postulated by Sismondi. The dictatorship of the proletariat is to be found in the writings of Babeuf at the end of the eighteenth century and in those of Weitling and Blanqui in the nineteenth century. Marx's labor theory of value is rooted in John Locke and in Adam Smith. The alienation of the proletariat was articulated by Max Stirner at least one year before Marx said it. (Berlin, 14).

Therefore, Marx's value lay not in the novelty of his ideas, but in the simplicity of principle and the comprehensiveness and attention to detail of his analysis and program. Second, Marx's program spoke to the actual experience of the people, both poor and rich, so it was not fanciful, but rather most powerful in the way that it dealt with their realities. Third, Marx's novelty was in his synthesis of German idealism, French rationalism, and English political economy, which explained many social phenomena hitherto unexplained because they were uncoordinated by any theory. Fourth, his ideas were coordinated and offered a systematic program for a revolutionary political party. He gave what Isaiah Berlin called "clear, unified answers in familiar empirical terms" to the theoretical problems that most exercised people's minds and formulated a practical program for them. Berlin thinks that therein lay the power and contribution of Karl Marx. (Berlin, 15f.) He wanted no more than to save the gullible masses from the knaves and fools who exploited them, even if he had to rescue them by force. His synoptic vision was of an "orderly, disciplined, self-directing" world that would rise from the ashes of the previous exploitative, capitalist, Christian one, which latter world was, to him, an irrational and chaotic place in which to live. Marx condemned society, not because its people were evil, but because they were bourgeois; their virtues were vices; their society was corrupt, tyrannous, and irrational. It had to be eliminated from the world for good. (Berlin, 19–21)

Marx and Hegel's Philosophy

The rational empiricism of the continent held that men and women were naturally good. Its proponents were in sharp contrast to the preaching of the day, which steadfastly maintained that humankind was vicious, that our nature had to be curbed. The new philosophers claimed that the churched laced their arguments with Aristotle's statement that some people are born naturally into the slave class. Such apodicticism galled the scientific community, among whom Marx wished to be numbered, whose empirical method precluded it from demonstrating with any certainty the inner essence of humanity. Rationalism held that it could know our inner lives with certainty. Theologians maintained that revelation had given them insights into human nature that transcended anything human methodology could muster. But the Enlightenment had thoroughly discredited the authority of both scripture and theology. So on both sides of the Channel the empirical view of human nature prevailed.

Further, the orthodoxy of the liberal class was that the church enlisted roguish princes to hold back the truth from the masses, which truth was the plinth on which contemporary liberalism stood: namely, that it is ignorance which impedes progress and causes both suffering and oppression. Hence secular modernity reemphasized the traditional Judeo-Christian doctrine that human nature was intrinsically good, thinking it was something new and quite different from what the prevailing religions held. It meant that people could grow into their full potential. Philosophers like Rousseau said that, left to themselves, people would pursue virtue and knowledge; that authority and privilege would give way to justice and equality; that cooperation would supersede competition. This was a semi-empirical rationalism, and its centerpiece was and is the cherished faith it holds in reason to explain and improve us and our environment. Bad preaching had been rooted in sin-laden theology. The reaction to it had set in, emphasizing humankind's innocence and goodness. Thus, the surd of evil found no place in classic liberal thought until after the carnage of World War I had forced philosophers, artists, and even the church to

9

rediscover sin and evil as necessary categories of human thought. English, German, and French boys had gone off to war with optimism and returned with the terrors of the machine gun and the dark night of modern bombardment. Theology would jettison miracle—the populace could no longer believe in a physical resurrection from the deaths they had seen; its German practitioners would, however, have to resurrect evil.

Marx fell heir to the optimism of the generations preceding World War I. Its view of human nature was much like the optimism of Hinduism's Vedanta, where one's divinity can be shaken loose only by shucking ignorance like a skin. These pre-Hegelians saw misery rooted in ignorance of nature's laws and the laws of social behavior. People had lived in this ignorance for so long that a lengthy process of education would be necessary to bring them up to standard. This would be something akin to Freud's "education for reality," which I discuss in-depth later on.[3] The education that these rational empiricists would offer was to be gained through the imparting of scientific principles. This in turn would produce an elite corps of enlightened people who would educate the masses. There was another corps, however, composed of unenlightened priests and tyrants, depending on the unenlightenment of the masses. In fact, they had fostered that privative state and even marinated their charges in it in order to maintain their own power over them. The obscurantist ruling elite exercised its sovereignty through an inflexible legal code by upholding and inculcating unfathomable mysteries with which to befog the masses, thereby retaining for itself its arbitrary authority. For these rational elitists, therefore, nothing supernatural could affect human nature. The intellectual climate and natural environment *entirely* account for one's ideas and behavior; and this can be verified by natural, physical hypotheses. When La Mettrie published *L'Homme-machine*, in 1747, it caused a sensation in France. It reflected an extreme mechanistic view of human nature, a view in line with, but more radical than, that of the encyclopedists Diderot, d'Alembert, Holbach, Helvétius, and Condillac. (Berlin, 37–40 passim) Nature had replaced God in the free-will controversy, where God foreknew all. Empiricists said that humankind is determined naturally; but if so, then it might be said that so are the elite educators, and then nothing could be changed, since matter in space/time determines all. But these latter considerations carried little weight in those days of heady empiricism. Nature's laws were ineluctable and unalterable, and knowing them wouldn't change anything, since it could not change anything. Human improvement could not come about by free decisions.

The intellectual crisis of the past century broke the power structures into two inimical camps. To the camp of modernity belonged the atheists, skeptics, deists, materialists, rationalists, democrats, and utilitarians. To the other, reactionary, camp belonged the theists, metaphysicians, and upholders of the status quo. The battle was joined over the issue of enlightenment versus the axis of clericalism and political tyranny. Thus, in Marx's time, the key issue for the radical intellectual was the liberal doctrine of the fundamental goodness of humankind.

The method of the day was the scientific one, in which verification could only be done by quantifying one's results. This shift from the soft rationalism of Scholasticism had been pioneered in the seventeenth century by Kepler, Descartes, Galileo, and Newton. It was absorbed best in the eighteenth century by Voltaire, who spearheaded the attack against political absolutism and its best ally, catholicism. Every freedom battle since has mined Voltaire for fuel; his was the very mind of liberation, whose heart was Rousseau; the latter was a preacher-propagandist of great genius. Rousseau glorified will at the expense of intellect. Many of the rebels in the world of art and politics in the nineteenth century used this seventeenth-eighteenth-century paradigm of Voltaire and Rousseau, which based its best hope on the omnipotence of education as the organ of freeing man's and woman's perfectibility. This is rational-empiricism at its height. Into this rattling lustiness for battle stepped Hegel in the early nineteenth century. (Berlin, 40–44 passim)

Hegel believed that the absolutism of the rational-empiricists was as bad as what it wished to replace; he especially belittled the unbounded acceptance of the scientific method as the only way to truth. He thought that the method was imperfect in science and disastrous if applied to history to discern its laws. (Berlin, 45f.) First, he saw how Galileo and Newton explained natural phenomena and how they replicate, but this in no way explained how they can and do change; i.e., the laws of empirical science cannot and do not explain history. If history has laws, they must be different from the physical laws of nature, since the latter do not give us acceptable answers to questions about change and development. Hence, real natural laws must include the laws of history in order to include all that exists. Hegel's paramount desire was to discover the principle of historical motion. (Berlin, 50)

Second, Hegel saw that an individual had character, temperament, and motives. He applied this insight to whole cultures and nations. He believed that the character each particular phenomenon revealed was a manifestation of a universal Idea or Spirit. This Spirit had evolved throughout the ages, passing through various stages. Spirit was, therefore, the dynamic factor in the development of peoples. Being so, it was a universal Spirit and was to be found in all individual phases of history and culture. His method was to look into the particular to find this universal Spirit. He violated the logic of this in making one religion the epitome of the All: Christianity was *the* religion and the other religions were truncated epiphanies of the Whole. It is a mark of the German mind that it characteristically looks for the universal in the particular. Such historicism locks the German mind into preconceived categories which demand that history be somewhat determined. As such, Augustine and his voluntarism was revived by Luther's predestination and updated by Hegel's historical determinism. Hegel's history was a science, and like its empirical cousins, it looked for the widest applications for its findings. Mathematics and physics must ruthlessly cast out the individual case as too variable to be trustworthy in looking for the universal law. Hegel, on the contrary, found that the individual was a manifestation of the universal. (Berlin, 51–53) As such, his "science of history" was really the art of hermeneutics.

Third, Leibnitz saw a pattern of progress inscribing itself in human affairs. Hegel subscribed to this seminal idea but with this difference: progress went through rugged clashes in ideas and history, and indeed in all phases of life. This would make wars and revolutions quite necessary as the universal Spirit moved us ever upward, careering us toward the ultimate progress of attaining the Absolute contained within the particular culture and each individual in it. Such dialectical clashes characteristically ended with the destruction of all the contestants. The continuity of history is broken thereby, and a leap to a new level is taken. At this new level the dialectical process of ideas and forces is begun again but by a new set of agencies that preceded it. (Berlin, 55f.)

Fourth, thought is reality become aware of itself. Both Engels and Teilhard de Chardin would take up this theme to limn out their views of matter on the move to self-consciousness. Fifth, the dialectic is a process of evolution in which clashing things are absorbed and resolved in a synthesis. History moves because of dialectical tension. Sixth, when Hegel applied his concept of history's struggle to produce the universal Idea to the race and individual nations, he found that "universal brotherhood" was out because some races and nations and the female sex were meant to be inferior in order to play out their role in the dialectical clashes that were necessary to produce the supernal Spirit. Both the Nazis and some contemporary Marxists have used this concept in their disdain for human rights. Each one's position in the scheme of things, therefore, is due to one's logically necessary historical position, which is one's proper nature. The laws of both physical beings and history are composed of Spirit and are, therefore, rational. One cannot oppose these laws; they are inexorable. All substances are composed of Spirit and are rational. The Spirit attains its perfection as it becomes more aware of itself. Philosophy is the Spirit becoming more self-aware. Applied to history, thought is the story of the Spirit becoming more self-aware. Hegel said that the philosophy of history is the history of philosophy. Hence, in becoming self-aware, people recapitulate nature, which cannot do its thinking for itself; they do this by self-analysis. In so doing, nature becomes more than conscious through its human vicars; it becomes aware that it is a self. This self-awareness manifests itself in societies improving themselves. Hegel said that matter is spirit at a lower, less conscious, brute level (Leibnitz) and is recalcitrant of its nature. Wars are, therefore, necessary to move matter forward. (Berlin, 56–59 passim) The influence this had on Engels was immeasurable. He began with a different postulate, admittedly. But his "matter" moving up to self-awareness and universalism (read communalism) is really Hegel turned upside down and inside out.

The despair of liberals after the failure of the French Revolution was answered by Hegel's faith in the reasonable laws of history and its inevitable progress. This despair meant that evil had beaten good; error had vanquished truth; and that humankind could not improve its lot. Hegel countered this by saying that one did not deflect history from its *predestined* path, nor did one speed it up or slow it down.

Marx was an empiricist from earliest times. One can see it beneath the surface of his philosophical view. His empiricism emerges when one sees him go after myths and irrationalism in any form, especially in religion, where he revealed his eighteenth-century materialism. But if he felt in tune with his empiricist age, he is Hegelian in spirit and was so from the beginning in this sense: our ascent is through our own labors, thus bringing all under rational control. He attacked Hegel's idealism but remained a devotee in some way. (Berlin, 60f.) To understand this one has to make a pilgrimage to the shrine of Feuerbach.

Feuerbach

A few months after Marx took his doctorate in philosophy, in 1841, Feuerbach published *The Essence of Christianity*. The book savaged Hegel's philosophical Spirit as a thinly disguised God. (Berlin, 78) Marx

13

had been quite enamored of Hegel's thought but had slowly come to the painful conclusion that it was no more than a thinly veiled idealistic Scholasticism and that his Spirit of the age was a tautology explaining the thing he set out to explain by that thing itself. The thing that stands out about Feuerbach is that he was a theologian and a materialist. It is daring for any Christian theologian to maintain a materialist ontology today, but in the nineteenth century it was nothing less than courageous. His anthropology pushed away from Hegel radically and gave both Marx and Engels a basis for their own materialism. Engels said that the young Hegelians all became at once Feuerbachians.[4] Feuerbach said that it was not Spirit, but the sum of material conditions of any time that was the driving force of history. Further, material distress caused men and women to seek solace in an inner ideal that was beyond this world and that would reward their pain forever with bliss; but this immaterial world of religion was a human invention. Whatever men and women lack on earth of goodness and justice they attribute to God and the world beyond, a God they worship and a world that they alone inhabit. The transcendent world and its deity are an illusion; analysis reveals that this other world is a product of humankind's material maladjustments. For Feuerbach, we are what we eat *(Der Mensch ist was er isst)*. By this crude materialism, Feuerbach explained us as an interplay of material forces; only the knowledge of these forces can make humankind master of its laws by being able consciously to adapt to them. Marx and Lenin were deeply affected by Feuerbach's statement that all ideologies, religious or secular, are attempts to give ideal solace for real (material) misery. Feuerbach's naive and badly written book *Theses on Hegelian Philosophy* had a telling effect on Marx, who found the theses refreshing but flawed: refreshing since he had concluded that Hegel had just been going on with words about words, not with words about realities, and Feuerbach corroborated his conclusion; more about the flaws in the book later. (Berlin, 78f.)

Feuerbach repudiated Hegel for basing his philosophy on religion, since faith and reason are incompatible. Mind is not, as Hegel would have it, perfectly at one with matter, since nature exists whether one is conscious of it or not. There is only illusion when one purports to represent anything beyond nature and people. This reversed Hegel's system: for "Spirit," Feuerbach inserts matter; for "God," he inserts man and woman. Hegel was wrong because he had been "putting the predicate in place of the subject and the subject in place of the predicate," a summation Marx would use in his "Critique of Hegel's Philosophy of Law."

For both, the idea reflects the world, not vice versa, as Hegel would have it. Marx advised philosophers and theologians to jettison their theories, since "there is no other road for you toward truth and freedom than this 'stream of fire'" (Feuerbach means just that in German). (Garaudy, 25f.)

Feuerbach's reversal of Hegel's system was but a way station for Marx. He would go further by inverting Hegel's method and system. Feuerbach had convinced the young Hegelians that, contrary to their conventional wisdom, Hegel was not only not opposed to the Christian religion, but that he also was an outstanding apologete for it. Marx thought that absolute idealism is the blood relative of religion. Hence, Feuerbach concluded, "If one does not renounce Hegel's philosophy, one does not renounce theology." Feuerbach thought that he had discovered the very essence of Christianity, thus the title of his most famous book, and retailed his find readily for all and sundry: the Christian religion had sundered soul and mind from body and Christians had made a god of their own souls. The nineteenth century was to follow this model with a docility somewhat amusing to us now. To think that any religion can be distilled to an essence is ludicrous, since religion is a mystery, a symbol system impatient of essences and absolute constructs. But Feuerbach's method and the conclusions it attained were of enormous influence during his time.

Thus, the nub of Feuerbach's critique of Christianity was that it was guilty of projection: God was the copy; people were the originals. This made the very notion of transcendence alienation for him. We created God in our image and likeness. Feuerbach was not the first to use this method of inversion; Voltaire had put it better when he said, "God made man in His image and likeness and man returned the compliment." But Feuerbach was infinitely more effective in the power he wielded over such men as Marx. Hegel had made people an alienation for God, but Feuerbach inverted this, making God the alienation of humankind itself. The very concept "humanity" was alienation to Feuerbach, since it made us an abstraction. God is the ideal we project into the heavens because of the schizoid state of human nature in Christianity. Feuerbach wanted us to be conscious of being a member of a species. Hence, "species man" was the universal he coined in place of the uninflected abstraction "man." Marx would pick up this notion and make capital use of it in his own theory. For Hegel, history's goal was the realization of God in us. For Feuerbach, it was our own realization when once we shucked off the projection-alienation that God is to us.

But Feuerbach did not go far enough for Marx; he failed to complete the

15

inversion and made it a reversal instead. He reversed Hegel's idealistic system into a materialistic one. Garaudy calls Feuerbach's system "naturalized Hegelianism," and I am inclined to agree with him. (Garaudy, 26f.) In his hands, Hegel's metaphysics becomes an anthropology; the dialectics of the Spirit now becomes the way nature works in history made dogma. Feuerbach's is a humanistic religion; it took the framework and mechanics of theology and installed a new spirit in the old theological body, an anthropology in which Hegel and the church had had a theology. Neither Marx nor Freud was completely to overthrow those religious paradigms, either. Both retained a religious framework and something of a religious intent in their teachings; the one held out a utopia and the other a sanation in place of salvation. Religion dies hard both as reality and construct.

In 1843 Marx completed his inversion of things in "The Critique of Hegel's Philosophy of Self Right" (also known as his critique of Hegel's philosophy of law). Here, Marx borrows Feuerbach's method of using materialism as a philosophical base to explain our loss of self (alienation). This is the problem of evil solved in a new way, reminiscent of Buddhism, in which humankind is not evil and has never had a fall. There, God is a nonissue; peace is the goal. God merely gets in the way, since people can cause their own Nirvana. Marx stripped God of the problem of evil and was left with the creature made good in God's image. Next, he completed the inversion by ridding us of the creaturehood that cried out for a creator; this need for the More that religion calls God is, for Marx, the root of alienation. Evil is not an offense against God; it is one against oneself and one's breed. It is the loss of the self in the alienation concept of God and the alienation of the self in a labor that strips one of one's role as creator, as worker. With Marx, the creature had become the creator; had found itself; had overcome evil by inverting everything that had taken its humanity away: God took the soul away in robbing the creature of responsibility to create; theology took the mind away by forcing humankind to be at one remove from reality intellectually. Where the Judeo-Christian tradition had found evil in an offense against God and neighbor, Marx had cut off the very possibility of evil as sin and left only human alienation from the self. Hence there was no need of a Savior—salvation would come in economics and politics; no need of priest, of bell, book, and candle; no need of prayer to suck up one's vitality. Marx had found himself, in stripping off these accretions, these alienations, and gotten to the nub of the problem of evil: alienation of the self by the very ways we

16

had solved it, or lived with it peacefully for two millennia. Now, that alienation would take care of itself in history's dialectical squiggles and violent discontinuities, such as class warfare and revolutions. Our role was to criticize and aid circumstances by changing them.

Both Freud and Marx went to the problem of evil as Original Sin— which is really only the problem of the human condition—in order to set up their new systems. As Luther had done, they reformed religion by addressing the problem of man's and woman's pain. Luther had it in the trappings of grace; the latter two reformers stripped humanity of God, and therefore of sin, and retrieved that humanity in the arenas of either economics-politics or the medical arts.

Marx's Move Beyond Feuerbach

Marx's paramount criticism of Feuerbach was that he was not radical enough; he had not done a complete job of it; he had not inverted the status quo, but only reversed it. In Thesis XI of *Theses on Feuerbach*, Marx says: "The philosophers have only *interpreted* [his emphasis] the world, in various ways; the point, however, is to change it."[5] Thesis I gets right to the heart of the matter when Marx says:

> The chief defect of all hitherto existing materialism—that of Feuerbach included—is that the thing . . . , reality, sensuousness, is conceived only in the form of the *object* . . . or of *contemplation* . . . , but not as *human sensuous activity*, practice, not subjectively. . . . Hence he does not grasp the significance of "revolutionary," of "practical-critical," activity. (Theses, 69f.)

It is praxis, not analysis, that is needed. Thesis II states that it is a purely academic matter whether this proposition or that one is true; not theory, but proof in doing something is the deciding factor in the question of truth. A thing is real or not as it works itself out in history, not in a footnote. Marx does not subscribe to any form of materialism that smacks of fatalism; his is no Nietzschean *amor fati* (love of one's fate) either. In Thesis III he says:

> The materialist doctrine that men are products of circumstances and upbringing, and that, therefore, changed men are products of other circumstances and changed upbringing, forgets that it is men that change circumstances and that the educator himself needs educating. . . . The coincidence of the changing of circumstances and of human activity can be

17

conceived and rationally understood only as *revolutionizing practice*. (Theses, 70)

Thus he jettisons La Mettrie's and Feuerbach's grosser historicist form of materialism for one in which humankind works out its future by freely helping what history is bringing about anyway. It is much like the classic evangelical doctrine of grace proposed by Luther and Calvin: we are predestined, but we are obligated to act as ones saved by grace too. Phenomenologically speaking, does one act so because one is God's chosen, or is one the chosen because one is beloved of God? It is a circular argument and much weakens both the Reformers' theology and Marx's philosophy, although it does not weaken the latter's main eschatological contention: we are on the move to something better, so "do something about it!" There is a strong principle of freedom in Marx's anthropology; and the fact that it is not a totally worked out doctrine in which one finds human freedom well articulated flaws his thought by trapping it in the cul de sac of historicism; but it does not destroy its value, nor has it seemed to detract from its influence in the world, much of which is presently Marxist.

I maintain that the outstanding feature of Marx's thought is the way he uses inversion as a methodological tool. He does this by using a logician's trick. Chiasmus is the logical schema that allows one to turn a proposition upside down and inside out. In Thesis IV, Marx chides Feuerbach for his incompleteness in this very matter:

Feuerbach starts out from the fact of religious self-alienation, the duplication of the world into a religious, imaginary world and a real one. His work consists in the dissolution of the religious world into its secular basis. He overlooks the fact that after this work is completed the chief thing still remains to be done. For the fact that the secular foundation detaches itself from itself and establishes itself in the clouds as an independent realm is really only to be explained by the self-cleavage and self-contradictoriness of this secular basis. The latter must itself, therefore, first be understood in its contradiction, and then revolutionized in practice by the removal of the contradiction. Thus, for instance, once the earthly family is discovered to be the secret of the holy family, the former must then itself be criticized in theory and revolutionized in practice. (Theses, 70)

Marx has flipped things on their backs here. Finding the secular once again, as Feuerbach had done so well, was only the beginning of putting down a firm basis for a program. The secular was in a dialectical conflict

18

with itself; it had more than one valence struggling for domination. The reality of the sacred, what Marx calls "the holy family," is the secular; Feuerbach knew this, but he did not create a program to rid one of the sacred illusion. He criticized it on paper and left it at that. Criticism rids one of religion by allowing the antithesis to the religious thesis to move beyond religion to a revolutionary synthesis, not to a theoretical synthesis, as Marx found in Feuerbach. Such a "theoretical synthesis" would leave a theological shell intact, which Marx knew could, as it had with Hegel before him, allow religion to return in a renewed state. This would make the last state worse than the first. At its best, religion deals only with the symptoms of the problem. A secularized situation that was not revolutionary was not one moving with history; it was dead in the water and would surely lead again, as it had with Hegel's critique of religion, to another religious illusion of a sort.

In Thesis V, Marx criticizes Feuerbach for stopping short again in desiring to move from abstract to *"sensuous contemplation"* (his emphasis); he failed to complete the motion, which would have been consummated in praxis, what Marx called *"practical* human sensuous activity."* (Theses, 71)

Marx assigns high marks to Feuerbach in Thesis VI for seeing the religious essence as the human essence; but he does not criticize the real essence once he finds it. What Marx means by this is that heurism (finding out what it is) is only half the job; the rest of it is getting past the abstraction, what Marx calls the "genus" human, to the species human. The genus allows one to deal with religious emotion as an abstract, isolated entity. It is not. Religious experience is a factor in human experience, which is a tissue of human relations. All Feuerbach achieves in getting to the genus is turning secularized humanity into "civil (egoistic) man." People are a "social product" for Marx (Thesis VII) and must be seen in the particular, culture-specific gestalt in which they live. Human nature is social, and "social life is practical" (Thesis VII). Criticism means, for Marx, going beyond the necessary methodological first step of what I have termed inversion—the first step of the chiasmus of turning things upside down and inside out—to get past the phase of correcting theory to the most necessary phase of criticism, which is the moment of praxis. This phase deals with the human essence, which Feuerbach knew was secular and not religious, in its humanity; and humanity is relational, collective, living in a specific time and place. Any relational human being is political; this is Marx's "species man," a phrase

19

he took from the first chapter of Feuerbach's *The Essence of Christianity* and will deal with again in his essay "On the Jewish Question."[6]

Theory should head naturally in the direction of praxis; when it becomes unhealthy it leads to further abstraction and mystery, and from there to mysticism (Thesis VIII); this is not the bedrock of politics and economics, but a holy fog, a theoretic chimera. Any materialism that does not understand the sensuous dooms the practitioner to a life in civil (egoistic) society. (And here, Marx means that practicality of doing something in solidarity with one's peers and knowing that that is what should be done and that one should be doing it, thereby saving theory with praxis.) (Thesis XI) To be human, to live in a human society, is to be socialized, to have a "socialized humanity" (Thesis X). Hence, Marx's parting shot at Feuerbach is the one he levels at all "liberal philosophers": he interpreted the world when he should have continued the process that ends by changing it (Thesis XI). (Theses, 69–71 passim) Marx's critique of all religious hermeneutics is the same as Nietzsche's: Christians talk too much and act too little.

Hence, for Marx, Feuerbach got to the theory of it fairly well: God is really our best side "in excelsis" and we are our own religion. Feuerbach converted things from theology to anthropology, but his consciousness was still illusory, since he remained trapped by the power of the Hegelian system, which was a false philosopher's consciousness. For Marx, it takes inversion to complete the process: one inverts after the first methodological step of finding the secular essence of humankind. Inversion takes one past one's meaning—which is a human meaning—into human life, which is a life of activity in concert with other human beings. This activity, in turn, flows back into theory to change one's philosophy to one based even more on one's humanness. The critique phase of the process is, therefore, antithetical to what one found in the theory phase; one negates one's secular essence in the sense that one gets to work, one does not sit on one's philosophical laurels like a philosopher or theologian. One "knows" one's essence in this action phase, not in the philosophical phase. In the theory phase, one merely glimpses one's humanness; in praxis, one experiences it. This demystifies religion and philosophy in what Marx calls "sensuous activity," in "practicality." It is praxis that is the synthesis phase of the dialectical process; and one arrives at it through the criticism of one's theoretical essence. It took great courage for Marx to say this, since Feuerbach's secularism was a monumental find in itself. But it did not afford Marx what he thought was consciousness of reality, which only came through an experience of oneself in praxis, in labor, in changing circumstances and not allowing oneself to flow with Hegelian calm with the tide of history. Feuerbach was a secularist, but a fatalistic one; and Marx would have none of that. Philosophy was at one remove from the real world, for Marx. Edmund Wilson quoted Marx's piquant quip to the effect that "philosophy stands in the same relation to the study of the actual world as onanism to sexual love." He would not become a Scholasticism, a philosophical mine for his followers. Late in his life he said to Paul Lafargue, "I am not a Marxist." (Bottomore, Intro., xiii, n. 2) He despised philosophies born in the head because they died there of dogmatic atrophy. He said in "Critique of Hegel's Dialectic," "Every skepticism is a concealed dogmatism." One could reverse it just as easily and say that every dogmatism is a concealed skepticism.

CHAPTER 2

The Celestial Refutation: Hegel Confronted

In "Contribution to the Critique of Hegel's Philosophy of Self Right," Marx said: "The criticism of religion is the premise of all criticism"; then, if one refutes celestial error, one refutes profane error as well.[1] The error Marx refers to would be not finding oneself. That was *the* search of the nineteenth century—what we shall call the human invention, in the Latin sense of "finding." If Marx found something to criticize in Feuerbach's anthropology, along with the helpful contribution the latter had made in that field, that criticism had to be based on his retention of the Hegelian mold, which was theological. The Feuerbachian shift had been from God to humankind, from theology to anthropology, from idealism to materialism; but it was not complete enough for Karl Marx. In "Critique of Hegel's Dialectic and General Philosophy"—written in 1844—Marx laid his axe to the roots: Hegel's philosophy was cryptotheology, no more than an apologia for religion.[2] Marx, then, skipped over the good found in Feuerbach to confront the latter's—and indeed his own—intellectual progenitor and mentor, who was Hegel. In doing so he vindicated Nietzsche's dictum that our convictions are our prisons. Religion had to be gotten at; it was the inner reality of Hegel's thought, as it was of all philosophy. The fulcrum of it all for Marx was criticism; Feuerbach's criticism had partially succeeded in his invention of our secular essence and wholly failed in not exploiting his gains by criticizing them and so coming to the consciousness of reality. Hence, Marx set out to finish the job by writing his essay on Hegel's dialectic and the whole contour of his philosophy.

Marx thought that Feuerbach's great contribution to knowledge was threefold: (1) He showed that philosophy was just religion developed by thought and, as such, merely another form of human alienation. (2) He founded "genuine materialism" and positive science by grounding his theory on human relationships rather than on the clash of antithetical ideas. (3) He opposed Hegel's third step—the negation of negation—and posited a self-subsistent principle in its stead; he took a principle that is "perceptible and indubitable" as his starting point, instead of Hegel's absolute Spirit, which was the epitome of abstraction. (Dialectic, 197f.) What all this meant to Marx was this: Hegel's process begins with a thesis on religion and theology, i.e., with the infinite, abstract, alienated substance. The antithesis to this is the finite, concrete particular, in which philosophy supersedes theology and religion, and the concrete and positive replace the abstract. The third moment, the synthesis of the clashing ideas, is the recrudescence of the abstract and universal; in other words, religion and theology return in a reformed state. Feuerbach saw the flaw here: that philosophy rids us of theology and then brings it back again. So Feuerbach stripped philosophy of transcendence (theology) and threw it away. His philosophy was one without the need for any transcendent categories to drain men and women of their human essence by the useless addition of the supernatural and its source—God. (Dialectic, 198)

Hence, Marx says, Hegel's philosophy is an *"abstract, logical and speculative* [emphasis his] expression of the historical process."* (Dialectic, 198) For Marx, this is not real history, but the story of human genesis; and for him, this is not going far enough because it is at one or more removes from real people. It is locked in someone's philosophical head rather than freed in the clashing flux of people's lives. It is only the beginning of the beginning, not the beginning of the end. Its continuance would be the praxis phase initiated by criticism—and neither Hegel nor Feuerbach went this far. Hegel's philosophical mind is trapped (alienated) within its own abstraction perfection. It is self-alienation performed by the very process of thinking abstractly in order to come to oneself, but it fails woefully, in Marx's estimation. (Dialectic, 200) The falsity of his consciousness is intrinsic to the thought process itself; for Marx, thought and falsity become tautologies in a philosophy of this sort. Logic does not deal in the coinage of one's concrete value (one's individuality), but with abstraction. Marx called this logic the money of the mind. It was a money that ignored one's real nature, since it was external to one's real nature. For him, anything abstract was external and therefore alienated from us.

Hence, only the positive, concrete type of consciousness can express our nature. If one wishes to become estranged from onself, one has only to oppose abstract, speculative thought to reality (sensible being); that is, thought becomes the subject and reality, the object. Marx's objection to this is that it reifies us: we become an object for our own thinking, when we are really subjects, human beings. One thinks not about oneself, but about something extrinsic to that, which one wrongly thinks is the self. This would be, in our psychological parlance, schizoid thinking; and this was alienation for Marx. (Dialectic, 201)

But here Marx retains a religious category. Alienation is what Original Sin refers to when it points to the human situation: we are alien to the self, to God, and to our neighbor. We have forgotten how to think. Religious *anamnesis* (remembering) is telling us the tale (gospel) not only of God's coming, but also of who we are. The one melds with the other. This *anamnesis* gives one true consciousness in returning one to the self. It is the negation of the negation of human nature that is Original Sin and, as such, negates the *amnesia* (alienation) of wandering through life at its best (philosophy), thinking that one had captured the real. This is hubris, and speaking theologically, Marx was on to it.

Hence, through Hegel's dialectic one appropriates, not the real self, but only an abstraction, a thought, and not one's alienated faculties. The dialectic of pure thought sees the object as an object of thought and the subject as self-consciousness. Marx rejected this out of hand. But if there is reification as loss of self, there is reification (objectification) as part of the process of negativity (dialectical process), in which one creates oneself by first losing oneself in an exploitative (alienating) form of labor. This loss of self in alienating labor is transcended in the finding of the real self in labor, which is the creative process in concert with one's species. One finds one's "species powers," meaning that one realizes that one is a member of a race; but one treats them first as objects and thereby loses the true self. Then one negates this loss in collective work and thus finds the self. In Marx's estimation, Hegel's greatest contribution in *Phenomenology* was, first, that he knew that one self-creates and, second, that it is a dialectical process. Marx refines the dialectical process radically, but Hegel, before him, knew that it was a process of negativity. (Dialectic, 202) Hegel said that one objectifies oneself through labor. This is the first step of self-negation; then one transcends the alienation to become oneself. The process of transcending the alienation is where Marx departs from Hegel. One finds oneself, not through a philosophy which would say one was God the Absolute Universal Spirit, but through labor, the circumstances of which were changed in finding that one is a member of a class. This finding of the species creativity is real consciousness; this in turn allows the labor and its fruits to produce and increase humankind. Hegel never envisaged such a humanistic circle in which we return to ourselves devoid of the Absolute; shorn of it, humanity shines forth *nudo e crudo*.

Marx on the Last Chapter of Hegel's *Phenomenology*

Hegel thought that the object of the human thinking process was self-consciousness, in which one knew or objectified the self. In referring to Hegel's epistemology, Marx would say that Hegel's men and women knew only the self and referred only to it, whether they were thinking about it or extramental reality. They were never in contact with either, in Marx's estimation, since they were embroiled in an epistemology in which the idea replicated the sensuous world and not vice versa—as Marx wanted it. Marx said that self-consciousness was a product of human nature, but Hegel would have it the other way around: consciousness created things, both the ego and the outside world. Thus, Marx said that all Hegel knew was a self produced abstractly; it was "purely abstract egoism raised to the level of thought." (Dialectic, 204) For Hegel, alienation meant only alienation of self-consciousness and no more. For Marx, alienation, as alienation of self-consciousness, was an expression of real alienation reflected in knowledge. Hegel thought that what Marx would later see as real alienation was merely phenomenal, and hence only an illusion. Marx rejected that illusion-based alienation. Hegel's whole phenomenology was based on that and he taught it *ex professo*. Marx said that he was after real alienation, not the illusory kind of the philosopher. For Hegel, self-appropriation—the finding of the self—is the return of the object to the self; to appropriate the self, it was necessary to reappropriate the object. In repossessing the object of thought, one came to own the self. But this was to "objectify" the person, who was essentially subject for Marx.

Reification—"thinghood" in Hegel's jargon—means the process of being the object through becoming one with all the moments of going out to the object. This makes the object "intrinsically a spiritual" being for Marx, wherein the self apprehends all the determinations as itself. Marx says that it is neither real humanity nor real nature which becomes the thing in Hegel's concept of self-consciousness. So, self-consciousness as "thinghood" is alienation for Marx. Thus does Marx reject Hegel's and all idealism. (Dialectic, 205) If self-consciousness creates an abstraction such as "thinghood" in its negation (alienation), then Marx says that it is not a real thing at all, neither independent nor external to the mind. It is a "mere construct."

Therefore, Marx says that all of Hegel's energy did not set up something permanent, but something apparent only for an instant. What Hegel achieves in doing this is not to establish something true and lasting; rather, he establishes the act of validating the self (it is "self-confirming"), and this is over in an instant. Such a person is "abstract man," and as such, Marx rejects him. Real humanity is corporeal for Marx. For him, the objects are really there; one does not create them, but one's mind merely confirms that they are there as "an objective, natural being." (Dialectic, 206) Marx says that his own philosophy is a naturalism or humanism and only it can "comprehend the process of world history," not Hegel's ideality and not Feuerbach's materialism. Naturalism—humanism—confirms whatever is true in idealism and materialism, however.

Hence, any being who is purely mental—non-objective—is a non-being for Marx. Man and woman are natural beings. "He is a being for himself, and, therefore, a *species being*," which means that one must express oneself—be authentic—in being and in thought. For Hegel, knowing means the negation of objectivity; to be objective is self-annulling. Marx rejects this "object" as a negative entity that is self-alienating; that is, to go out makes one exist "out there," and this means that one becomes alien to the self. Therefore, Hegel's arguments are an assemblage of the illusions of speculation, and this for two reasons: (1) consciousness is at home in its object and not offended by it—alienated—as Hegel says it is; Feuerbach says that consciousness is at home in its object, and Marx agrees with this; (2) Hegel's criticism is false criticism—just apparent and not real—and this leads Marx to his first major criticism of religion. (Dialectic, 207–10 passim)

Marx's Critique of Religion

When one has arrived at self-consciousness one has done so by negating the spiritual world (superseding it, in Hegel's terms); by finding that it is a "product of self-alienation, he then finds a confirmation of himself in *religion as religion*." (Dialectic, 210) For Marx, this is the root of Hegel's "*false* positivism" and "apparent criticism." Feuerbach rightly says that

26

Hegel first posits religion; then he negates it; and then he reestablishes both religion and theology. This is a compromise on Hegel's part. He waffled on both religion and politics, and his argument failed precisely here, in Marx's estimation. In the third and sixth steps of his phenomenology, Hegel implies that self-conscious humanity "recognized and superseded the spiritual world . . . then confirms it again in this alienated form and presents it as his true existence; he reestablishes it and claims to be at home in his other being . . . thus is at home with unreason as such." Marx says that if Hegel were correct, then a life of knowledge or one in law or politics, for example, would be that in which one lived a life in contradiction to itself; it would be self-negation, a dead end, not just dialectically, but also in reality. So, Marx says, when one knows oneself in religion, it is not the true self that one knows, but alienated self-consciousness. Religion, then, does not confirm Marx's self, since consciousness of *his* self is his essence, and one does not know this reality in religion. Hence, Marx says that religion must be abolished and superseded if one is to know oneself at all in reality. (Dialectic, 210f.)

Therefore, for Marx, the negation of negation should confirm true being (reality) by getting rid of illusion; but Hegel confirms illusory being, or self-alienating being, even as he tried to deny (negate) it. Religion does not exist outside our minds. But Hegel's mind is the quintessential religious mind for Marx; it is far more brilliant than other minds, but prototypically religious, and it turns itself into a real subject, a thing existing within us. This is definitely not so for Marx.

Marx thinks of religion as no more than a moment in philosophy—a philosophical mode—as it moves along in its dialectical processes. These modes do not perdure long, but dissolve and engender another mode. This mode in turn does not exist in isolation from its roots and from what it engenders. (Dialectic, 212f.)

Hence, religious existence is, for Marx, a philosophical moment in the philosophy of religion, just as political existence is a philosophical moment in the philosophy of politics. None of these things exists apart from Hegel's dialectics. Therefore, they do not exist outside the mind; so they are not real, they are illusions. Thus, Marx rightly says that if his only religious existence is to be had when he is doing the philosophy of religion, then no actual (extramental) religious experience, and, a fortiori, no actual religious people, exists. For Marx, Hegel's negation of religion is really the rejection of a category of thought, not that of a real extramental being. Thought imagines itself to be a sensuous reality. But it is not so. Religion is, therefore, a moment of thought for Marx. Hegel's critique of religion is of something he self-projected, not something "out there" in its own right. Religion never touched reality in Hegel's philosophy, as far as Marx was concerned; what it touched was "dogmatics" as an object of thought. The ultimate confirmation that the religious person finds in Hegel's construct is, likewise, an experience out of touch with reality. It experiences nothing "out there," but only something "in here," something that one creates by the self and for the self. Marx rejected this completely. He wanted us to be in touch with reality, and reality was sensuous, empirical. It was not idealism, then, but positivism that undergirded Marx's philosophy, his metaphysics.

As we all know, Hegel's dialectics was a process of thesis, antithesis (or negation), and synthesis (or the negation of the negation). The final phase made something positive of the second, negative phase. Hence, something of good is saved from the two previous phases in the third and final synthetic phase, which brings the positive out of negating the negative. This is the critical phase of Hegel's dialectical thrust toward the real. He calls this moment supersession. Here, the alienated (negated) thing is reabsorbed into itself; objective being is appropriated by the subject. Marx follows this dialectical process with the docility of a believer; this leads him to the most critical point of his critique of religion: atheism. The negation of religion is the negation of its heart, which is God. And what comes forth is not Hegel's renewed religion, but Marx's "theoretical humanism" on the one hand and communism on the other—an anthropology and a politics where before there had been theology and a sociopolitical structure flowing inexorably out of a religion that preserved the power elite who exploited the poor. Communism negates the egoism of "civil man's" private property, and atheism negates the egoism of his private religious experiences, which cut him off from his species. Both communism and atheism, then, afford one true consciousness: that one is a member of a species, that one is aware of one's solidarity with one's brothers and sisters. This negation of both religion and private property returns us to ourselves; we take possession once again of our true human life. Alienation is, thus, negated in humankind's emergence to reality. So the annulment of religion ultimately produces what Marx called practical humanism, a "humanism mediated to itself by the annulment of religion." (Dialectic, 212f.)

The thesis Marx uses to negate Hegel's philosophy of religion is his rejection of Hegel's concept that the mind is in touch with reality when it is a religious mind. His antithesis is the negation of religion by means of his practical humanism, which renders religion null and void, since people have finally become themselves and won't want to leave their newfound humanity. Marx begins the second stage by, quite simply, saying that, in religion, the mind is only in touch with itself, not with the real. Thus, the negation of religion is the first stage of humanism. To turn that negation into something positive, it is necessary for a third movement—a supersession—to happen in order that we be allowed to finish the process of self-creation. The negation of the negation criticizes the newborn humanism as only a reaction to religion; the gist of the criticism is that the neonate is a negative human being, as yet. More has to happen to finish the process of self-creation and turn the person into a real, positive human being. Marx calls this "self-originating positive humanism." Therefore, both atheism and communism are in touch with reality, which, for Marx, is the reality of anthropology on the one hand and the reality of economics on the other. The illusions of Hegel's abstractions alienated humankind from itself. The one took away one's humanity through the egoism of religion. The other took away one's nature by alienating the fruit of labor from the laborer. In both religion and bourgeois capitalism, human nature was passive; it was something one received, not something one achieved by one's efforts. Not so with Marx. Human nature was the end-product of humanistic striving to overcome false consciousness and egoism. Marx wanted no part in a static view of our nature. We are active and dynamic. Hegel's dialectical process revealed this to Marx, but his own ruthless honesty was necessary to allow him to tear away the dogmatic skepticisms that he felt had fed humankind its illusions for so long a time. Hence, for Marx, atheism and communism were not a return to a "primitive simplicity," but the first historical epiphanies of human nature. (Dialectic, 213)

Hegel's negations had not inverted things to get at truth and reality, so Marx set out to flip things over on their backs and turn humankind into something humane. Because the negation that produced us was based, not on Lockean empirical knowledge, but on Hegelian abstractions, Marx saw it as a process confirming the unreality of religion and private property instead of the reality of humankind. Hegel was dealing with the symptom, which was religion, not the illness, which was humankind not in possession of itself as a human and economic entity. For Marx, God and private property constitute the loss of the self. Marx criticizes Hegel's logic, since the latter thinks it is truly human simply because it moves one

29

into the divine, absolute Spirit where the knower realizes oneself as God; one becomes absolute self-consciousness in the realization that one is divine. Marx maintained that our real nature becomes a symbol (predicate) for an unreal person and unreal nature itself. So people, who are really subjects for Marx, become inverted into a predicate object for Hegel. Human nature becomes a mystical relation in which the self never emerges from itself; that is, the subject becomes the object, which is negated, only to become the subject again. But Marx says it is an absolute subject (God) that Hegel has created, and this is "an unceasing revolving within itself." In Marx's estimation, it becomes a "subjectivity reaching beyond the object"; and transcendence is out for Marx.

For Hegel, our real expression is an abstraction, which makes it a negation in Marx's estimation, and he rejects it as being literally unreal. The next phase of Hegel's dialectical search for human nature, the logic of which ends with humanity becoming the absolute, is the negation of the negation phase of the process. Marx thinks that the person who emerges is vacuous. Hence, he says, concrete, sensuous self-objectification is, therefore, "reduced to a mere abstraction, [to] absolute negativity." Hegel reifies this abstraction to give it the appearance of an independent being. But Marx says that that is all it is, an appearance. He concludes that Hegel's person is not a reality at all, but only an *ens rationis*, a logical being made out of whole cloth. Hegel has detached the human spirit from "real spirit and real nature." (Dialectic, 214f.) Hence, Hegel's real contribution to philosophy, in Marx's estimation, is to conclude to determinate, general, fixed thought forms. These thought forms are divorced from nature and spirit; that is, they are illusions. In this way does Marx conclude that God, too, is an illusion. Here, Marx gives the highest accolade to Hegel in seeing the latter's construct as the ultimate God-concept, and in doing it in, Marx feels that he has done in God. But all he has achieved is to disprove Hegel's *notion* of God, not *God*. If Hegel's thought is circular, beginning with humankind and ending with the apotheosis of human nature, then Marx's thought is guilty of the same in beginning with Hegel's God and ending with, not humankind, but the negation of Hegel and thinking that that is humankind. In negating Hegel, Marx retrieved us; that is his achievement—and it is no mean achievement. He destroyed Hegel's idealism and gave us an analytical tool with which to strip away the culture-specific notions of religion, man, woman, economics and so on. This was quite a breakthrough, but to think that he has destroyed God in wiping out the illusion of God is an act of hermeneutical hubris on Marx's part. To think that negating Hegel is to set up a real anthropology is to stop when the job is half finished. Man and woman are secular, but what does that mean? Marx never says, because he negates transcendence, which consists in asking and solving just such questions. He cuts himself off from the concluding anthropological questions, contenting himself to stay in the foyer rather than admit the possibility that there was a house behind his critical entranceway.

His critique of Hegel is devastating when he says that the latter's "absolute idea" has, itself, to be superseded. It has to abandon itself and go on in an endless skein, ultimately beginning the whole thing all over again from scratch. This process of moments negating previous moments so empties us of reality that we arrive at what Marx calls the exact opposite of human nature. Thus, he would say that the category of the supernatural is not only otiose, but also mischievous. For Marx, Hegel has shown that his logic is "nothing for itself, that the absolute idea is [also] nothing for itself, that only *nature* is something." (Dialectic, 215) Further, Hegel's absolute idea is, for Marx, an intuition, i.e., an abstraction without empirical foundation or content. It is no more than a hunch. Abstraction, then, became an abandonment to intuition. Marx says that Hegel moves from logic to the philosophy of nature, which is no more than moving from abstraction to intuition. The philosopher, driven by lack of content in his idea, went from the abstract to, not a conclusion, but an intuition. This is totally unacceptable to Marx, who would have only verifiable science, not romantic religious intuition parading as philosophy. Hegel as thinker is alienated from himself because his thought is alienated "from his natural and human life." So, "the abstract thinker who had committed himself to intuition, intuits nature abstractly." Not only is God an *ens rationis* in Hegel's thought, but so is nature itself. If this is so, then so is humankind itself only a figment. Marx is an anthropologist in carrying out his critique of Hegel and religion—the critique of the one is the critique of the other—and the loss of human nature is an unforgivable crime. Marx rightly indicts Hegel for it. Hegel's logical creatures "shuttle endlessly back and forth in [themselves] . . . [but are] simply *abstractions* from natural characteristics." (Dialectic, 216f.)

Religion and Hegel: The Critique Continued

In 1844, Marx continued his critique of Hegel, and, a fortiori, of religion, in writing "Contribution to the Critique of Hegel's Philosophy of Self

Right." In it, he starts to focus his sights directly on religion, rather than indirectly, as he did in his criticism of Hegel's dialectic. Marx begins by delivering himself of the unforgettable aphorism "the criticism of religion is the premise of all criticism"; and if one refutes celestial error, one has refuted profane error. (Contribution, 43) Marx's method is to begin to shape his answer by properly shaping the question—to frame the one well is to go far in accomplishing the other.[3] He begins by stripping away the heavenly, the transcendental, and the sacred. In their place he leaves the earthly, the sensuous, and the profane; in this way he means to find human nature. He does that at once in the second critical essay on Hegel, in which he says that humanity found only its own reflection in its search for the supernatural. And this reflection is a "non-human being" that is a semblance of reality, not the real thing. Hence, he sees God as the imago hominis (image of humankind) and not vice versa. He has inverted things at once and thereby shaped the answers that will flow from his defenestration of God.

The basis of his criticism is that men and women make religion and not vice versa. When we are lost and have not found ourselves, our consciousness is religious consciousness, which Marx says is "an inverted world consciousness" produced by the state and society, both of which are "an inverted world." Further,

> religion is the general theory of this world, its encyclopedic compendium, its logic in popular form, its spiritual point d'honneur, its enthusiasm, its moral sanction, its solemn complement, its general basis of consolation and justification. It is the *fantastic realization* of the human being inasmuch as the *human being* possesses no true reality. The struggle against religion is, therefore, indirectly a struggle against *that world* whose spiritual aroma is religion.

Religion is a halo around the world's suffering, changing not a bit of it, but merely "sanctifying" it with the false consciousness of giving it an incorrect—unreal—meaning. Therefore, religious criticism is a critique of the suffering in "this vale of tears." Marx goes on to make one of his most unforgettable and telling statements:

> Religious suffering is at the same time an *expression* of real suffering and a *protest* against real suffering. Religion is the sigh of the oppressed creature, the sentiment of a heartless world, and the soul of soulless conditions. It is the opium of the people. (Contribution, 43f.)

32

Thus, he damns religion at its best with faint praise. It is a noble but illusory protest about the human condition. Marx knew that religion had set out to confront the human condition; that, indeed, the starting place for religions is the acknowledgment and confrontation of our pain—with God's aid in theistic religions and just on one's own power in Buddhism and Vedanta Hinduism. Marx knew that religion purported to be about the human condition, but he rejected the claim, since it does not do anything important or lasting about our sad estate. Instead, it merely narcotizes one with religious peace. And when one awakes from the religious dream, the world is just the same. Religion does not change anything. Marx's religious criticism, then, intends to denude one of one's illusions and thereby allow one to regain one's reason, "so that he will revolve about himself as his own true sun." The center of Marx's world is humankind, not God or the supernatural. (Contribution, 43f.) Religion is what happens to one when one knows no better. Marx means to establish no truth; history does that by itself. He means only to declare what history is doing; that is the truth and he is its prophet. History will establish the "truth of this world" by demythologizing it of the supernatural world. It comes down to a battle between history and the supernatural, or history and myth, or, in the terms of the Catholic and the Protestant Reformations, between the natural and the supernatural. The role philosophy plays in this drama is as a servant for history; it shows self-alienation in its human mode once the self-alienation of the sacred has been stripped away by criticism. History is doing it, but philosophy shows what is being done; criticism does not so much change things as keep out of the way of the changes that take place inexorably. Religion and false consciousness, like bourgeois capitalist systems, stand in the way; so criticism shows them for the illusions they are. Marx opposes economics to the human situation; this means that he opposes it to Original Sin. Philosophy becomes, then, an examination of conscience.

He concludes: "Thus the criticism of heaven is transformed into the criticism of earth, the *criticism of religion* into the *criticism of law,* and the *criticism of theology* into the *criticism of politics.*" Criticism secularizes all without so much as evoking a bit of human passion in the critic. He says: "Criticism is not a passion of the head, but the head of passion." (Contribution, 44) Marx's inversion, brought about by employing the rhetorical device chiasmus as his methodology, becomes both a philosophy and a pamphleteer's cudgel for him. But one wonders if it does not suffer from overkill, causing Marx to fall into the same trap that he saw Hegel fall into: namely, playing epistemological head games—and all questions of philosophy ultimately become epistemological in German philosophy. It appears that Marx used words in a procrustean way to force realities like human rights, which were too fractious for his system, into rather pat solutions. Marx had set up a paradigm, and paradigms are, by definition, major problem-solving models that more or less force problems into their boxes in order to solve them.[4] Over and over again we shall see him invert things with a well-turned chiasmic phrase that flips them upside down and inside out. I will return to the question of inversion when I take up the "Jewish Question," later in this chapter. Suffice it to say that Marx's system makes the totality of the sacred give way to the profane, God to humankind, theology to politics and economics.

Religion is often used to impart its benediction to gross injustices. For Marx, society is a series of fragments that are in adversary relationships, the parts of which "are forced to recognize and acknowledge this fact of being *dominated, governed* and *possessed*, as a concession from heaven." The critic, then, must awaken consciousness and exacerbate his own and his contemporaries' shame by publishing it; and oddly enough, "the nation must be taught to be terrified of itself, in order to give it courage." (Contribution, 46f.) Germany is leaving its past, and Marx says that it should be done gladly by all Germans. This is so since "the last stage of a world-historical formation is comedy. The Greek gods already once mortally wounded in Aeschylus's tragedy *Prometheus Bound*, had to endure a second death, a comic death, in Lucian's dialogues." (Contribution, 50) He opposes the peoples of prehistory, with their myth life, to the posthistorical Germans of his day, with their philosophical life—the one lived in myth and the other lived in a philosophical fog, an intellectual illusion. So, the alternative is to abolish philosophy; this will mean no loss, since "you cannot abolish philosophy without realizing it." (Contribution, 50) His praxis philosophy, put into action politically in Germany, did just that; in abolishing philosophy he and his colleagues installed a new philosophy in the very dissolution of the old one. The theoretical philosophers held that no abolition was necessary; Marx thoroughly disagrees with this. Hegel's flaw is in his restoration of philosophy (which is a code word for religion) in the third stage of the dialectic, instead of leaving it lie, destroyed.

Praxis is the real world for Marx; it is a world of material force in which "the arm of criticism cannot replace the criticism of arms." This means that only material force can overthrow material force. Theory becomes a material force when it takes power over the masses; this means that even theory is a praxis when it becomes an agent for change, for living in the flow of world history. Marx says that the only way theory can become praxis, and take power over the masses, is to use ad hominem arguments; for him, these radical arguments are the very roots of reason. The roots of people are themselves; so to get at humankind one must go to the roots. Reason strikes at the real person by criticism, by ad hominem arguments meant to expose the realities of injustices and the reality of the flow of history, consciousness of which is reality consciousness. We are rooted in ourselves. Telling us that abolishes religion and takes possession of the masses. Criticism is a praxis in this first movement of Marx's program; but in being practical (political, conscious that one is a "species person," a member of a class), one has exposed one's human roots. Religion falls because it is no longer needed; its theory held the masses when they did not see the way the world really moves, or better, the way the real world moves. Seeing it frees us from the trammels of religious theory in the praxis of politics and economics; this seeing in praxis is, itself, a theory. Hence, praxis abolishes the deductive, preconceived theory of philosophy and religion and in its fall establishes a new theory.

Therefore, in Marx, German theory is radical because it abolishes religion: "the criticism of religion ends with the doctrine that *man is the supreme being for man*. It ends, therefore, *with the categorical imperative to overthrow all those conditions* in which man is an abased, enslaved, abandoned, contemptible being." (Contribution, 50–52 passim)

Germany's theoretical emancipation took place during the Reformation, when "Luther shattered the faith in authority by restoring the authority of faith. He transformed the priests into laymen by turning laymen into priests. He liberated man from external religiosity by making religiosity the innermost essence of man." (Contribution, 53) Thus, Marx thought Protestantism posed the problem correctly even though it did not solve it. The laity struggled, not with the external priest, but with their own internal priestly nature. Luther had done in his day what Marx found in his day was the right method for facing up to the problems: invert all things; laicize and secularize them—and the one is really the other. The monk had made all Germans into their own popes, thus emancipating all—the privileged princes, the priests, and the laity, together. Emancipation of this kind would secularize all things and in so doing free property to be confiscated, not only the property of the church, but that of lay society as well. (Contribution, 58)

Marx chose the proletariat—the class that owned nothing but its *proles* (its children)—as the representative class that embodied all the evils of modern society. These people had "radical claims" and were "a total loss of humanity . . . which can only redeem . . . [themselves] by a total redemption of humanity." The praxis of Marx is his critique of religion, and the critique of Marx comes to its climax in what he says is the program for the proletariat. This class has been denuded of all private property, and this is no bad thing. It should be the state of all in principle, which is theirs in fact: all things should be held in common, since this one class holds nothing as its own. Philosophy, then, finds its matter in the proletariat, and the proletariat finds its thought in philosophy. Thus, "the emancipation of Germany will be the emancipation of man. Philosophy is the head of this emancipation and the proletariat its heart. Philosophy can only be realized by the abolition of the proletariat, and the proletariat can only be abolished by the realization of philosophy." (Contribution, 59) Religion's fall is simultaneous with the fall of the false consciousness of metaphysics, thus freeing history to liberate humankind's nature: both economics and humankind become communitarian in the process. We become in history what we are by nature: species persons aware by praxis, by experience, that we are members of the human race.

Marx's Critique and His Sociology of Knowledge

In his Thesis VII on Feuerbach, Marx says that it is not religious sentiment that produces men; it is men who produce the sentiment.[5] Marx's sociology of knowledge plays a heavy role in his thought, and particularly in his criticism of religion. In the essay he wrote in collaboration with Friedrich Engels entitled "German Ideology,"[6] Marx states a key concept: "Consciousness is therefore from the start a product of society, and it remains such as long as men exist at all." Further, a person's first consciousness is an overpowering one in which one submits to one's surroundings as to a god. This nature "worship" is determined by the form of society and the society, by the nature worship. He adds, "It is not consciousness that determines life, but life that determines consciousness." (German Ideology, 74f). And history

36

does not explain practice by the idea but explains the formation of ideas by material practice. Accordingly . . . [it is] not criticism but revolution that is the motive force of history as well as of religion, philosophy and all other forms of theory. [And] . . . history does not end by dissolving itself in "self-consciousness" as "the spirit of the spirit" but that there is present in it at every stage a material result . . . that circumstances, therefore, make man just as much as man makes circumstances. (German Ideology, 78)

We must rediscover history in this principle of knowledge. Further, the religious conception of history is one that "supposes religious man as primitive man from whom all history proceeds, and in its imagination it sets religious fantasy production in the place of the real production of the means of subsistence and of life itself." (German Ideology, 80) Hence, Marx and Engels state that religious consciousness is a false consciousness; and real consciousness is a sensuous one, i.e., one taken from the experience of life in the world. Marx blasted Feuerbach for this very failure: "The chief defect of all hitherto existing materialism—that of Feuerbach included—is that the thing (Geganstand), reality, sensuousness, is conceived only in the form of the object (Objekt) or of contemplation (Anschauung), but not as human sensuous activity, practice, not subjectively." (Marx and Engels, Thesis I, 69)

This sensuousness is used in the furtherance of Marx and Engels' sociology of knowledge in the "Manifesto of the Communist Party." In it they say:

What else does the history of ideas prove, than that intellectual production changes its character in proportion as material production is changed? The ruling ideas of each age have ever been the ideas of its ruling class . . . that the dissolution of the old ideas keeps even pace with the dissolution of the old conditions of existence.

And:

There are, besides, eternal truths, such as Freedom, Justice, etc., that are common to all states of society. But communism abolishes eternal truths, it abolishes all religion, and all morality, instead of constituting them on a new basis; it therefore acts in contradiction to all past historical experience.

The old social consciousness cannot vanish except by the dissolution of class antagonism.

As the parson has ever gone hand in hand with the landlord, so has Clerical Socialism with Feudal Socialism. Nothing is easier than to give Christian asceticism a Socialist tinge. . . . Christian socialism is but the holy water with which the priest consecrates the heart-burnings of the aristocrat. (Marx and Engels, 88)

Marx says that religion

is the self-consciousness and self-feeling of man, who either has not yet found himself or has already lost himself again. But *man* is no abstract being, squatting outside the world. Man is the *world of man*, the state, society. This state, this society produce religion, *a perverted world consciousness, because they are a perverted world*. Religion is the general theory of the world. (Marx and Engels, 263)

Robert Nisbet states that Marx based this theory of religion on Feuerbach, who maintained that suffering or false teaching impelled us to project what is basically human onto God. Marx said that economic forms are the basis of life, not religious ones. His parting shot was, "The demand to give up the illusion about its condition is the demand to give up a condition which needs illusion."[7] Marx's sociology of knowledge has, thus, relegated religious knowledge to an epistemological "Fantasy Land"; it is not only a knowledge of nothing that exists in the real world, but also a pernicious knowledge. It can hurt people, since it is knowledge derived, not from the benign world of the goodness of liberal priests, but from the perverted world of religion, politics, and economics in which they dwell. One's world forms one's consciousness. The program he proposes is to change that world so that consciousness will be changed. It is not only a political-economic praxis that will change the world to a just place in which knowledge reflects reality, but an educational praxis as well. When a Marxist regime takes over a country, therefore, it educates the populace to its version of reality. It is much like Freud's desire to do the same for his elite cadre. However, unlike Freud, who totally repudiated Marx's utopianism as being an illusion, it is to be an elite of the proletariat. The reality has shown Freud to be correct: the proletarian elites of the Soviet Union, China, North Vietnam, and Cambodia have distinguished themselves for feathering their own nests and turning their countries into charnel houses in the purges necessary for this educational phase of the revolution.

Marx's sociology of knowledge came down firmly on the side of one's thought processes being a product of one's culture and environment. One changed thought, however, not with another thought, as Hegel had sought to do, but through praxis. Change the world and one's thought changes perforce.

The Jewish Question

In 1843, Marx wrote two essays in answer to Bruno Bauer's assertion that the Jews, lagging one stage behind the dominant Christian culture, needed to be baptized in order to be liberated and catch up with the rest of society. The first essay was *"Die Judenfrage"* (The Jewish Question). The second was titled *"Bruno Bauer, Die Fahigkeit der Heutigen Juden und Christen, Frie zu Werden"* (Bruno Bauer, The Capacity of Contemporary Jews and Christians to Become Free). In both, Marx hoped to put behind him not only the Jewish Question, but also the question of religion itself. After writing these essays he did not labor much longer on the question of religion. Most of what he had to say of moment on the question was written by the end of the next year; most of what he had to say on religion at all would be over by 1850. Thus, already in 1843, Marx thought the "Jewish Question" was a non-problem. He refused, in fact, to be plagued with Jew-baiting garbed in the respectability of academic robes as the "Jewish Question." This latter problem had oppressed Disraeli, Heine, and Lassalle all through their careers. He had no time for it in his.

Marx's treatment is not as brilliant and profound as were his critiques of Hegel and the latter's religious philosophy. These two essays were somewhat shallow and dull by comparison, but they tie up the package of his religious criticism, so I shall outline what they have to say in order to complete the treatment of Marx on religion.[8]

The whole problem of the Jew is the problem of humanity for Bauer and Marx. The Jew sought political emancipation so as to be able to function in the newly wrought secular societies, the best of which were England and the United States. Germany and France posed special problems, since they had been, for centuries, professedly Christian states. Both Bauer and Marx sought to make the Jew not only assimilate; they wanted him to disappear. *This* is the problem not only the Jew but any religious person faces in the wonders of the new secular humanism: How to live as man and woman, and how to live religiously—problems that are still unsolved and that are perhaps unresolvable.

Marx's method, again, was to turn theological questions into secular ones; wherever there was God, Marx made a human; wherever the sacred, he made it profane; wherever the civil, he made it political; whichever religion, it became law; wherever theology, politics; wherever heaven, earth; wherever magic and supernatural (i.e., religion), history. He applied this method to religion and its *Heilsgeschichte* (Salvation History) and concluded that it was superstition; so religion turns history into superstition and Marx would invert it, turning religious history into secular history.

Marx opens "The Jewish Question" by restating Bauer's assertion that the Jews demand what the Christians haven't gotten for themselves: freedom. No German is free. Bauer barbs the Jews for asking the Christians to abandon their religious prejudice when the Jews wish to retain their own—any religion is a prejudice. It is well to watch both Bauer and Marx fit the question and then dispose of it. By using prejudice in the contemporary denigrating sense of narrowness and mindlessness, instead of the medieval one of the root of one's transcendental consciousness—forming one's ideas of the one, good and true through the inculcation of a particular ideal—he throws the debate into his own court and all but wins it at the outset. Already the Jew is reprobate for having a prejudice. (The Question, 3) Bauer adds that no Christian state can emancipate any Jew until it gives up its Christianity and becomes politically emancipated itself. (The Question, 4)

All that the Christian state can do is what it has been doing: namely, allow Jews the privilege of cutting themselves off from the mainstream of German life in their ghettos. Thus, Christians must make Jews particular (ghettoed) and Jews must make themselves foreigners to their German neighbors. The essence of the Jew is being a chosen people. This must be foresworn before they can shuck off their alienation. Marx quietly quotes his old mentor, Bauer, waiting to spring the trap on what he considered a good, but flawed, train of thought. So, Marx quotes Bauer to the effect that Jews cannot demand emancipation on the grounds of religion, since theirs is "the mortal enemy of the state religion"; nor can they demand to be citizens, since Germany, as yet, had none; nor can they as human beings, for there are none in Germany.

Bauer then launches into his critique of Judaism. Like Marx after him, Bauer solves the question by posing it correctly. Thus, the proper study of the Jewish Question is the solution of it. He says that the solution in brief is: "We have to emancipate ourselves before we can emancipate others." (The Question, 5) The Jew has been in constant religious conflict with the

Christian. The way to obviate that is by making religion, as such, impossible. Bauer then uses the common nineteenth-century argument drawn from Darwin and applied to anthropology. Religion is but a state in human development; and he hastens to add, we are beyond that stage now. The dialectical forces at work are religious prejudice and political emancipation; Bauer stipulates that the state must become as emancipated from religion as the Jew is from Judaism. He says that if the Jew were to become a citizen, it would be a second-class one, since the citizen is a universal person and the Jew is, by nature, a particular (egoistic) one. (The Question, 5)

Bauer criticizes France, which was then in the midst of a national political debate over the emancipation of the Jews, for offering only the appearance of freedom, while, in fact, the Jews have none. And the Jews, for their part, would have to foreswear their Jewish observances—in particular the sabbath—in order to participate in matters of state and fulfill their obligations to it. Both Jew and Christian demand that they retain the privilege of fulfilling religious obligations when they conflict with state functions. Thus, all religious privileges must be taken off the law books and any observance become a strictly private matter. To abolish both the Jewish and the Christian sabbaths would effectively abolish the respective religions. Bauer concludes that the Jew in particular and people in general must renounce their religion to be emancipated as citizens. (The Question, 7)

Marx moves in here to radicalize the debate. Bauer doesn't go far enough in asking who should be emancipated. Marx would ask, "What kind of emancipation is involved?" In sum, Marx will argue that Bauer's mistake was to negate (criticize) only a Christian state and not the state as such. Bauer asked whether the Jew had the right to ask for emancipation. Marx uses his inversion device to ask "the converse question: from the standpoint of *political* emancipation can the Jew be required to abolish Judaism, or man be asked to abolish religion?" (The Question, 8) He says that Germany has no political state, since it has not secularized as yet. It has only a theological state, so all questions of criticism reduce one to going around in theological circles. Thus, when the Jewish Question is asked, it is always resolved within a theological paradigm. France is better equipped to ask the question but not much better. Because it is a constitutional state it poses the problem from a constitutional paradigm; but it possesses only a semblance of secularity. It is the United States that

41

serves as Marx's model secular, religionless state in theory and practice. Only there does the Jewish Question become "a truly *secular* question." (The Question, 8f.)

Bauer's critique fails when his question persists in being theological. The United States has ceased to take a theological attitude toward religion and has become emancipated from it. It takes a political attitude toward it, allowing criticism to become truly political (secularized and humanized) rather than theologized. Marx reveals himself as holding to an ideal in recognizing the goodness of the U.S. position that "no one in the United States believes that a man without religion cannot be an honest man." (The Question, 9) I shall return to this in chapter 3; suffice it to remark on his love for basic human decency. He remarks on the preeminence of religiosity in the United States but notes that no constitution, state or federal, imposes that on anyone. But wherever religion persists in a state, even privately, it is a revelation of that state's lack of full secularization. Marx calls it "secular narrowness." He constantly opposes the universal "species man," aware of his bonds with his brothers and sisters, to the particular, egoistic "civil man," who, at his best, is merely out for himself and his class.

Marx sets up his thesis at the same time as he criticizes Bauer. "The *political* emancipation of the Jew or the Christian—of the *religious* man in general—is the *emancipation* of the state from Judaism, Christianity, and *religion* in general." (The Question, 10) In order to be free, the state must recognize no religion, "affirming itself purely and simply as a state."

But the political emancipation of the state does not free the individual human from it. In the secular state, one attains the freedom to be a universal, i.e., political, human. In one's private life, however—if it be religious—one is a civil person. In being so, one loses one's species nature to the degree that one is religious. Political life cannot emancipate the core of the individual; only people can free themselves, and that only be renouncing religion to free their human cores to become what they are by nature: communal beings. (The Question, 11–13 passim) Civil society is a sink of egoism, a *"bellum omnium contra omnes"* (a war of everyone against everyone else). It is one class against another, one set of vested interests against opposing interests. Religion is fissiparous; the fragmentation of society into sectarian groups is an example of how strictly private religion is. The United States is the prime example of Protestantism—which is the Christian religion for Marx—in operation. It has what he calls an infinite capacity to fragment, thus weakening society. Thus, he makes the sacred versus the profane dialectic into one in which the political realm wars on the civil, privatized one. (The Question, 14f.)

Therefore, Jews must go through the same routine as do Protestants and any citizens: they must decompose into Jews and citizens. Religion must be destroyed in the same way that one destroys private property; whether it takes the tax gatherer or the executioner to do it, it must be done. The perfection of the Christian state is the atheistic state in fluxing through the dialectical oppositions Marx calls "permanent revolution." The core of religion is humankind, and that remains the reality of both religion and state. Thus, no Christian state is a real state; only a fully secularized state can truly be called a state. The core of the Christian is man and woman, and thus the core of any so-called Christian state is merely man and woman, not Christianity. Hence, any state that professes itself as Christian accepts as the core of humankind a chimera, an illusion, not a secular reality. Any such state is a "hypocritical state." Christians say that Christian states are perfect, but Marx calls them imperfect because "religion is its basis." All that Christians in such a state can have is "a political attitude towards religion and a religious attitude towards politics. It reduces political institutions and religion equally to mere appearances." (The Question, 17)

Bauer says that the Christian state demands that one submit to the authority of the Bible, to the supernatural, thus abolishing the secular and even the state itself. In a secular state, the nation would find its true existence in its leader. But in the Christian state, God imposes the leader and in doing so alienates that person from the people. Law becomes a direct revelation rather than the work of the people of the state. Local interests take over, and privileged classes must arise to care for them. Such a state would have to become like the Catholic Church, which Bauer sees as fully potent, reducing its members to "myrmidons," i.e., subordinates who execute orders without pity or protest. Criticism would put such a religious state into irresolvable conflict between the sacred and the profane. The only person in a Christian state who counts is the king, set apart—alienated—by God and essentially different from them. Hence, the "religious spirit cannot be really *secularized*." (The Question, 20) The dreams of Christians for human sovereignty are no more than fantasies in a Christian state, but they become realities in a fully secularized state. In such a state, religion becomes withdrawn and devoid of any terrestrial consequence; this is because it is purely an affair of the heart and thus essentially apart from the real workaday world. Thus, Bauer concludes, political emancipation would emancipate the state from religion, stripping it of its privileged status. (The Question, 20f.)

Marx rejects Bauer's criticism as missing the point. Bauer says that emancipation for the Jews would come in their emancipation from Judaism. Marx says, however, that the Jews never fully leave Judaism and that their political emancipation is not their human emancipation. The Jews demand civil rights without leaving their religion. Thus, they act politically while remaining Jews. Marx says that this is a logical impossibility. Political action can only come about by those who are humanly emancipated, not merely politically free; and really, they are no more than the appearance of free persons when they retain their Judaism. (The Question, 21) The Jews, as Jews, have no civil rights and cannot demand them, since they cannot act politically as yet. Only secularized persons can act politically because their cores have been cleansed of the dehumanizing taint of religion. Marx imposes on the Jews the necessity of undergoing a secular baptism in order to assimilate. In this he is no better than the Christians he opposes in their efforts to be "Christian" toward the Jews— i.e., to evangelize them.

Bauer says that even if the Jews can acquire civil rights in becoming politically emancipated, they cannot acquire the broader "rights of man." Marx allows Bauer to career through the French and North American documents on human freedoms in order to show that the Jews can't give what they don't have. If the rights are inalienable, they are so only by nature, and the Jews haven't attained their nature until they undergo the secular right of passage, expunging not religious Original Sin, but the Original Sin that is religion. No Jew and no Christian can confer such rights, since both are religious and in the state of "sacral sin," which can be removed only by secularization. Bauer says that one must sacrifice the "privilege of faith" in order to acquire human rights. The Jews can't acquire these rights, which were only discovered a few years before—in the 1790s in France and a few years before in the United States—since they did not participate in the struggle to discover and win them. Thus, the idea was not innate, although both the *Declaration of the Rights of Man* and the American Constitutions of Pennsylvania and New Hampshire declare them to be inalienable. Marx and Bauer see such rights— especially the right to be religious—as emanating from a civil soul, not a political one. As such, human rights are in need of a radical critique, which both Marx and Bauer are giving them. Human rights confer civil rights, and the latter are essentially egoistic. Hence, the rights so beloved

44

of both French and American societies are merely manifestations of unredeemed bourgeois and Christian souls. If the Jews want them, what they want is as tainted as what they would have to leave to get them, namely, their Judaism. (The Question, 22–31)

It seems to me that Marx is trying to set up a state that doesn't recognize what really is meant by the theological category Original Sin, which really is not a sin at all, but a code for the human condition. It is endemic to the Marxist mentality, particularly the humanistic one, that it comes down firmly on the side of the innocence of human beings by trying to strip away the pernicious accretions of Judaism and Christianity of every stripe to get at what Rousseau and both the French and the American founders of modern democracy affirmed: that there is an innocence at the core of our nature. Where Bauer and Marx diverge from the republicans is in their affirmation that that nature is communitarian and not individualistic; that humankind in the pure state is a "species man," not a civil one; that "he" is at "his" deepest level aware of and desirous of being "for the other fellow."

In his second essay on the Jewish Question, "Bruno Bauer, The Capacity of the Present-day Jews and Christians to Become Free," Marx again applies his method of inversion of the religious categories of God, man and woman, theology, and so on so he can convert them into secular ones like man, woman, law, politics, and economics. He cites Bauer for erring in making the question of the religions a religious question. Bauer fashioned his question in terms of salvation and made political emancipation seem like salvation. It is a secular problem, however, and to posit it as such allows the situation to be seen devoid of religious illusion. (Second Bauer, in *Early Writings*, 32f.) Thus, "the critical study of the Jewish is the answer to the Jewish question." Put in purely secular terms, the Jews, and a fortiori Christianity—a Jewish derivative—come down to this: the profane basis of the Jews is "practical need, self interest." Their worldly cult is "huckstering"; their worldly God is money. For the age to be free of the Jewish "hustle" and their "money-god," we would emancipate the world of not only the Jew, but also the Christian and the Christian's secular arm, the banker. Marx wants to emancipate the Jews by making the "Jew impossible." Thus, "in the final analysis, the *emancipation* of the Jews is the emancipation of mankind from *Judaism*." (Second Bauer, 35)

Marx uses the rhetorical device of chiasmus to invert and convert things into his reductionistic categories. A muscular sociology followed his good insights into the evils of nineteenth-century capitalism, and once inside, he pulled the walls of the religious edifice down about him. He could not abide religion, any religion, because it made for fear and servility. Capitalism was a good scapegoat, and tying it to the Jew and the vulgar bourgeois Christians who abounded in the Europe of his day gave his trenchant pen dominance over his good sense. One cannot wipe away religions with the swipe of a pen any more than one can do so to sex or sunsets. So over and over he uses the pamphleteer's tricks to secularize the question of the Jew and the Christian. He is quite unkind to the Jew in this brief essay; one would think him anti-semitic if one did not know that he fought for Jewish rights in Germany. What he hated in them he hated in the Christian: mercantilism. He pronged the Jews for fostering it in the Christian and the Christian for bettering the Jews at their own game. No one left the arena unscathed by his invective. This essay is a simple and clear example of his methodology applied to religion, but it is in no way up to the level of the essays on Hegel's philosophy. Marx was running out of steam as far as the question of religion was concerned, and it shows here. The religious question was irrelevant by the mid-1840s. He wanted to get on with more serious questions, like how one could set up a new economic order for his already secularized world. Religion was irrelevant, again, since once secularized one need not retrace that ground again lest one suffer rhetorical overkill; and this he does in Second Bauer.

A few examples of his literary and emotional excess should suffice here. "The monotheism of the Jews is, therefore, in reality, a polytheism of the numerous needs of man, a polytheism which makes even the lavatory an object of divine regulation. . . . The god of *practical need and self-interest* is *money*." (Second Bauer, 37) "The god of the Jews has been secularized and has become the god of this world. The bill of exchange is the real god of the Jew." (Second Bauer, 37) "Christianity issued from Judaism. It has now been reabsorbed into Judaism. From the beginning, the Christian was the theorizing Jew; consequently, the Jew is the practical Christian. And the practical Christian has become a Jew again. . . . Christianity is the sublime thought of Judaism; Judaism is the vulgar practical application of Christianity." (Second Bauer, 39) Thus, his "criticism is not a passion of the head, but the head of passion." (Contribution, 46) He wrote from great passion in as passionless a way as possible; here, however, it flows over into his work, lessening its impact to a great degree, especially when one places his invective against the infected spot of Germany: anti-Semitism, a spot that would consume not only Jewish bodies, but also German souls only two generations after Marx's death.

The quiet intellectual finishes his essay, replying to Bauer that the Jewish Question, and a fortiori the whole religious question, is irrelevant. Jews were not a religious or ethnic entity any longer, but an economic one forced by history into usury and other ugly occupations. Jewish, Christian, and general emancipation would come in Europe when the conditions of false consciousness were removed. Baptism of the Jews would only substitute one set of chains for another; it would be a liberal ploy to endow all people with human rights, which rights are for civil, not political (species), man and woman. After this essay, Marx refused to address the question for most of the rest of his life, even though he had aided the Jews of Cologne earlier on. God was a non-issue for him, just as it was for earlier (Theravada) Buddhism. If Buddhism is the atheism of Hinduism, then Marxism is the Buddhism of Christianity. God would be interesting to both if people weren't suffering intensely. Buddhists see us as a house afire. And one does not ask, "Who built the house" when it is burning. One gets out. So Buddhism becomes a praxis for peace. Marx's insistence on flipping the question on its back and dealing with its underside as its very solution is not an answer so much as it is an experience; and the essence of both Marx's thought and Buddhism is an experience gained through doing something about one's real conditions. Buddhism vectors hard toward enlightenment as to one's real conditions, which are good and peaceful amid the garbage of everyday life. Marx, too, holds out a hope for better times through the samsara (painful fluxes) of dialectics, twisting and turning one toward that better day. Eschatology is there in Marx; it has returned through his criticism. But it is one without God. Why?

Marx's Atheism

Before he was a socialist, Marx was an atheist; that is, by the time he had left his high school Christian pieties and entered the University of Berlin, he had become an atheist. That would put it at age eighteen, at the earliest. His atheistic statements were nearly all made when he was a young man, i.e., during the 1840s. He said little about it in his later years; this is largely because the roots of the ills of his society were economic, not religious. Religion was merely a symptom of those ills, so to treat it would be to act as one removed from the real problem. Militant atheism was not central to his agenda later on; that centrality was given to economics and politics and to a praxis with which to bring about the revolutionary conditions that would overturn the sick society that had birthed him.

Simply put, for Marx, religion was an enslaver; so it had to go. Servility and submission to authority were the poles of his antipathy for religion. [9] But even more than religion, it was the nineteenth-century church that galled Marx. It was kind in its steely way, but it was paternalistic in its authoritarianism. The overriding emotion of the churchgoers of his day was fear of God, guilt for sins, and a servile submission to rules, as well as individualism in piety. This led to fear becoming cowardice, guilt becoming abasement, obedience becoming servility, and individualism becoming egotism. Humanity is free and self-determined and takes as its guide reason alone. (McGovern, 246, 250) It came down to this: freedom versus servility and reason versus authority. These were the shapers of Marx's atheism. He was not out to destroy God, but to establish free people. Feuerbach said that religion was a projection and an abstraction. Primitive humans projected their fears onto a personified sun or sea or mountain and this became God. Now we project love, power, and all our best traits onto an imagined God. He finished by saying that we had given away all our best attributes to an imagined God, thereby alienating ourselves from our true worth. But if Feuerbach and Bruno Bauer were influential, it was Greek materialism that did most to form his atheism. Marx's doctoral thesis on the natural philosophies of Democritus and Epicurus conformed him to the main line of so much of materialist thinking of the past century. He was taken by the freedom shown by Prometheus' courage in becoming fully himself when he stole God's fire. Although punished for it, Marx felt the state of pained freedom was infinitely more valuable to Prometheus than was servitude to the gods. That, for him, would be "truly impious." (McGovern, 247)

Religion negated us; for Marx, it was to be a case of either God or humanity. Further, even the proofs for God's existence offered him, at most, evidence that we were conscious; they proved our existence, not God's. So one could not be free and be religious; the assertion of King Wilhelm IV of Prussia that his subjects were his "children" and that they must trust him, since he was God's representative, clinched it for Marx. At its best, religion was a manifestation of human misery. (McGovern, 249) At its deepest, religion was shallow. At its most real, it was a poultice for actual misery compounded of the desire for God and the human projection that God was there. God wasn't; man and woman were. The program would not begin with a political revolution. The problems

48

were economic; these were the real conditions of humankind. When men and women knew that they were members of a race in the very changing of those wretched conditions, then, and only then, could political revolt be put in motion to change the rest of human inequities.

If atheism was an abstraction, communism was not; it was a praxis—a plan of action. The philanthropy of the former was abstract (unreal) because it was not a praxis; the philanthropy of the latter was real because it was an orientation to action. Atheism was merely the reality factor in one's assumptions. The religious assumption was creationism, but Marx said that it did not explain humanity or the world; science could and did take care of that. Marx's assumptions were, then, scientific. (McGovern, 249) If the world created itself, then so did humankind. Religion was just too passive for Marx; communism was based, then, on a dynamic anthropology in which humankind was no longer the *imago dei* (God's image), but *deus* "Himself." When humankind was established in a communist state, atheism would be superfluous. (McGovern, 274) Marx's essay "Private Property and Communism"—in *1844 Manuscripts* —is illuminating on this. Marx thought that his was a vision devoid of the illusion of religion, i.e., devoid of illusion per se. But this was his greatest illusion, to think that he thought without illusion, without ideology. History has proved how ideological—how religiously dogmatic—his hypotheses became. The praxis proved to be just as much an explanation fetish as Marxism was. It was a feast of hermeneutics. His was a reductionist fetish; capitalism's was one of egoism; that of religion, as he rightly saw, was of passively receiving one's world and one's nature.

In "The German Ideology," Marx says that religion or any ideology, including atheism and politics, is of secondary importance, since society is molded by the production of human goods, material or otherwise. Conditions have shaped religion, politics, and economics, not vice versa, so both Marx and Engels do not criticize religion as a cause of real conditions—changing human conditions will take care of that for them— but as an ideological force justifying the status quo at worst and lodging an impotent protest against it, at best. (McGovern, 251) The church was long ago destroyed as a force for real protest, but even in its present vegetative state, Marx felt constrained to score it for lining up with monopolistic capitalism in attempting to enforce the Sunday closing laws; this was in his latter years. (McGovern, 253) Thus, both Marx and Engels criticized religion as an ideological force hindering the change of humankind's real conditions.

Both Marx and Engels assumed that their system was based on bedrock science, an assumption not borne out by present-day science. Their view of economics was based on their view of history, and their view of history was based on their view of matter. I think that it is here that their science and anthropology have their strengths and weaknesses. The weakness of their science is that Engels rejected the second law of thermodynamics (the phenomenon of entropy, in which a congealed, complexified, and convergent matter would cool off and, ultimately, fall apart) in the face of an enormous body of scientific evidence to the contrary. He rejected that scientific law for his quasi-religious faith in the ultimate convergence of humanity and matter in a solidarity approaching utopia. Both the atheism and the religious critique of Marx cannot be treated without, at the same time, placing it alongside the same aspects of Friedrich Engels' thoughts; for if Marx was the fire of the movement, Engels was its engine; if Marx was its prophet, Engels was its philosopher.

Summing it up, Marx is not as radical as he thinks. The mold in which he operates is a religious one. He says, "Just as . . . so" (The Question, 11); the "just as" is the frame of reference, and it is a religious one. So the state is like Christ, a liberator. Thus, Marx had completely secularized history by ridding it of God and God's religions' superstition to free the state and humankind in history, but in doing so his secular body had a sacred paradigmatic soul. To do this, Marx flipped the sacred/profane dichotomy on its back and negated the sacred underpinnings outright. We became essentially profane: "Man, in his most intimate reality, in civil society, is a profane being." He views the distinction between political and civil humanity as essentially a secular one. In this he is, I think, essentially correct. When religion makes all sacred, nothing becomes sacred. Such pansacralism pulls the rug out from under legitimate sacrality. Luther's rebellion was essentially along these lines; God had made it impossible for anyone to live. God and the church had frozen us into inactivity by driving out the creativity from our creaturehood. Marx and Luther realized that unbridled sacrality makes humankind exist as a symbol for something higher—religion, God, the holy—thereby defrauding (alienating) human nature of its essence, which is the imago dei (image of God); and God is an ultimate who exists for the God-self. Both reformers knew that we are unlimited and autonomous, although not infinite. We are like God, and religion had for too long impeached the likeness in the name of its own autonomy and unlimited (sacred) character. It was a battle of ultimates, and Marx saw only one way for us to be liberated: invert things intellectually and, *in praxi*, revolt. This would clear the air and allow history its proper latitude. He did religion a favor in this, since the basis of religion is matter, the secular stuff of our human experience; Christ is God become matter that can think and feel and live forever. The French say that the heresy of the truly noble is spiritism, not materialism; this is especially true when the materialism is grossly egotistic. But when religion becomes a spiritual egotism, it, too, is a heresy, and the reaction of the noble is a humanistic materialism to free the human spirit *in*, not *from*, matter. This is the benefit I see in Marx's revolt. More on this later.

When Marx says that religion is strictly apolitical, he means that it has no worldly goals. He splits religion off from the mainstream much as a fundamentalist Christian would. His reason for holding this is that in sum, "it is an affair of the heart withdrawn from the world, an expression of the limitations of reason, a product of arbitrariness and fantasy, a veritable life in the beyond." (The Question, 21) Marx is a pure Hegelian in making the essence of religion a thing of the heart. Here his criticism of religion is essentially the same as Hegel's, since both elevate religious emotion to the status of concept—Hegel eschewed dogma and miracle, reducing Christianity to feeling. But it was a feeling that was at the service of philosophy. Thus, religion became the servant of the philosopher's idea and purely a private matter as feeling. Marx felt free in according this much validity to religion, since he had effectively made it into a philosophy—and he could handle an idea with a counteridea. He constantly inverted ideas and wiped away the one that was prickly and needed more attention than a philosopher could give it. Philosophy deals with ideas like essences and universals. It could hardly spend its energy on emotion, especially a transcendental one. Karl Lowith states it thus:

> The final sentences of *Glauben und Wissen* are a culmination of this exaltation of religion to the level of "philosophical existence"; they transform the death of God into a "speculative Good Friday." The historico-empirical "feeling" that God himself is dead, this infinite grief "which forms the basis for the religion of the modern era" [Lowith quotes Hegel], must be comprehended as a "component of absolute freedom."
>
> This distinction, and the consequent exaltation of religion out of the form of feeling and imagination into that of the notion, are the means by which Hegel accomplishes his positive justification of the Christian religion, and

at the same time his criticism of it. The ambiguity of this distinction forms the background for all post-Hegelian criticism of religion; it even produced the breakdown of the Hegelian school into a left and right wing.[10]

Marx's criticism was a process of reduction and inversion: reduce religion to something less grand, to something one can handle, to something secular, to its causes or functions. Make God a god and we become divine. Rid the debate of the sacred by wiping out history. For the Christian, the holy is history and history is the holy. But the job of pulling the rug out from under sacred history was left to Hegel. Miracle and myth went out with dogma in Hegel's critique of Protestantism. This simplified Marx's work. Because salvation history was, for him, merely an emotion, and as such merely a chimera, history and the world belong only to man and woman *qua tale*—and people as such are political and historical; but religion is neither.

Thus, sacred/profane became political and civil. The values and affect content of the sacred became those of the secular. Marx flipped the categories back on themselves. The logic follows a pattern of inversion through conversion, in which God becomes god and we attain divinity. It is not unlike the Christian dynamic spoken of by Augustine, in which "God became man so that man might become God." But Marx's meaning is radically different from that of the saint's. The apotheosis of the Marxian person was done totally without a Theos—and here is the problem, no matter how much good Marx's anthropology did in cleaning Christianity's man-and-woman-weighed-down-by-God. Man and woman, by definition, are empty of meaning without creaturehood. Marx had to fill up this void by making humankind self-create.

Thus, the basis of Marx's criticism is that we make religion and not vice versa. He calls it his irreligious criticism. And what we can make, we can unmake. The consciousness of humanity, when it is lost or has not found itself, is religious consciousness. Religion is self-consciousness (how the Buddha would revel in Marxist dialectic and its aphorisms!): "Religion . . . is an *inverted* world consciousness" produced by the state and society, which are an "inverted world" themselves. Religion derives from the mythopoeic level of humankind. Marx and Hegel knew this. Hegel got rid of the supernaturalistic interventions of God (miracles) in order to retail religion to a less believing Germany. Marx and Bauer had demanded that both the Jew and the Christian read Strauss's life of Jesus, which reduced Jesus to myth. Marx went further. He got rid of the whole content of religion, but he unconsciously and unwillingly, retained the paradigmatic soul of religion by pouring his critique into a Christian liberationist mold. History brings freedom as Christ the Liberator would bring it, if only it were true. Religion is the "aroma of the world," and Marx's critique fought to free us of that pernicious myasma. Hegel and Strauss captured the German imagination by saying that religion was largely a product of human *mythopoesis*. Marx went further than Hegel, Strauss, and Feuerbach—or even all put together. God was a product of human *theopoesis* and humankind a product of *autopoesis*.

CHAPTER 3

Marxism's Mantras for the Oppressed

In considering Marx I found it necessary to say that he is not understandable without seeing him over against Hegel's critique of religion. In this chapter I shall show that the Marxian critique of religion is a combination of his and Friedrich Engels' thought. Thus, Marx took from Hegel the form of his thought, dialectical, while rejecting the content of the latter's philosophy. Feuerbach added a radical humanism to Marx's thinking. But it was Friedrich Engels who finalized what we know today as Marx's critique of religion. Engels was the philosopher of dialectical materialism, the theory that Marx opposed to religion.

The critique that Marx and Engels leveled against religion is still mordant because it "bit" deeply into the heel of religion's hypocrisy, its alignment with the forces of obstruction and oppression all over the Western world. However, it has become shallow, since it is today a critique of an ideology with another ideology, of an illusion with another illusion. The assumption on which both Marx and Engels built their system—and on which their credibility lay—was that their theories were based on science. Their dialectical materialism was a "portrait" of history outlining how things were. History was moving ahead, careering violently, with its dialectical twists of revolutions and wars, toward a solidarity that would last. History's simples were a mixture of matter evolving toward an ultimate unity; matter as it moved to sensibility; matter as it moved to consciousness, and then to self-consciousness, reaching its apex when it could break out of its isolation to attain solidarity with other thinking unities. However, this flew in the face of the scientific fact of entropy. This "flight" was not the leap of illation, in which reason moves from one idea to another and thence to the logical consequences of its journey. Rather, it was the leap of faith, and not scientific in the empirical sense at all, in which one verifies one's thoughts in the laboratory, ending by quantifying them. It was the product of two men hoping in a dark place against the vicious surds that would devour them. It was a trust in the goodness of things. It was, therefore, a faith of sorts; a secularist faith in the sense that Wilfred Cantwell Smith uses that word; an openness to the goodness of both people and things. Marx and Engels "knew" as people of faith "know" something, and what they knew was that people would come together, since matter was coming together and would stay together. If the critique of both men was reductionistic, since it tried not only to explain religion by its origins and functions, but also to "explain it away," their materialism has exerted a lasting influence on the world. Religion has taken note of the deep insights of Marx and Engels into its sins and flaws, and instead of toppling of its own weight, it seems to be renewing itself with an anthropology that has a secular shell suffused with a view of God formed both by sacred tradition and the Marx-Engels critique. Freud says that all questions are an aggression; and those of Marx and Engels are an aggression to which our culture and church could not but succumb; such questions as they asked are the stuff of philosophy. Their answers, their materialistic philosophy is one of the two hopes of the world: the one is God and the other, Marxist faith in the "throes of matter." In the West it is either the incarnationalism of Christ or the incarnation of man and woman in Marxism that is our hope. It is not, then, atheism, which is the heart of Marx and Engels, for they knew that atheism itself was an ideology if pushed beyond its fragile and temporary usefulness. The heart of Marx and Engels' thought is a communitarian humanism, a noble incarnationalism that bespeaks a faith in what *is*. Nietzsche would later say, "Will what is," and both Marx and Engels did just that in their own philosophic way.

Materialism: Humanism, Not Crass Libertinism

In *Ludwig Feuerbach*, Engels chides Feuerbach both for his failure to progress beyond the "shallow, vulgarized form . . . [of] . . . the materialism of the eighteenth century" and for being, at bottom, hooked by Hegelian idealism, which became unscientific in not following evolution, or at least being open to it in the way he throttled science with his dialectical method. Thus, he said, Feuerbach was untrue to the facts of

55

progress described by "geology, embryology, the physiology of plants and animals, and organic chemistry."[1] Engels felt that the materialism of the eighteenth century was too mechanical: "This exclusive application of the standards of mechanics to processes of a chemical and organic nature . . . constitutes the first specific but at that time inevitable limitation of classical French materialism." If French materialism was too mechanistic for Engels, it also failed to comprehend the universe as a process, "as matter undergoing uninterrupted historical development." In Hegel's thought, all this led to what Engels called "the absurdity of a development in space, but outside of time." (Feuerbach, 373) In Germany, Engels felt that this failure to understand history, together with scientific materialism, led to "vulgarizing peddlars." Hence, Engels criticizes Feuerbach, not for his materialism, but for not being advanced enough in it. Engels thought that, at bottom, he was an idealist (Feuerbach, 375): "The real idealism of Feuerbach becomes evident as soon as we come to his philosophy of religion and ethics. He by no means wishes to abolish religion; he wants to perfect it." (Feuerbach, 377)

For Engels, the crasser forms of matter will eventually become subtle, thinking, willing, and even loving: in a word, human.

> We simply cannot get away from the fact that everything that sets men acting must find its way through their brains—even eating and drinking, which begins as a consequence of the sensation of hunger or thirst transmitted through the brain, and ends as a result of the sensation of satisfaction likewise transmitted through the brain. The influences of the external world upon man express themselves in his brain, are reflected therein as feelings, thoughts, impulses, volitions—in short, as "ideal tendencies," and in this form become "ideal powers." (Feuerbach, 376)

His notions of materialism are not open to libertinism, nor are they to pander to the cretinous among us:

> By the word materialism the philistine understands gluttony, drunkenness, lust of the eye, lust of the flesh, arrogance, cupidity, avarice, covetousness, profit-hunting and stock-exchange swindling—in short, all the filthy vices in which he himself indulges in private. By the word idealism he understands the belief in virtue, universal philanthropy and in a general way a "better world," of which he boasts before others but in which he himself at the utmost believes only so long as he is having the blues or is going through the bankruptcy consequent upon his customary "materialist" excesses. It is then that he sings his favourite song, What is man?—Half beast, half angel. (Feuerbach, 377)

Was he then professing atheism, as some of his detractors said when they imposed on him the conclusion, *"Donc, l'atheism c'est votre religion!"* (Well, then, atheism is your religion)? He rejected that claim, so often to be made by those who would impose religious paradigms or even content on his thought. He says that to say this is an etymologist's trick. They say that we derive our term religion from the Latin *religare*, which means "to bind." And religion means a bond between two persons. So wherever there is that bond, there is religion. But if atheism is a bond like that, then atheism is Engels' religion. "No," he goes on to say, "if religion can exist without its god, alchemy can exist without its philosopher's stone." (Feuerbach, 378) Atheism is not his religion. I would think, if anything is, and he would not admit to any religion, that materialistic (secularistic) humanism is. It is eisegesis—reading one's own categories into those of another—to see atheism as a religion in his case. Atheism is a state, a philosophical moment on the way to W. C. Smith's term "positive secularism," which is, again, an opening to the goodness in people and things. Matter and people are the things, and not matter most foul (for the denigration of which he scored priests) but matter most noble: as man and woman. (Feuerbach, 378)

Both Marx and Engels accuse Duns Scotus of eisegesis in forcing a theological answer to his own question: "Can matter think?" But neither criticize him for posing the question. They begin their answer in their essay "The Holy Family" by saying:

> The first and most important of the inherent qualities of *matter* is *motion*, not only *mechanical* and *mathematical* movement, but still more *impulse*, vital *life-spirit*, tension, or, to use Jacob Boehme's expression, the *throes* (Qual) of matter. The primary forms of matter are the living, individualizing *forces of being* inherent in it and producing the distinctions between the species.[2]

The idealist is not an angel; the materialist is not a beast. Matter, as Teilhard de Chardin would put it, is "ambiguous, unquiet, the combined essence of all evil and all good."[3] As Heraclitus would put it, matter is a flux—something constantly on the move, always changing; and Engels knew this. His *Anti-Duhring* says this about matter's throes:

> We see the picture of an endless entanglement of relations and reactions, permutations and combinations, in which nothing remains what, where and as it was, but everything moves, changes, comes into being and passes away. . . . This primitive, naive but intrinsically correct conception of the

world is that of ancient Greek philosophy, and was first clearly formulated by Heraclitus: everything is and is not, for everything is *fluid*, is constantly changing, constantly coming into being and passing away.[4]

What Engels had done was to place Marx's materialism in an evolutionary schema, giving it both meaning and push. Matter moves on to thought in an "eternal cycle," a cycle in which "every finite mode of existence of matter . . . is equally transient . . . wherein nothing is eternal but eternally changing, eternally moving matter"; it is the cycle of evolution "in which the time of highest development, the time of organic life and still more that of the life of beings conscious of nature and of themselves, is just as narrowly restricted as the space in which life and self-consciousness come into operation."[5] The mechanical motion of the spheres becomes transmuted into light and heat, into, in other words, "another form of motion, in which it can once more be stored up and become active." (Nature, 53) Thus, mechanical motion becomes energy, and energy becomes matter in motion once again, as the cycle renews itself. This cycle moves inexorably to the complexity of energy in motion, which we call sentience. This in turn becomes consciousness, and when this sufficiently complexifies so that it can bend back on itself in a sentience that knows it is both sentient and conscious, we have human thought, the apex of the process of the self-creativity of the universe in the self-creation of humanity. Thus, he had junked the old teleology, in which one is created by God, for one in which matter is eternal, moves in cycles and according to laws that necessarily produce the thinking mind. Humankind is, therefore, self-creating, and "the old teleology has gone to the devil." (Nature, 262) God has been rendered otiose.

The mechanism of the age comes under Engels' fire for making the evolution of the thinking human brain a matter of chance. It is not: "the truth is that it is the nature of matter to advance to the evolution of thinking beings, hence this always necessarily occurs wherever the conditions for it . . . are present." (Nature, 278) There is, therefore, a teleology in evolution: it moves up to human thought; but it is a necessary teleology. Humankind must come about, even though Engels knows that the conditions necessary for this are present on only about three planets, which he leaves unnamed. For humankind, freedom is to know these laws and grow into them through the agency of thought.

Scientists in the so-called natural sciences study matter in motion, not just mechanical motion, but qualitative (living) motion. The nature of things is determined by the type of matter that is in motion. Mechanical motion produces "sound, heat, light, electricity, magnetism," and these forces pass over into the realm of forces in which the influence of one over the other causes chemical changes, a higher form of motion. Chemistry leads us toward an organic complexification, prepared in the arena of history, which culminates in organic nature. Thus, the various sciences deal with a hierarchy of motions and must necessarily arise out of one another. (Nature, 329–31 passim)

Matter contains in itself all its possible mutations, from the grosser forms of mechanical motion, through heat, light, and energy, which jumps on to the lower one-celled animals on up through the more differentiated forms of matter like the vertebrates and, ultimately, to humankind itself. Matter is constantly finding this ability to mutate and move upward. Engels says that if it could not perform this process of evolution through differentiation over and over, matter and motion would have to be mortal, but of their nature they are not. Matter is immortal, and motion is indestructible. Further, matter and motion are not to be construed as being merely quantitative; both are qualitative entities. It is "unthink-able" to him that matter should lose its *dunamis* (power) and *energeia* (activity), and so forfeit the motion necessary to transubstantiate me-chanical motion into higher, qualitatively better, forms. Matter, if such were possible—which it is not—would be partially destroyed. (Nature, 50)

Further, motion comes about because of the attractions and repulsions that material bodies and energy fields have for each other. It is a law of nature that each attraction has an equal and opposite repulsion. Thus, the law of conservation of energy, which goes, "the sum of all attractions in the universe is equal to the sum of all repulsions," corroborates an axiom of ancient philosophy. (Nature, 95f.) These laws of motion and change (evolution) Engels terms "an absolute law of nature." (Nature, 299) But this physical law is no less a law of thought for Engels in which "the laws of thought and laws of nature are necessarily in agreement with one another, if only they are correctly known." (Nature, ibid.) Hegel had it that mind creates extramental reality, but Engels holds that it is matter which moves up to create mind. So, if one's mind works correctly, it knows the matter in motion exterior to it and the laws that govern it. This is not only the epistemology of Engels, but that of Lenin too. Ideas are copies of reality. The world is objectively real and not a product of the mind; and that world is knowable.[6] With all these epistemological axioms does

Christian philosophy agree—especially Roman Catholic philosophy as classically conceived by Aquinas.

In the outline plan of *Dialectics of Nature*, Engels both reveals and stresses the Hegelian shape of his thought. Dialectics are conceived of as "the science of universal inter-connection . . . [whose main laws are] transformation of quantity and quality—mutual penetration of polar opposites and transformation into each other when carried to extremes—development through contradiction or negation of the negation—spiral form of development." (Nature, 27) But for Engels, dialectics are not, as Hegel would have it, the laws of thought. He faults Hegel for forcing nature into thought; it is the other way around. Nature is dialectical; it shows opposites penetrating each other; it evolves through the negation of the negation; quantity is transformed into quality. Hegel's idealism has it the wrong way around; it is nature that is dialectical and thought that reflects nature. Qualitative change can occur in nature only by the addition or subtraction of matter in motion (energy). Thus, any qualitative change comes about either through an exchange of chemical composition or the clashing of different quantities of energy (motion) or both. The quality of any body cannot change without the addition or subtraction of matter in motion. Hegel's dialectics appears not only rational, but Engels calls it "rather obvious." (Nature, 84)

For example, when heat changes into mechanical motion, or vice versa, the quality is changed, but the quantity remains constant. The change, however, "of form of motion" takes place always between two bodies, one of which loses a precise amount of heat (one quality) of motion while the other body gains a definite amount (quantity) of motion of another quality—mechanical motion, electricity, or chemical decomposition. This holds for organic compounds and living bodies of a higher form also. (Nature, 85)

In nature, all things penetrate their opposites. It is senseless to conceive of mind being split from matter in the Hegelian sense, which sense is an anticlassic dichotomy typifying Christian thinking. People are one with nature but have forgotten it because of philosophies like Hegel's and religions like Christianity. Matter is alive; on the move; interpenetrating its opposites; changing quality for quantity and back again to leap constantly forward to thought and unity. History will allow us not only to know our unity with nature, but to feel it as well. It is "senseless" and "anti-natural" not to know of this unity and live with it. The natural consequences of all this should have us living in working and home conditions that are socially acceptable. They are not. The potato blight in Ireland consigned one million Irish to their graves. The scientific achievement of the Arabs, which allowed them to distill alcohol for the first time anywhere, ultimately proved a blight for the American Indians. The machines invented to facilitate labor have been used by the bourgeoisie to enslave those same laborers. (Nature, 243–46 passim) Not knowing the dialectical, ultimate results of actions has led the first generation of inventers to misuse their marvels to the detriment of succeeding generations. The knowledge of nature's dialectics should allow one to see how things interpenetrate so that one can see how history wishes class antagonisms to go by the board in a society reflecting nature, a solidarity of thinking matter on the move. Therefore, the *eternal laws of nature* also become transformed more into historical ones." (Nature, 315) But the process of becoming historical is a messy one. One hypothesis is battered about by muscular newfound facts. If one were to wait for hypothesis to become law, nothing would happen. Science (thought) is dialectical like the rest of nature. Engels concludes with reference to the way chemical rays appear to ants. He says that no one will ever have the final answer to this problem, and he adds the barb, "Anyone who is distressed by this is simply beyond help." (Nature, 318–20)

It is a natural law that opposites interpenetrate. Things are relative, as Hegel said: positive and negative have meaning only in relation to each other. All thought becomes polarized, just as all natural things become polarized. Things move toward their opposite poles, so no scientist or philosopher can maintain one-sidedness and be worthy of his or her discipline. The law of noncontradiction, in which a thing is equal to itself $(A = A)$, has been chipped at, bit by bit, by the physical scientists, with the effect that it is no longer tenable as such; but philosophers hold on to it nonetheless. This law has given way, since "identity and difference— necessity and chance, cause and effect, the two main opposites, . . . treated separately, become transformed into one another." And then "first principles must help" us. (Nature, 287) Scientific absolutes must give way to the irrefutable fact that identity and difference are not irreconcilable poles but one-sided ones representing the truth "in their reciprocal action, in the inclusion of difference *within* identity." (Nature, 286) After this reconciliation of opposites is recognized by philosopher and scientist alike, and only after, can first principles such as "$A = A$" be brought in to say something about both thought *and* extramental reality. Nature (history) is not a smooth concatenation of things, but a series of necessary discontinuities. But Engels says that there are no leaps in Nature, since history is totally composed of leaps. (Nature, 358) One would think that leaps would be something irregular, not expected, rhythmic; but history (Nature) is a saga of leaps evolving from a lower to a higher form. Thus, the dialectics of Nature are these qualitative leaps to qualitative states, themselves leaping and jerking on their way toward thought and unity. This is a process of moving "from the wholly conditioned through the partially conditioned to the absolutely free."[7]

As for infinity, Engels says that there is both "bad" and "good" infinity. What he calls good infinity begins in this way: he affirms that one can only know the finite, since "only finite objects enter the sphere of our knowledge." But he says that this statement needs this amendment: "fundamentally we can know *only the infinite.*" (Nature, 310) One's knowledge is of the individual; this in turn is raised to particularity, and this is then raised to universality "in seeking and establishing the infinite in the finite, the eternal in the transitory." He goes on to say, "The form of universality, however, is the form of self-completeness, hence of infinity; it is the comprehension of the many finites in the infinite." (Ibid.) Knowledge of the infinite, therefore, has a set of obstacles to be overcome: what is knowable is the infinity of knowable matter—in all its forms; the knowers are an infinity of finite minds working out this infinite knowledge with fallible results. Thus, Engels says, "the cognition of the infinite is therefore beset with double difficulty and from its very nature can only take place in an infinite asymptotic progress . . . [so] the infinite is just as much knowable as unknowable, and that is all that we need." (Nature, 311) This is his notion of "good" infinity. True infinity is the progress of organisms in history, culminating in human self-consciousness.

Nature has about it an infinite complexity somewhat negated by the "bad infinity" of space and time. Engels chides Hegel for this concept of bad infinity: "According to Hegel, infinite progress is a barren waste because it appears only as *eternal repetition of the same thing:* $1 + 1 + 1$, etc." (Nature, 314f.) The end of the earth can be foreseen because progress is a dialectical process of progression and regression; but the earth is only a globe among many in the universe. Hegel failed in seeing his philosophy as the crowning point and end of history. Engels chides him for this bit of unscientific hubris. It is motion, or the law of the change of form of motion, that is infinite for Hegel: "it included itself in itself." Thus, Hegel's limitation of infinity by space and time is "bad infinity," since there is a perception of infinity there, all right, but it is "smitten with finiteness." Such perceptions occur for Engels only one at a time; thus their finiteness. What does Engels think about limited infinity? What of "good infinity"? How does his concept of eternal, self-creating matter, of a self-creating humanity as its culmination, jibe with the law of entropy, which has the universe cooling off and falling apart for good? He denies entropy but bases his humanistic, communal philosophy on an empirical (scientific) foundation. What do we make of this? The most obvious thing about life is that it tends toward death, a death that does not reconstitute itself as life for the dead individual—there is no resurrection here. (Nature, 386ff.) But the totality of life is passed on and does not and will not die out. In the face of entropy, which sees things running down, the clock—wound so meticulously at its creation—having run its course, should cease to run, but Engels has it run *in aeternitatem* (eternally). All this smacks of religious language, the language of faith. It bespeaks a belief in, a trust in, the goodness of things, in the sense that they will not let him down; that people and things had revealed their potential and the joy amidst the sadness, he opted for joy in the face of overwhelming scientific evidence to the contrary: both we and the universe die. His is a hope, against scientific fact, that the clock will run "world without end, Amen!" No physicist denies the law of entropy any more than any will deny the law of gravity. If one does, what does one put in its place? Engels hopes against entropy. It is his creed:

> It is an eternal cycle in which matter moves, a cycle that certainly only completes its orbit in periods of time for which our terrestrial year is no adequate measure, a cycle in which the time of highest development, the time of organic life and still more that of the life of beings conscious of nature and of themselves, is just as narrowly restricted as the space in which life and self-consciousness come into operation; a cycle in which every finite mode of existence of matter, whether it be sun or nebular vapour, single animal or genus of animals, chemical combination or dissociation, is equally transient, and wherein nothing is eternal but eternally changing, eternally moving matter and the laws according to which it moves and changes. But however often, and however relentlessly, this cycle is completed in time and space . . . we have the certainty that matter remains eternally the same in all its transformations, that none of its attributes can ever be lost, and therefore, also, that with the same iron necessity that it will exterminate on the earth its highest creation, the thinking mind, it must somewhere else and at another time again produce it. (Nature, 54)

What Is It?

What I have outlined of Engels' thought is not to be considered apart from Marx's ideas: they go together. Marx authored a theory of class struggle with his political and economic writings; Engels, a theory of dialectical materialism that served as a framework for Marx's thinking. Whereas Marx saw history in economic terms, Engels saw it in evolutionary and scientific ones. During Marx's lifetime he and Engels showed little difference in approach, but after Marx's death Engels made his departure for more evolutionistic grounds. This is to be added to his and Marx's earlier thoughts on anthropology. The two complement each other. Thus, our time spent on Engels and his materialism. It is part and parcel of the Marxist critique of religion, negatively speaking, and of its outlook on the world, speaking positively. Engels fashioned Hegel's insights into something scientifically evolutionistic, something based on a dialectics found in nature, not something made up between one's temporal plates, as he thought Hegel had done.

What their combined Marxism looks like is detailed well for us in R. C. Zaehner's book *Dialectical Christianity and Christian Marxism,* referred to earlier. In "The Holy Family," Marx and Engels said that the proletariat and wealth are opposites that form a whole, this since they are complementary opposites. The positive side is this: private property maintains itself and the proletariat in existence. The negative (complementary) side is: the proletariat is bound to abolish itself and its opposite. The owner conserves; the proletariat destroys; this is the contradiction, the negation. The proletariat will execute the sentence that wage labor pronounced on itself by the very fact that it brought wealth into existence. Thus, the bourgeoisie had enslaved the proletariat with the machine and the petty bourgeois state. (Zaehner, 39–41 passim) When the tension between these opposites becomes unbearable, an explosion must come that will cause the opposites to disappear, giving way to a social equilibrium. Both Marx and Engels believed this to be so, agreeing with Heraclitus that "what is at variance agrees with itself. It is an attunement of tensions." Thus, the ultimate synthesis is inevitable, historically speaking. The bourgeoisie produced its own grave diggers, and the proletariat will inevitably win, according to "The Communist Manifesto," written in 1847–48 by Marx and Engels.

Engels said that capitalism will ultimately lead to state capitalism, which will render the bourgeoisie superfluous. The state will take control of production and then abolish itself in favor of the individual, who would then be free. Thus, when the state dies out, a free society will be born. One becomes free of the tyranny of the dialectic of history and Nature by willing it. The necessity of history enslaved the worker; now history becomes a matter of a free choice. Engels calls this "the ascent of man from the kingdom of necessity to the kingdom of freedom." (Zaehner, 42–45 passim) Hence, Marxism's strength lies in the difference between Marx's and Engel's complementary attitude toward the purpose of the cosmos: one is prophet (Marx), the other is mystic (Engels). There is messianic hope here; it is the time of the liberation of the mind and spirit. Evolution, the philosophical expression of which is dialectical materialsim, is "one great act of giving birth," as Paul would put it. Zaehner says that there is much make-believe here, the kind that kept the Jews going for millennia, as they waited for the Messiah. Marx's hope is in a linear time frame and can sustain humankind in its eschatological stretch for the *optimum*. (Zaehner, 46f.) Engels' hope is couched in the categories of a philosopher with an evolutionist model: history was a process, an extension of evolution into human consciousness, governed by immutable laws that are not cyclic, but linear. This law careers us toward a higher plane: the classless society. Both Engels and Teilhard de Chardin agree that evolution is "the progress from the wholly conditioned through the partially conditioned to the absolutely free." Both see quantitative leaps become qualitative; that is, the process goes from dead matter to life, from life to consciousness, from consciousness to self-consciousness. But now humanity is ready for another leap: to collective consciousness, the denial of what Marx called "civil (egoistic) man." This is the theme that Zaehner says is central to all religions worthy of the name namely, "this is not I." (Zaehner, 47–50) For Buddhism, it is the snuffing out of the candle in the coolness of nirvanic peace; for Christians, it is the grain of wheat dying so that it might bear fruit (John 12:24). In his *Anti-Duhring*, Engels has a parable that bears striking resemblance to the Johannine text:

> Let us take a grain of barley. Millions of such grains of barley are milled, boiled and brewed and then consumed. But if such a grain of barley meets with conditions which for it are normal, if it falls on suitable soil, then under the influence of heat and moisture a specific change takes place, it germinates; the grain as such ceases to exist, it is negated, and in its place appears the plant which has arisen from it, the negation of the grain. But what is the normal life-process of this plant? It grows, flowers, is fertilized and finally once more produces grains of barley, and as soon as these have ripened the stalk dies, is in its turn negated. As a result of this negation of

the negation we have once again the original grain of barley, but not as a single unit, but ten, twenty or thirty fold. (*Anti-Duhring*, in Zaehner, 52f.)

This means that the individual must die to personal goals, merge with his or her contemporaries in a common effort to build a new life in a free association of men and women.

There are no absolutes in Marxist dogma—although one might tell this to its Marxist exegetes around the world; both freedom and necessity are relative. But Engels said that the ruling class interpreted both. True freedom can come only when all classes cease through a historical negation. This is an immutable law of Nature, binding even on human-kind. Nature tends to the classless society, and freedom will come through this tendency to classlessness. Engels said that Nature is not unreasona-ble, and reason never unnatural. Matter is one and the same in all these changes. (Nature, 55) In this, Engels hews along the row set for him by his mentor, Heraclitus, whom Zaehner calls a mystic and a seer. This One appears for Engels, as for the scientists of his day, as the laws of Nature. They are the Ultimate or Absolute appearing among us. Law is reason in Nature, and humankind's job is to find out these laws and collaborate with them. Nature's laws are the finite searching for the eternal, the absolute, the infinite. (Nature, 311) So if we can achieve Nature's goal, a classless society, through the negation of the negations, we can achieve infinite knowledge through collective effort. Man and woman come from matter, and mind, from man and woman. Hence, Engels says that dialectical evolution is from both the kingdom of necessity and the kingdom of freedom; it is also an ascent from ignorance to knowledge and from individual knowledge to collective knowledge. Things are a tissue of interconnections for Engels, a series of processes bound by these bonds into a whole human person. People never rule Nature; they belong to it. (Zaehner, 54–57)

Engels said that matter is living, is life itself, since it cannot die because of its eternal nature. Of life and death he says:

Death is either the dissolution of the organic body, leaving nothing behind but the chemical constituents that formed its substance, or it leaves behind a vital principle, more or less the soul, that then survives *all* living organisms, and not only human beings. (Nature, 387–88, in Zaehner, 58)

Some vital principle (soul) survives the dying. There seems to be a World Soul, then, left behind after the death of all organisms, not just man and woman, and all individual minds merge with this World Soul. In this,

Engels seems not to have progressed much beyond the Greek *Nous* (World Soul), with the exception that the ancients were idealists and he was a materialist; the core idea is the same, the constitutive stuff just different. Thus, matter is a unity converging in a complexity so subtle that it is capable of knowing that it was a person, and it was a member of a class:

Matter bent back upon
itself in complications
so happily intimate
that it knew
its own folds
in flashes of
intelligence.
By dint of earth's own light
it hovered upon its scrolled mass
and found its name
(Evolved to Truth)
had suddenly seen
not just itself in God,
but God devolved upon his molecules
so they could cry,
"I'm He"
in full-spate incarnation.[8]

Matter would not only not cool off and pull away from thought's convergences and molecules' adhesive persistencies, but it would also perdure; it would pull men and women together in that unity of humankind that has obdurately survived as only an ideal: community. Engels believed that a life principle would survive and disbelieved in entropy. The belief in the one is religious; the disbelief in the other is unscientific, since to reject the imperatives of entropy flies in the face of secularism's assumptions that reason had figured it out, that probability had slanted us on a vector of coolness that would unravel our community and our very molecular chains. Engels believed in reason's insistent push toward communalism but rejected reason's obdurate and cogent assertion that it would all fall apart in ice-cold randomness. Matter, then, had to be more than a creature; it had to be its own creator.

Thus, we see immortality in some form and the flight from the reasoned conclusions holding for entropy; all this smacks of religion. It is tiresome to "baptize" Engels and Marx with facile assertions about their religiousness. It has been done so often before—and quite unsuccessfully.

With that in mind as a caveat to both me and you, what have we here with Engels?

It appears to be a secular faith in the goodness of things and history. It is a contrived vulnerability to be open to a bit of irrationality because one's dream demands it. God is superfluous in this vision of an eternal linear push upward toward a knowing unity of human matter. It is a faith in history, a trust in the ultimate goodness of the sanguinary torques and dialectical discontinuities as history pushes forward over the corpses of its defeated classes. Engels has devised a way of dealing with the problem of evil (theodicy) in which the *Theos* (God) is irrelevant and the *Dike* (judgment) is made that all shall be providentially well. Religion begins when man or woman faces up to the human situation of pain and sorrow, what the Hindus call *Duhkhd*. In theistic religions this happens at God's instance—when God calls people to face life responsibly and aids them to do it. In nontheistic religious forms, like Theravada Buddhism, Vedanta Hinduism, and Taoism, one faces up to the dialectical tragedies by oneself and in the Self. But it is religious nonetheless. Such religion is bedrock empiricism. It bases itself on experience that it can bring about itself—through the application of the proper technique, stripping off the *illusion* of ego, leaving an immediate experience of one's goodness in the midst of imposing empirical evils. What is stripped away is what Marxists would call ideology and Hindus and Buddhists, ignorance *(avidya)*. In the eastern religions this gains one immediate access to an intuition of the deep and abiding peace within. The foyer of this religion of Isolation (Hindu, Buddhist, and Taoist) is an expansive state in which one intuits not only one's materiality, but one's unity with all things as well. At this juncture it is a matter of hermeneutics what name one shall attach to the experience. Some have called this overpowering, but transient, experience God. Then all things become gods. This is the pantheist hermeneutics. Others, open to the goodness of materiality, have called it the One: Heraclitus. This opens one up to a World Soul *(Nous)*, and the Greeks took this opening gladly. Vedanta Hindus said that this was not religion yet, but merely its propaedeutic. Real religion lay beyond what Raja-Yoga could induce: the euphoric intuition of matter and one's unity with it called Nature Mysticism, or a mysticism of matter. Some, like Engels and Teilhard de Chardin, have fashioned a mystical vision of matter on the move. Here is a long, but worthwhile, quotation from Chardin's *Hymn of the Universe*, which exemplifies the sort of thing Engels is referring to:

The man was walking in the desert, following his companion, when the Thing swooped down on him. From afar it had appeared to him, quite small, gliding over the sand . . . as a pale fleeting shadow like a wavering flight of quail over the blue sea before sunrise or a cloud of gnats dancing in the sun at evening or a whirlwind of dust at midday. . . .

The Thing seemed to take no heed of the two travellers, roaming capriciously through the wilderness. Then, suddenly, it assumed a set course and with the speed of an arrow came straight at them.

And then the man perceived that the little pale cloud of vapour was but the centre of an infinitely greater reality moving towards him, . . . the *moving heart of an immeasurable pervasive subtlety.* . . .

A great silence fell around him.

Then, suddenly, a breath of scorching air passed across his forehead, broke through the barrier of his closed eyelids, and penetrated his soul. The man felt that he was ceasing to be merely himself; an irresistible rapture took possession of him as if all the sap of all living things, flowing at one and the same moment into the too narrow confines of his heart, was mightily refashioning the enfeebled fibres of his being. And at the same time the anguish of some peril, more than human, oppressed him, a confused feeling that the force which had swept down on him was ambiguous, unquiet, the combined essence of all evil and all good.

Teilhard then says that the two travelers were ascetics and contemplatives, but the Thing (matter) would not let them alone, even in the wilderness. It begins to speak:

You called me: here I am . . . I am on you, for life or for death. You cannot go back, you cannot return to your everyday comforts and your untroubled worship. Once you have seen me, you can never forget me: you must either be damned with me, or I shall be saved with you.

[Know that] he who *touches me never knows what power he is unleashing*, the wise fear me and curse me . . . because I am the essence of all that is tangible, and men cannot do without me. . . .

Nothing is precious save what is yourself in others and others in yourself. In heaven all is but one. In heaven all is but one. . . .

You thought that you could do without me because the power of thought had been kindled in you! You hoped that the more carefully you rejected what can be touched, the closer you would be to the Spirit . . . "Yes, and [in so doing] you very nearly starved." . . . Never say, "Matter is accursed, matter is evil," for one has come who has said, . . . "Life shall arise out of death," and again, uttering the final promise of my liberation, "This is my body." . . . No, purity does not mean separation from the universe but an ever deeper penetration into it. . . . *Purity is a chaste contact with that which is the same in all.* (Chardin, in Zaehner, 1–10 passim)

Teilhard found matter so refreshing that it became a seductress for him. It tempted him to worship it, so he found that he had to walk a tightrope over the chasm of this temptation, but walk it he did. Matter was his truth, and he could not but follow it, or better, follow *in* it. Teilhard would not succumb to the pantheist's temptation to call his unity with the One a god. Engels had no problem; his context was not theistic at all. He had carved a nontheist ambience for himself and those who would follow his truth. If it was not a faith in God, then what was it? It was Nature Mysticism—a secularist's recognition of an accession to his unity with matter; an openness to and trust in the goodness of all things (of all matter). An experience which is the response to that most radical dual human experience: the experience of the self as fallen, unworthy, evil, broken, and weak, coexisting with the experience of being pure and good and of being grounded in a foundational affirmation that one's core goodness was also the dwelling place of God. Engels eschewed the more difficult road of looking at God to take the material road to unity and wholeness, past one's brokenness. As do the Buddhists, he made God a non-question, but unlike the Buddhists, the whole human ego was the question he chose to pursue, very much in the tradition of the West. Buddhists are even more radical than he is, however. They find God otiose, but the ego, pernicious. Engels found God pernicious and the self essential. His negation of the ego was of the civil, selfish ego. His encomium was for the corporate person-for-others. He had taken doctrine apart and followed what it pointed to: a revelation of God's self and our self. Therefore, his writing is not scientific, but it is religious myth writing in the secular idiom: flashy, brilliant at times, quintessentially modern in its sadness for the loss of God and the sad joy of living alone with one's wounded brothers and sisters. It is secular mythology, since it follows what I consider the essence of myth: a more radical "telling" of our self than doctrine does. Myth points with an immediacy to the self as fallen, in need of something integrating. Marx and Engels addressed the reality of man and woman, which was an anthropological reality composed of economic, political, and material simples. Marx supplied the sociological assay of the fall and the eschatological possibility of healing. Engels supplied the myth language in the rubric of scientific (empirical) language. The tip-off is his refusal of entropy. Here he moves into something religious. And this I feel I must explain, since it is the essence of my hypothesis about humanistic Marxist thought.

Elsewhere, I have defined Nature Mysticism as a preternatural experience in which the ego expands to identify with all things and thus to unite with its objects in a way that carries it beyond space and time, beyond good and evil, an experience in which immortality is assured and in which no god is necessarily involved. Because it is a unitive experience, it is a mystical experience in which one is aware of one's intimacy with one's environment, or in which one's material side becomes aware of itself. But it is not *necessarily* religious.[9] Engels' experience with matter was not a "graced," supernatural experience in which one is the recipient of the self-donation of God, which divinizes one. His was an experience in which he humanized himself by doing away with the illusions of God. Its thrust was to rediscover or recover humanity, not directly by "killing off" God—that had been done by Hegel before them with his "speculative Good Friday," in *Glauben und Wissen*[10]—but by bypassing God. The rediscovery of humanity was such a thrill that it caused Engels' mind to expand to include all men and women, and all matter incorporated vicariously in them, in a unity with himself. This unitive experience with the human person as matter is the essence of mysticism, defined as a unitive experience with a person or a principle. The expansion of the ego united the knowing subject with the object (thought reflects reality) so that the knower somehow knew himself in knowing others. This scotched out the possibility of Hegelian idealism, in which ideas create the world. Engels' unity was one in which we were created by that unification of matter that was evolution; we were self-created by knowing the laws of evolution and following them; which laws antedated any knowledge of them on our part. So this expanded consciousness of the real—the illusionary consciousness of nineteenth-century religion—was the first step in his Nature Mysticism.

It was a preternatural experience, second, because in discovering historicity, and using it as a method so sedulously, Engels inserted humankind into the world for good. Further, we were created *in* the world *by* the world, i.e., by an eternal matter. But science merely told him that matter *is*, not that it was eternal or that it would be eternal. On the contrary, science told him that it would cool off and come apart in an apocalypse of entropy. Engels refused this, putting his historic consciousness onto another plane: faith. He did not just think; he also felt. He was in the realm of the metarational, of something quasi-religious. Man and woman participated in space and time in a new way. This was one of the glories of Marx's and Engels' historicity; but their humanity had an eschatology about it too. They had an hypothesis about the future and

71

proclaimed it in a nonrational, i.e., nonempirical, way. They predicted the future as would a prophet who had knowledge not based empirically, but on a "revelation." Engels and Marx loved matter and would not let it go; they loved man and woman in their cosmic evolutionary unity and would not let this go. This is putting historical man and woman both *in* and *beyond* space and time. As Engels said, scientific absolutes must give way to the irrefutable fact that identity and difference are not irreconcilable poles, but one-sided poles representing the truth "in their reciprocal action, in the inclusion of difference *within* identity." (Nature, 358) This means that good and evil have been reconciled (inverted), as well as space and time. Good and evil are categories meaningful only within time; one can do good or evil only within space and time. Remove them, remove God, and they run together. This Engels did. When time gives way, one swells with omnipotence, feels above good and evil, sees the good in every evil and the evil in every good. Marx had been the prophet of evil in the good, spiking the liberal clerics for committing evil in keeping the status quo as they tried to push for what would later be called the "social gospel." When space gives way to its opposite, one feels everywhere, i.e., united with all people and things indiscriminately. This is what frightened Teilhard; one had to worship this feeling of being "deity-like." It frightened R. C. Zaehner no less when Aldous Huxley said that his mescaline experience had united him with all things and was a surrogate for religion. Arthur Rimbaud, too, had drug experiences of what he later knew as Nature Mysticism, but his desire was to go through hell to get to God, i.e., to reconcile, invert, opposites. What he first thought was the experience of the God of his first communion was revealed to be only his ego. On his death bed, Huxley admitted the same to his wife: he had not experienced God, but only his own inflated, happy, temporarily healed ego. William James' experiments with nitrous oxide (laughing gas), too, allowed him to distinguish between healthy and sick religion. The unhealthy was the desire to get into Nature Mysticism's reconciliation of opposites and operate out of it. It was too dangerous. Huxley, too, called this underside of the euphoria that he had known "downward transcendence." Engels had discovered something, all right, and it was quite potent. It held out a happiness as an experience, a meaning in the sense of a teleology. Men and women were coming together. He had rediscovered a healed self in the mess of the reality at the bottom of the evil barrel of reality; and the reality took great courage getting to. To do it, both he and Marx had to jettison God and religious structure, to feel the nakedness and sadness that are the unhappy sequelae of a totally existential healing process. Religious language had short-circuited humankind. The human situation could not be gotten at. To call our state one of Original Sin meant nothing but "laying a trip" on the innocent who weren't there *in principio* when the god and the first men and women walked the earth in the cool of a Semite's oasis evening. Getting rid of all this myth demanded that the vacuum be filled; the soul, too, abhors a vacuum.

All I have outlined thus far filled that void: a preternatural experience, overcoming the loneliness of Original Sin (original alienation) with unity—although never with men and women, but with matter. Engels was wrong; Nature Mysticism cares not a fig for people, only for things and experience—a feeling of omnipotence to satisfy the God-urge. Then omnipresence filled the loneliness again with the ability to be everywhere and miss nothing going on in the busy, fluxy knowing matter that is humankind. And now immortality is secured by Engels, not in a personal way—Engels found that "tedious"—but in a metapersonal way. All things, including the life principle, perdured.

Last, no God or god is involved here necessarily. It is not necessarily a religious experience either, since one does not always have to face up to the responsibility of being human; one does not have to face up to the pain. One can achieve this experience through drugs. Then an euphoric expansion carries one beyond the ego to unite it with all things—again, never with all, or even any, people. It can be an escape from a dull and meaningless life, as it was for Huxley. This links up with the feeling of omnipotence and of being beyond good and evil. Teilhard feared this; so did William James and Zaehner. So do I. The experiences of the sixties are proof; Charles Manson and his vicious brood were "into" the form of mysticism in which wickedness became virtue and considered murder an act of high virtue. But if no God is there necessarily, one could be; however, it would be more than wishful thinking to see one in Engels' thinking; it would be eisegesis at least and delusion at most. Many have failed in this attempt to "baptize" him against the meaning of his words—which is his will. I believe that it is a nontheistic Nature Mysticism that Engels describes. As a politics and economics, it is nonreligious, since it faces up to the reality of the dialectics of pain with a program and an experience: the experience of unity as an eschatological promise of the cessation of class pain. His economics and politics borrow somewhat shamelessly from the religious and mystical side in accepting the "beyond good and evil" inversion. Of course, one can say that this was arrived at by applying the methodology of inversion spoken of earlier; this is true, but not all the truth. The experience of Engels, his vision of matter on the move to unity and a classless society, gave this rather ruthless inversion of values a legitimacy. It was the "book" written down after the vision went away, and Engels was its mystical amanuensis, fusing the twin sources of his and Marx's gospel of materialistic humanism into something so telling that the world would read it and take something of hope from the marriage of their "faith" in the new eschatology of humankind on the move, without God, to a better life.

My definition of Nature Mysticism is only a descriptive one, not an exhaustive philosophical one. But it is one that I use to get the feel for phenomena, and I find it workable. Engels put the finishing touches on his and Marx's critique of religion, and it has more than the feel of mysticism and religion about it. I applied my definition to it and conclude that it is a nature mysticism. Put together with Marx's anthropology, which cleared the Temple of ideological views about God, their thoughts on religion are not so much an attack on it as a cry of the heart against bad theology, against falsifying the human vision with unhistoric, limited language and calling it doctrine. This work of Engels and Marx so cleared out the Temple that, where God had stood, there now stood a human being freed of the illusions of many bad theologies.

Thus, Marx and Engels' critique form a humanism. This is the end of the line for them both, since their method is empirical and can only leave us with the palpable; and the most palpable creature is Nature's best: man and woman. Theirs is, then, a critique leaving us with an anthropology. This is the method at its best. On the negative side, they reduced religion and humankind by explaining religion by its origins and its functions. Things are always more than where they came from and what they do; so are people; so is religion. They did not explain religion so much as explain it away with their hermeneutics of suspicion. The first moment of their philosophy, their anthropology, left us with an economic and political human being freed of the accretions of "bad religion," freed to be a human being. Engels added a religious orientation and much religious content to Marx's materialism by making dialectical materialism into a foyer for religion in his Nature Mysticism. This was a statement that life (thinking, communitarian matter) was antecedent to its explanation, be that theology or philosophy. Engels and Marx taught us that theologies are dreams turned illusion when they, not life, become primary. Marx and Engels, therefore, turned us back to our lives as the antecedents to our methods, which is the right end of the stick, or to put it in Jesus' terms, "the sabbath is the servant of man, not man of the sabbath." Freud and Nietzsche returned us to life as antecedent as well—the former as a psychological entity, the latter as a philosophical-theological one.

As Nature Mysticism has its expansive (solidarity) form of unity (transcendence), so has it its contraction (downward transcendence, diabolic) form. This latter is the side of Bakunin and Lenin, the revolutionaries, and of Sartre, the philosopher-litterateur; all offered a Nature Mysticism in which violence became a purifying influence in one's life and in society. Violence was to become a beautiful angel of death for those chosen for it by the laws of history. It was dialectics become executioner; the revolutionary was the mystic placed beyond good and evil because he was beyond space and time—the arenas of morality and human decency. Both Teilhard, the scientist, and Zaehner, the Catholic Marxist, realized that the expansion phase of Nature Mysticism made one "less sociable," which was an odd phenomenon, for Engels and Marx said that the laws of history would make one more social and thereby more sociable when struggle had given way to a submission to the laws of history. This was their light; but Teilhard, the evolutionist—ever open to dialogue with Marxist evolutionists—said that giving himself to the consciousness with matter afforded would bring him only darkness:

> I wanted to see whether, as the vast hopes aroused in my heart by the "cosmic awakening" suggested, I could simply by surrendering to it reach the very heart of things, whether, by losing myself in its embrace, I could rediscover the soul of the world. Ardently and with no holding back I made the experiment, unable to imagine that the true could fail to coincide with this enchantment of the senses and this deadening of pain. And so it was that the more I allowed myself to flow ever closer towards the centre of primordial consciousness, becoming ever more expanded and dilated, the more I came to realize that the light of life was being darkened within me. For one thing, I felt less sociable.[11]

Thus, Marx and Engels' criticism freed man and woman from the trammels of a blind and hypocritical Christianity—blind to the poor and hypocritically saying with Christ, "they would always be with us"—and released people now capable of human life (praxis) because of their anthropology got by this critique (theory). The mysticism of Engels opened one not only to the expansion of communalism, but also to the worship of the expanded ego; it also opened one to the reconciliation of good with evil and to so many of the evils performed by their disciples in

Europe and in Asia in the name of the dialectics of history and justice. Their critique of religion could so easily become a religion of critique—an endless, insane circle enveloping one in the no-exit road of historicism. Their expansive Nature Mysticism could become the downward transcendence of inverting evil and good.

Part II

FREUD'S CRITIQUE OF RELIGION

CHAPTER 4

Religion as Illusion

To be born is to leave paradise forcefully, forsaking the amniotic peace of one's mother to begin fending for oneself. One's first knowledge is a pain, a wail of anguish. Knowledge makes a bloody entrance with us all; and it was no less so for Sigismund Freud (later shortened to Sigmund), born on May 6 in 1856 in Moravia, Frieberg, which is now part of Czechoslovakia. His mother, Amalia Nathanson—a descendant of the famous Talmudic scholar Nathan Charmatz of Brody, Poland—was only twenty-one at the time of his birth. She was the second wife of Freud's father, Jacob, who was forty-one and a grandfather at Sigmund's birth. He was her firstborn, and she adored him. She and an old Catholic nanny were to supervise Sigmund's childhood years.

Freud seems to have been mildly religious as a youth; at the very least, he knew the Jewish customs and festivals. His mother taught him these rudiments when he was six years of age. Also, he read the scriptures, which affected him profoundly, both positively and negatively, in the way he was to do science in his adult life. His acerbic Catholic nanny taught him something about Catholic piety as well and even took him to Mass. These experiences of a somewhat vapid Catholic ritualism and the daily onslaught of small-town anti-Semitism made Christianity utterly incredible to him. Despite the positive religious influences that attended his formative years, the young Freud seems to have had neither any belief in nor any need of God in his life. Immortality held no charm for him.[1] Jewish ritualism utterly repelled him, and he shunned it whenever he could, which was most of the time. Jews, their culture and company, however, were not only a comfort to him, but almost a passion; he loved everything about them except their religion. For the rest of his life, though, Freud, the nonbeliever, would spend much of his scholarly time working out his hermeneutics of the religious phenomenon. He finished the final draft of *Moses and Monotheism* in England shortly before his death, in 1939, at age eighty-three. He seemed incapable of leaving religion alone.

The age into which Freud was born was, like that of La Mettrie, one in which materialism was the thing. The bourgeoisie felt that any learned person should put little, if any, stock in religious belief. Freud was not immune to these influences. For both him and his age, religion had nothing to do with science. Matter and its combined forces explained the world and all in it. God was otiose at best, pernicious at worst. Like Marx before him, Freud was influenced by Feuerbach's materialism. The latter saw the scientific revolution coming; it would be a time that would "dissolve the Christian world-view in nitric acid." (Kung, 3) Atheism was the norm for the bourgeoisie, which had strayed from both Christianity and the church. And the assimilated Jew was not immune to this middle-class phenomenon.

Feuerbach's materialism supplied a basis for Freud's materialism and his psychoanalysis. Freud's studies of anatomy and physiology early on fostered in him a "medical materialism" that was rooted in Feuerbach's view that each physician was a materialist by nature. Feuerbach taught a material view of secularity and raged against the idealistic-spiritualistic psychology and prudery of his day. In this he helped to open up the way for the investigations that Freud and his contemporaries would make later in the century. Hence, the foundation was laid by the rather crude but revolutionary brick masonry of Feuerbach, who brought to completion the natural scientific materialism of the nineteenth century. (Ibid.) This scientific method became a world view in which people believed, replacing entrenched views of religion, politics, and philosophy. All this led to Freud's atheism and the radical materialism of his younger days.

When he went to university, Freud became captivated by the study of physiology. He linked this to the laws of conservation of energy and entropy, which were so basic to nature that he thought that, by applying them, he could explain the human mind physiochemically. Hence, Freud scotched out the very possibility of philosophical idealism as well as the Aristotelian and Scholastic view of an immaterial soul inhabiting the human body. Freud determined that man and woman were to be explained chemically and deterministically. Things worked in us like the water studies of the previous century, which stated that water tensed, that this tension was released in some physical way, and then that the water returned to its previous state of quiescence. This became, for Freud, a theory of psychic energy in which a person was charged with energy (energetic cathexis), became excited, and then displaced the energy (countercathexis), thus returning the subject to peace. (Kung, 15) Psychic energy was a physical phenomenon and followed the laws of physical bodies. All psychic phenomena were within the sense world and were wholly determined because of it. Like Engels, Freud came to "believe in" scientific laws and methods but with this difference: his medical work gradually led him to give a psychological meaning to physiological phenomena. (Kung, 19) His first work on religion, done in 1907, was titled "Obsessive Actions and Religious Practices." Here, he was of the opinion that the very roots of religion were pathological; they described "a universal obsessional neurosis." (Kung, 11) Throughout his career he would not deviate from this seminal position.

Thus, physiology had given way to hermeneutics. Freud had begun his interpretation of religion, and it was one that was devastating in its consequences. It was not that his critique was so potent scientifically; it was not. In fact, many of his theses drawn from the anthropology and history of religions of his day haven't stood the test of more rigorous research. But his insights into religious illusions and into the roots of neurosis in religious people was so much on target that they caused knee jerks of outrage among religious people everywhere. It took many people quite a long time before they could view his intuitions calmly and see how much health he held out to them with his almost clairvoyant hunches about what was going on in their minds and hearts. His method of healing and his way of getting at their darkness, especially the darkness that so easily combined with unhealthy religion, form the basis of not only much of modern psychiatry, but of religious spiritual direction as well.

The Origin of God and Morality

> God at bottom is nothing but an exalted father.
> —Freud, *Totem and Taboo*

In his practice as psychoanalyst, Freud noticed a certain pattern among neurotics: their religious life was less moral than compulsive; men and women were frozen by fear to do or avoid things. Reason played no role here. Further, the God of the religious seemed very much like everything they wanted in a father. God seemed a figment created in the secret recesses in which men and women shaped their wishes. When he read the writings of ethnologists and historians of religions, Freud's "hunch" was bolstered by their hypotheses. These disciplines overturned the popular Judeo-Christian view of human origins, that our forebears had fallen from a paradise in which they had enjoyed an embarrassment of preternatural gifts to a low state in which their embarrassment now lay in their poverty of being all too human. Darwin had refuted this Augustinian view of the fall with his theory of evolution. Man and woman had begun humbly and moved upward. If they moved from the less sophisticated and well-developed states to the higher and more complex states, then, the conventional widsom of the nineteenth century concluded, so did religion move with it from the less developed to the more highly developed. These studies corroborated Freud's hunch about the origins of things. Thus, he concluded that his neurotic patients shared something very much in common with primitives in their religions: fear and helplessness before reality. This is the origin of religion, in Freud's view. It is a manifestation of a primitive and uncultivated level of human nature. All are afraid of the dark future awaiting them, so they create a sphere they call "the holy" to deal with it. This sphere is peopled by a citizenry unrivaled by, and higher than, men and women, and it is tended by an All-High father figure whom they call "God." Freud knew the workings of the neurotic mind, and he read that into religion and used the findings of ethnologists and historians of religions to bolster his intuition that human affectivity was a tissue of ambivalences: one loves and hates, fears and needs (desperately), seeks and avoids one's father and mother and their surrogates.

I begin this study of Freud's critique of religion with his theses on the origin of morality. After I complete it, his thoughts on God should be more easily understood. For Freud, the moral life is not based on reason, but on a figment of fear found universally, but called by ethnologists taboo, after an originally Polynesian concept. Freud wrote about this in the second chapter of *Totem and Taboo*, titled "Taboo and the Ambivalence of Emotions." In Polynesia, taboo means two things: either the sacred and consecrated or the uncanny, dangerous, forbidden, and unclean.[2] In the West, we have only the notion of "the holy" (*sacer*, Latin; *agos*, Greek; *kodaush*, Hebrew) as an analogue, but it is a poor one alongside the richness of the Polynesian concept. Taboos offer no justification; they just are and are perceived as such. There is no rational basis for them either, and no moral theological system seems capable of gathering them into its organizing arms. No one knows where they originated; they do not seem to have come from any god; they just are and must be obeyed. The sources

Freud cites for his theses on the origins of morality are W. Thomas' article in the eleventh edition of the *Encyclopaedia Britannica;* Wilhelm Wundt's work on religion, myth, and primitive psychology (*Volkerpsychologie, Religion und Mythus,* published in Leipzig, 1905–09); and the work of the first Oxford ethnologist, E. B. Taylor (1871), who wrote about the evolutionary development of religion. The latter maintained what became dogma for the rest of his century and flowed over into the next: that religion developed upward in a straight line, passing through various perceptible stages; that its origins survive among contemporary primitives and may be studied to give us scientific knowledge about our own human genesis. Freud accepted this and would have us look to "our primitives" if we would see how religion began. The pattern the Taylor-Freud thesis describes looks like this: we began with animism, in which all people and things are instinct with soul; next we moved up to polytheism and then on to monotheism. (Totem, 34) With Thomas, Freud said that "sanctity" meant, in some way, "uncleanness." So to violate a taboo meant that one had violated its sanctity and had thereby become unclean. In Polynesia, the obverse of taboo is noa, which means "ordinary." Taboo, then, means "forbidden and dangerous." Taboo is the power hidden in a person or thing, or it can come about by being imposed by a priest or dignitary. Taboo functions automatically; it avenges itself in our internal lives, without fail. Later, society, too, would avenge infringements of any taboo. Violators themselves became taboo but might become normal again through penance. Persons or things charged with taboo are filled with a power called mana, which is somewhat like electricity, in that it can be passed from one person or thing to another by the merest contact. Kings and chiefs have this power, which can also be invested in things, which in turn become repositories of the power. One cannot address kings and chiefs directly, but only through the mediatorship of one having greater mana than oneself. Mana, therefore, is the genus from which the species taboo is derived. Thus, conditions like menstruation, childbearing, and puberty are taboo states. Taboo affects persons, states, and even places, imposing interdictions on any violator with its automatic, irrational and imponderable power. (Totem, 29–30, passim)

Freud thinks that the roots of our moral imperatives are to be found in the notion taboo. With Wundt, he says that kings, priests, and chiefs "exercise an especially effective taboo and are themselves exposed to the strongest taboo compulsion." The sources of taboo are deeper than economic powers and the privileges of the upper classes—Freud rejected the

Marxist analysis ab initio; instead, "they begin where the most primitive and at the same time the most enduring human impulses have their origin, namely, in the fear of the effect of demonic powers." The taboo was the "objectified fear of the demonic." But later this fear detached itself from demons and became autonomous. It became "the compulsion of custom and tradition and finally the law." (Totem, 34; 307 of Wundt) Therefore, Wundt theorizes that underlying all morality is fear of the demonic. "Psychic persistence" keeps taboo at the root of contemporary custom and law, according to Wundt. But Freud won't accept fear of demons as a psychological explanation of anything, since demons don't exist. If they did, it would be different. Freud considers them in the same category as the gods and God: they are the product of the psychic powers of humanity. So he concludes that humans, not gods or demons, create taboos and all moralities; that the moral is the reasonable imposed on conduct to guide it to perfection, or to keep it from working harm on one's neighbor.

In the early development of the phenomenon and concept taboo, the sacred and unclean are in undifferentiated states. There, taboo is an apt word for the intermediate stage of the demonic, which, by then, has come to mean "don't touch!" It bespeaks a dread of contact. Later, the sacred and unclean would become differentiated, but dread of contact adheres to both the sacred and the unclean, even though they develop in opposite directions. It proved to Freud that, originally, both spheres were in agreement. The object, when touched, avenged itself because of demonic power inherent in it. Later, awe and aversion were the two emotions connected with the holy and the unclean. (Totem, 35f.) Wundt says that one can see the separation coming: "It is a general law in mythology that a preceding stage, just because it has been overcome and pushed back by a higher stage, maintains itself next to it in a debased form so that the objects of its veneration become objects of aversion." (Totem, 36; Wundt, 307)

Freud concluded that compulsion neurotics suffered from a "taboo disease." He warned, however, that the similarity might be superficial. The origins of both compulsion prohibitions and taboo are unmotivated and enigmatic. They just appear and must stay because of the invincible anxiety that violation is sure to be punished—someone will suffer something unknown for a violation. The heart of both taboo and neurosis is, therefore, "don't touch"—it is a touching phobia. It may be either a physical or a mental phobia; the two blend following the movement of what Freud calls "displacement." Thus, an obsessive prohibition tends to be extended from one realm to the other so that, in Freud's words, the whole world comes to be "embargoed." To touch one who is unclean from a taboo is to become unclean oneself; it is that contagious. (Totem, 37f.) Both the physical and the mental realms involve excessive restrictions and renunciations in life. Part of one's violation uncleanness may be removed by penances or purifications, expiations or defense reactions; the most common is washing with water, as in lustrations. (Totem, 40) In the background of Freud's thought is, obviously, the Jewish and the Catholic purification rites of his day, which exercised such power over people. For instance, circumcision and baptism release one from demonic power and change one into a cleansed person and a child of the religious and personal family. Freud sees these rites as roots for both religion and compulsion.

Compulsion is characterized by ambivalence; the neurotic both loves and hates the object of the compulsion. This state demands that one seek surrogates, since the two currents are so localized that they cannot meet, and the first level is now repressed and unconscious anyway. Freud says that it is a law of neurosis that obsessive acts serve the impulse coming ever closer to the forbidden act; that is, one is compulsed about something religious because one wants to do the opposite, the forbidden act. He says, "The basis of taboo is a forbidden action for which there exists a strong inclination in the unconscious." He maintains that the center of both neurosis and the infantile wish-life is to be found in the earliest taboos: don't kill the totem animal, and don't marry or sleep with forbidden women. It is important to remember this linkage throughout his critique of religion; the neurotic and the infantile are wed in the religious soul, even the best of them.

Thus, the nub of taboo is "the propensity to arouse the ambivalence of man and to tempt him to violate the prohibition." (Totem, 44f.) The violation arouses envy and tempts others to do the same. Touching is the first act in taking possession of or using a person or thing. (Totem, 46) Freud bases his proofs that compulsion and taboos share more than similarities on that part of Frazer's *The Golden Bough* titled "Taboo and the Perils of the Soul." (Totem, 50; in Frazer, Part II, 1911 ed.) It is well to remember this source, since it and Freud's other sources will come into play during my assessment of Freud's critique.

Freud goes on to analyze taboo. First off, an excess of anxiety led to the taboo ceremonial. In fact, excess is the tip-off that one is neurotic; an excess of tenderness and hostility, in alternating moods, is typical of neurotic behavior. The tenderness originates where there is also an excess of hostility, i.e., where there is an ambivalent attitude. "The hostility is then cried down by an excessive increase of tenderness which is expressed as anxiety and becomes compulsive because otherwise it would not suffice for its task of keeping the unconscious opposition in a state of repression." (Totem, 66f.) Freud says that today's privileged persons are often the objects of deification, while there is also heavy unconscious hostility against them. The people distrust the privileged just as they once did kings and nobles; and they surround the celebrity with concomitant taboos: one wishes to touch but cannot; one wishes to violate but must not; one wants to participate in the mana of the famous merely by the sympathetic magic of rubbing against them.

The savage elevated the king to a level at which he was responsible for the cosmos and could be killed when things went wrong. Neurotics act the same with delusions of persecution; the president is responsible for one's woes. For Freud, the prototype for the neurotic is the child-father relation. (Totem, 66f.) The neurotic sees the persecutor as a surrogate father. In the taboo ceremonial for the elevation of a king, Freud finds that among the people there is love-hate ambivalence toward the king, making his life all but unbearable. Neurotics have both conscious tendencies and unconscious countertendencies that are suppressed but that meet and tend to satisfy one another. The compulsive act, therefore, is only nominally a protection against the forbidden act. In reality, it is a repetition of the forbidden act: for example, repetitive washings may really be masturbatory activity. (Totem, 68)

Both taboo and neurosis punish the king-father for his omnipotence in the very veneration that his subjects offer him. There is an ambivalent attitude toward the dead, for one fears that the dead become demonic. One tries, therefore, to hide from the dead. Thus, the two feelings noted both in taboo and in neurosis are tenderness and hostility, and when applied to the dead become both mourning for them and satisfaction that they are dead. With primitives, the process adjusts itself by projecting the unknown inner hostility onto demons in the outer world. Freud will later say that with us, the projection is onto the modern local or national demons, such as political or religious enemies. (Totem, 83) The essence of what he is saying is that the seething and intolerable angers that one falls prey to are taken care of, allowing one to function in the world, by blaming Commies, "fags," Jews, Catholics, and so on, instead of facing up to one's inner darkness.

Freud posits two sources for every act: (1) the systematic and (2) the unconscious, but real, origin. Thus, each act judged by consciousness has a patent and latent origin. The projection of one's own evil impulses becomes the world system for the primitive and, by extension—since religions and their adherents are primitive and infantile, in Freud's eyes—for the neurotic (read "religious person"). Freud is building a case for making religions the collective—and legitimated—repositories for our individual lunacies. He uses Wundt's research to say that, in the history of religions, evil demons are older than good ones; they also dominate them. Freud extrapolates from this and comes up with the assertion that the origin of the demons seems to be the dead, since they were seen as the spirits of long-dead persons. Primitives dealt with the evil spirits by rendering them benign through appeasement.

The ambivalence of the holy at its roots may explain the present consciousness that is secular and lumps the divine and demonic together—all is spirit or all is matter. Wundt sees the roots of the holy as the sacred and unclean. In this, I submit, he is wrong. The world is not sacred and profane; it is divine or demonic. The roots of the holy have reasserted themselves in these eschatological categories today. The re-emergence of contemplation and mysticism among Catholics and hot mystical fundamentalism among Protestants and Shi'ite Muslims manifest the millennial appearance of religious extremes that crop up in religions at the end of a period of time (like a millennium), thought to bring both an end to time and an appearance of God in the world. One wonders why only evil impulses are seen by Freud as the engine of primitive religions; it doesn't coincide with even the linguistic facts. God and Demon are linguistically undifferentiated in the Sanskrit and the Persian *Raksha*, which was an evil force on the Persian side of the mountains and a good one on the Indian side. Freud's use of his sources is suspect, to say the least, and as I will demonstrate later, his sources have been discredited in the light of today's scholarship.

Wundt sees taboo as rooted in and meaning demonic and not to be touched. It was only later that the two became differentiated. Freud says that taboo was ambivalent from the beginning, and that it stems from an emotional ambivalence. (Totem, 89) He tries to prove it linguistically by saying that many words in the *Ur* languages included their opposites. A slight difference in pronunciation of the ambivalent word gave them the two meanings, according to Freud's linguistics, which doesn't hold water in the view of contemporary linguistics. Whatever word one uses, taboo as category vanished from society in the West, which severely weakens Freud's theory that conscience and taboo originate in the same way; for example, a "taboo sense of guilt" is by his reckoning a "taboo conscience." He will extend this to religion to mean that the religious conscience is at best primitive and at worst infantile, obsessive-compulsive, and therefore irrational. It is based on illusion, not reality. There will be much truth in what he says, but it will be the truth he saw in neurotic patients who happened to be religious, hence the truth of an individual, not the systematic truth that he tried to portray in his corpus of books against religion. Both religious people and religions can become sick; true enough. But he tried to show that they evolved—which has yet to be demonstrated; the opposite seems more likely. And he tried to demonstrate that he had construed the sick individual correctly and had constructed a systematics to articulate his hunches into the individual's soul and mind. I will demonstrate that his healing system works for the ill, but his systematics of religions is false and amateurish, based, not on history, but on the fancies of the infant discipline history of religions. So when he concludes that "conscience is the inner perception of objections to definite wish impulses that exist in us . . . [and this] does not have to depend on anything else, that it is sure of itself," he means that conscience is a fabrication of the overheated religious mind. He goes on to say that savages who violate a taboo feel the same reproaches as do moderns who violate their conscience, this without ever having met a modern savage, let alone studied one professionally. He goes on to say, "Taboo is a command of conscience, the violation of which causes a terrible sense of guilt which is as self-evident as its origin is unknown." (Totem, 90) Again, he categorically condemns the millions of healthy religious persons who form their consciences quietly and rationally and without the slightest trace of obsessive behavior. This is because the religious studies of his day were reductionistic and aided him in his nineteenth-century prejudice and because his practice was heavily devoted to lonely, neurotic females for whom he had compassion but little liking and respect. In condemning conscience to the taboo heap, he relegated woman there as well. When he says that the origin of conscience is unknown, he hoists himself on his own petard; he is endeavoring to uncover the roots of conscience—in primitive religion—to demonstrate that religion and its God are not plugged into reality.

It seems probable to Freud that conscience is rooted in ambivalent feelings, just as taboo is, that one has a conscious feeling and a counter-feeling in the unconscious. Conscience, therefore, is rooted in two contrasting feelings. Compulsion neurotics are painfully conscientious, which is a reaction against the temptation hidden, but active, in the unconscious. This in turn becomes a guilt, which grows as the person becomes sicker. (Totem, 90f.) Further, guilt contains much anxiety (conscience phobia)—the fear points to unconscious sources; "when wish feelings undergo repression their libido becomes transformed into anxiety." (Totem, 92f.) Guilt contains the unknown, which is the motivation for the rejection. Prohibition is based on what people want to do, and taboo is expressed mainly in prohibitions. The desire frequently is unconscious, especially the desire to kill, and is revealed in the dreams of normal people as well as in those of the sick. Therefore, Freud assumes that the taboo and moral prescript aren't superfluous in the matter of killing, since the desire to kill exists irrefutably in sick and well alike. Through displacement, an unconscious impulse arises ostensibly unconnected with its conscious cousin. Hence, taboo and moral laws are similar but different psychologically.

Next, Freud analyzed the neurosis in question. The impulse to kill is repressed, and the neurotic translates it into the fear that another, most often a loved one, is in danger of being punished for what the neurotic wants to do. He explains the dynamics of what many call "smother love." Hitting the mark and explaining the experience of so many who have dealt with the compulsed, he says, "The neurotic . . . acts as if he were altruistic, while primitive man seems egotistical." The psychology of punishment is that the punishers have the same impulses as those they punish. The "mobility" of the neurotic is a fear of one's own death displaced to a beloved person. The process runs thus: an evil impulse toward the beloved is at the basis of prohibition. It is repressed through some prohibition. Displacement substitutes a beloved as object for one's virtuous hostility. Then the fear of one's death emerges from a wish for it. Tender altruism compensates for "brutal egotism." The neurosis is disguised by overcompensation. (Totem, 94f.)

The touch taboo is similar to a neurotic touching phobia, which is connected to a prohibition against sexual touching, which is "deflected and displaced." Hence, egotism plus eroticism become a touching neurosis; that is, there is more of sex than of social relations in a touching neurosis. Freud feels that neuroses are much like cultural achievements—although distorted: hysteria caricatures art; compulsion neuroses caricature religion; and paranoiac delusion caricatures philosophical systems. His thesis is that "neuroses are asocial formations; they seek to accomplish by private means what arose in society through collective labour." The root of neurosis is a flight from the real social world to a fantasy world that is pleasurable. (Totem, 96f.)

Freud moves on in his analysis of religion and neurosis into a chapter titled "The Omnipotence of Thought," which is an analysis of magic, sorcery, and its likeness to religion. He says that it is the essence of totemistic thought to be unconcerned with any distinction between the contents of mind and extramental reality. He accepts without question the hypotheses of Wundt, H. Spencer, J. G. Frazer, A. Lang, and E. B. Taylor. Their hypothesis on religious development is tied to one of anthropological evolution. The first stage of religion was one of *animism*, which is a myth stage in which humans saw everybody and everything inhabited by spirits. The next stage is what they call the *religious stage*. The contemporary stage is the *scientific* one. Animism is not per se a religion but contains the stuff from which religion was formed: myth, which was based on animistic foundations. Magic and sorcery come into play in this most primitive level of religion, and Freud maintains, not without reason, that it persists to this day. The animist becomes the magician forcing his will on reality to change it; and the sorcerer either charms or terrifies the spirits so that they become pliant to his wishes. In this, the animist becomes master of all he sees and doesn't see. (Totem, 102) S. Runach maintains that both magic and sorcery are a strategy the primitive finds not only useful, but necessary. But Freud, following Mauss, construes both as merely techniques; know the correct rite or formula and the mind moves both matter and spirit. (Ibid.) Sorcery treats spirits like people and tries to persuade them to follow one's will. So it uses intimidation, deprivation of power, and subjection to one's will as it would with anyone one wished to persuade. Magic is essentially different from sorcery, since it is not concerned with spirits. It is an earlier religious form than sorcery—and a more important one; it exists where nature had not yet become spiritual. E. B. Taylor said that magic is based on an assumption that "mistakes an ideal connection for a real one." So, in magic, one uses the name of a ghost to frighten it away. (Totem, 103, n. 8) In magic, one assumes telepathy throughout, whether one is causing rain or indulging in sexual intercourse, to ensure a good crop. Frazer calls the production of rain through magic homeopathic or imitative magic. (Totem, 106)

The notion of contagious magic is based on contiguity—one keeps the bow that wounded one in a cool place so the wound will not become inflamed. Therefore, contiguity and imitation are the bases of magic, and both are the foundation for the metaphysical outlook of the "primitive": that the real-out-there is controlled by the mind. One is tempted to say that it looks very much like Hegel and all idealism, mutatis mutandis. What Freud and the early historians of religion meant by the imitative factor in magic is pretty much what Eliade means when he talks about redoing or recreating the cosmogonic-healing acts through ritual. Ritual is really liturgical mimesis by which one's intention is to link up oneself and one's client umbilically to the gods and giants that once walked the earth in a time of primordial innocence. Freud calls this mentality "madness." Frazer agrees with Taylor that "men mistook the order of their ideas for the order of nature." Hence, if one controls thought, nature follows along pliantly. Freud and the others he reads don't accept this as being the essence of magic, but merely the path it travels. Contagious magic presupposes the imitative form. Hence, Freud concludes that our wishes impel us to use magic. The child and the primitive satisfy the wish through play and imitative representation. When he comes to criticize religion he will call it emotively and intellectually infantile, looking for a "Father" in the sky to tend to the world's injustices and madnesses, never growing up to the human darkness implied by mature and responsible behavior. One should watch, however, how he works the evidence to suit his ready-made logic: what the child does is not what the adult does; what the primitive does is not what the modern should do. He overlooks the staying power of mime and rite, concluding that it is there but quite otiose. One can just as easily conclude that it is there and meant to be there; because one must become mature and responsible in order to be human in no way demands that one not be mythical as well.

Freud then begins to embroider his notion of religion onto the one he accepts concerning primitive magic and sorcery. He says that prayer is in three stages: (1) primitive, in which the emphasis is on the wish itself and not the means of its fulfillment; (2) the second stage, in which the emphasis falls on the means; and (3) the third stage, when skepticism arrives and one begins to repress and demand that belief is necessary for the conjuration to work; that is, he says that prayer without piety is useless. So Freud sees prayer as fitting into the framework of magic; for example, "My words fly up, my thoughts remain below./Words without thoughts never to heaven go." (Hamlet, Act III, Scene 4) (Totem, 108–10 passim) Therefore, both primitive religious culture and contemporary religiosity overestimate the power of thought to control the real world.

Space and time conjoin in thought. There are two principles of association in the magical mind: similarity (which becomes imitation in later rites) and contiguity. Thus, similar plus similar equals one is in contact with the world one wants to control. Also, thing next to thing in the mind and extramental reality become, through contact, efficacious in bringing about the wish. Therefore, thought is omnipotent in the magical mind.

In seeing the magical and pious mind fitting into the same category, Freud commits two capital blunders: first off, conjuration may well be the proper term for magic, but modern religion impetrates in prayer. The one forces the result, the other begs it and in no way believes that the force of its will has any power over the mind and will of the Almighty. There is an essential difference here. The Christian, Jew, Muslim, and Hindu wait for grace—outside help—to do the job. The magician does it himself, having god as agent. Second, Freud compares a healthy scientific attitude with the worst of Christianity and Judaism; then he compares that with magic and says that religion and magic fit together as one. Von Harnack's principle was that it is wrong to compare the best of one's own against the worst of one's adversary. This Freud seems to do. So he errs both as a historian of religion and as a scientist who delves into religion. In both errors he seems to miss the different internal states involved in the one who does magic and the one who prays healthily.

Freud states that the same dynamic is operative in the neurotic mind as that viewed in the magical one; thought is omnipotent in both. Thinking makes it so. Freud sees this dynamic as diseased, always. He fuses the disease with the dynamic, the thing (malady) with its way of making something; this is the same trap that Frazer and Taylor fell into and that Freud noted and earlier avoided: that the essence of magic and the omnipotence of thought are different. Omnipotence is the way that magic travels, not its essence.

Freud says that the "thinking makes it so" dynamic of the primitive magician is also to be found in the mentally wounded. He calls it superstition and states that all compulsive neurotics have the same superstition. (Totem, 112) The thought is the basis of the symptom, not the experience. "The primary obsessive actions of these neurotics are really altogether of a magical nature. If not magic, they are at least anti-magic and are destined to ward off the expectation of evil with which the neurosis is wont to begin." The evil expected was death. Freud accepts Schopenhauer's idea that the problem of death is at the root of every philosophy. The neurotic displaces this onto some trifling thing. Compulsive neurotics protect themselves by formulae, just as magicians use incantations. Freud believes that these compulsive acts began as spells against evil wishes and ended up as substitutes for "forbidden sexual activity." (Totem, 113f.) He places the omnipotence of thought concept in a schema in which animism becomes religion from which science developed. Animism sees the self as omnipotent; religion, and the religious person, sees God as omnipotent but doesn't really give up its own omnipotence, since one controls the gods by one's own wishes. Freud says that science rids one of omnipotence and that one submits "to death as to all other natural necessities in a spirit of resignation." (Totem, 115)

Both primitives and neurotics are narcissistic and feel themselves omnipotent through the medium of thought. This is a state of solipsism, in which one says, "I alone rule the world through thought." It is based on a refusal to admit death as a fact. (Totem, 117) Freud finds the development of the psyche passing through three stages of thought: animism, religion, and science. Animism is the narcissistic stage; religion is the stage of parental dependence; and science is the stage of independence. Only in art does Freud see a semblance of thought omnipotence left. The artist began, for Freud, as a religious-magical figure. In their use of magic, primitives imposed the structure of mind on the outer world. Freud views modern piety as an attempt to incorporate animism into the soul in the same way. (Totem, 118f.)

Freud says that the creation of spirits was humankind's first theoretical achievement. Spirits sprang from the taboo source, just as the moral law did. Taboo is the font of the law and the spirits. But spirit is a reflection of the inner psychic life. "The thing which we, just like primitive man, project in outer reality, can hardly be anything else than the recognition of a state in which a given thing is present to the senses and to consciousness, next to which another state exists in which the thing is latent." (Totem, 121f.) The unconscious exists alongside the conscious. Spirit is the ability to recall what has gone from conscious perception. The "real bearers of psychic activity" form the unconscious. The stages that are preliminary to psychology are superstition, anxiety, dreams, and demons. (Totem, 126)

Therefore, for Freud, morality is rooted in taboo, and its dynamic follows the laws outlined by the ethnologists for taboo. Primitives, neurotics, and religion follow the same irrational—and destructive, for moderns—paths. Now Freud turns the gimlet eye on God, seeking God's roots and trying to find just how God functions in both religion and the individual mind.

He begins his analysis of the God-phenomenon by rooting it in totemism. In sum, Freud maintains that humankind's relations with God are analogous to, and rooted in, the totemic (and therefore infantile) ambivalence of feelings that the individual or tribe had toward its totem animal or thing. This thing or animal is a living—religious—symbol of the tribe. The human person and the totem are one genus; the devotee does not distinguish between the totem and other members of the tribe; they are all an undifferentiated whole. (Totem, 135) The totem protects them, and in turn they do not kill it or reap it. They eat its flesh only rarely—solely on ceremonial occasions that demand communion with one's totem. (Totem, 139) The very name of the tribe, in fact, derives from the totem. Hence, totemism was a religion of mystic union with one's totem that formed one's social relations with the tribe and with externs. (Totem, ibid.: cf. Frazer's "Origin of Totemism" in the *Fortnight Review*, 1899).

Now, Freud offers us a trove of his intuitions, beginning by saying that the neurotic child identifies quite easily with animals and has ambivalent feelings toward them—both stroking them and wishing to kill them at almost the same time. (Totem, 170) The animal is the father to the totem clan. This is important in Freud's critique, since he says that God is father and we the dependent, father-needy—read infantile—children who create the Father chimera. The clan lays down two imperatives regarding its totem and its extension, the clan: (1) don't kill the totem animal and (2) don't misuse, or even marry, one's own womenfolk. Incest is an enormously important and complex taboo. Freud noted that Oedipus violated both rules. (Totem, 171)

He makes copious use of W. Robertson Smith's *The Religion of the Semites*, published in 1889, to flesh out the rites and internal dispositions of totemic sacrifice. Freud accepts his assertion that altar sacrifice loomed large in totemic religion, as in all religions: "its origins must be traced back to the very general causes whose effects were everywhere the same." According to Freud—who accepted Robertson Smith's thesis in its entirety—the root meaning of sacrifice was the same everywhere. Freud's docility before nineteenth-century apodicticism makes him seem naive by our present standards, but one should remember that these sciences were new and that their hypotheses confirmed many of the prevailing wisdoms, especially one's "down on" religion. Originally, sacrifice was meant to reconcile the clients with their god or to render the deity benign. Only later did it come to have another, and secondary, meaning: self-denial. (Totem, 172f.) Social fellowship between the god and the god's clients was the root meaning of worship. Sacrifice consisted of the things that people ate, like cereals, flesh, fruits, wine, and so on. Later, flesh—which was the "food for the god"—became too repugnant to the client. So blood became the deity's diet; later, it was replaced with wine: "the god and his worshippers are communicants, thus confirming all their other relations." (Totem, 173f.) The two became of one substance. Robertson Smith says:

> There is not the least doubt . . . that every sacrifice was originally a clan sacrifice, and that the killing of a sacificial animal originally belonged to those acts which were forbidden to the individual and were only justified if the whole kin assumed the responsibility. Primitive men had one class of actions which were thus characterized, namely, actions which touched the holiness of the kin's common blood. (Totem, 176f.)

The god and the clan were one community. Freud says that Robertson Smith, "on the basis of much evidence identifies the sacrificial animal with the old totem animal." The "holy death" was justified on the grounds that it was the only way communion could come about. (Totem, 178f.) Both he and Freud stress the sacramental nature of the sacrifice and communion.

A holiday, for the totemists, was a day in which the cruel killing and eating of the totem animal was prescribed; the solemn strictures against this were lifted for a day by a law that was equal in power to the taboo against it. In psychoanalysis, the totem animal is a substitute for the father. The animal is killed, yet mourned; it is an ambivalence that Freud sees in all human feelings of moment, especially religious ones. Freud explains the essence of the idea in this way:

> They undid their deed by declaring that the killing of the father substitute, the totem, was not allowed, and renounced the fruits of their deed by denying themselves the liberated women. Thus they created two fundamental taboos of totemism out of the *sense of guilt of the son*, and for this reason these had to correspond with the two repressed wishes of the Oedipus complex. Whoever disobeyed became guilty of the two only crimes which troubled primitive society. (Totem, 185)

Freud takes the myth pattern of the primal patricide from the history of religions of his day. It is this deed on which the ambivalent attitudes of primitive and modern religious people are based. "If the father had treated us like the totem we should never have been tempted to kill him." (Totem, 187) Every religion, according to Freud, contains this primal deed as one of its characteristics.

> The totem religion had issued from the sense of guilt of the sons as an attempt to palliate this feeling and to conciliate the injured father through subsequent obedience. All later religions prove to be attempts to solve the same problem . . . they are all . . . reactions aiming at the same great event with which culture began and which ever since has not let mankind come to rest. (Totem, 187)

He goes on to say:

> The ambivalence attached to the father complex also continues in totemism and in religions in general. The religion of totemism included not only manifestations of remorse and attempts at reconciliation, but also serves to commemorate the triumph over the father. The gratification obtained thereby creates the commemorative celebration of the totem feast at which the restrictions of subsequent obedience are suspended, and makes it a duty to repeat the crime of patricide through the sacrifice of the totem animal as often as the benefits of this deed, namely, the appropriation of the father's properties, threaten to disappear as a result of the changed influences of life. . . . A part of the son's defiance also reappears . . . in the formation of later religions. . . . The socially established prohibition against fratricide is now added to the prohibition against killing the totem. . . . Society is now based on complicity in the common crime, religion on the sense of guilt and the consequent remorse, while morality is based partly on the necessities of society and partly on the expiation which this sense of guilt demands. (Totem, 187–89)

Next, Freud follows two themes of religion away from their primitive sources: what motivated the sons to kill the father and the relations of the sons with the father. (Totem, 189f.) His thesis is:

> that god is in every case modelled after the father and that our personal relation to god is dependent upon our relation to our physical father, fluctuating and changing with him, and that god at bottom is nothing but an exalted father. Thus the totem may have been the first form of the father substitute and the god a later one in which the father regained his human form. (Totem, 191)

The bitter feeling toward the primal father stemmed from his unapproachable power. Both acrimony and tenderness for the father grew together in the "primal horde," which killed its father. But culture changed, and as it did the original equality of each tribal member was lost. So Freud and Robertson Smith hypothesized that the change saw the elevation of some heroic tribal members to the level of a deity. The tendency was to "revive the old father ideal in the creation of gods. . . . That a man should become a god and that a god should die, which today seems to us as an outrageous presumption, was still by no means offensive to the conceptions of classical antiquity." (Totem, 192) The father appeared in the sacrificial ceremony as victim and as god. The son's ambivalent emotions appear here as well; he is tender toward his father-ideal, yet vicious in killing him. The rite commemorates this ambivalence and continues it. The primal father was deposed in death and reinstated triumphantly in ritual. All this becomes stylized later in the rites of religion. (Totem, 193) The two feelings that perdured in subsequent religion were the defiance of the son together with his sense of guilt. Defiance and guilt are the ambivalences that Freud finds in present-day religion. In Christianity, the guilt flowing from the first sin could be atoned for only by the death through sacrifice of another human. (Totem, 198) Freud concludes:

> Thus in the Christian, mankind most unreservedly acknowledges the guilty deed of primordial times because it now has found the most complete expiation for this deed in the sacrificial death of the son. . . . In the same deed which offers the greatest possible expiation to the father, the son also attains the goal of his wishes against the father. He becomes a god himself beside or rather in place of his father. The religion of the son succeeds the religion of the father . . . [thus] the totem feast is revived . . . the sons thereby identifying themselves with him and becoming holy themselves . . . [thus] the Christian communion is a new setting aside of the father, a repetition of the crime that must be expiated. We see how well justified is Frazer's dictum that "the Christian communion has absorbed within itself a sacrament which is doubtless far older than Christianity. (Totem, 199, much of it taken from Frazer's *Eating the God*, 51)

Freud saw this primal crime leaving "ineradicable traces in the history of humankind and must have expressed itself the more frequently in numer-ous substitutive formations the less it itself was to be remembered." (Totem, 200) The tragedy's hero had to suffer and die, since he had taken on the guilt of the others. The chorus in Greek tragedy had caused the problem for the hero, but they "exhaust themselves in sympathy and regret, and the hero himself is to blame for his sufferings." So Freud concluded:

(1) The beginnings of religion, ethics, society, and art meet in the Oedipus complex. This is in entire accord with the findings of psychoanalysis, namely, that the nucleus of all neuroses as far as our present knowledge of them goes is the Oedipus complex . . . that ambivalence, originally foreign to our emotional life, was acquired by mankind from the father complex, where psychoanalytic investigation of the individual today still reveals the strongest expression of it. . . . (2) We base everything on the assumption of a psyche of the mass in which psychic processes occur as in the psychic life of the individual. We allow an emotional process much as might have arisen among generations of sons that had been ill-treated by their fathers, to continue to new generations which had escaped such treatment by the very removal of the father. (Totem, 201–3)

Our unconscious has an apparatus that allows us to untangle all the substitutions for the primal deeds that humankind has left embedded in custom, law, rite, and myth. So, "by this method of unconscious understanding of all customs . . . which the original relation to the primal father had left behind, later generations may also have succeeded in taking over this legacy of feelings." (Totem, 204f.)

Freud says that we passed on the primal wisdom that one should not do things like breaking the killing taboo. This creates a sense of guilt. The neurotic picks up the dynamic and twists it so that one becomes "guilty," not for real crimes, but for psychic ones. "It is characteristic of the neurosis to put a psychic reality above an actual one and to react as seriously to thoughts as the normal person reacts only towards realities." (Totem, 205) Each "over-good" person had, therefore, done something early in life for which he or she was guilty. This perversity antecedes the supermoral personality it later generates. In the neurotic, there may be no deed for which one is guilty. But thought is the same as deed: the one substitutes for the other. (Totem, 207)

Thus, Freud had given his scholarly explanation for the origin of God and guilt in *Totem and Taboo*. Original Sin was to be explained by a Greek myth, Oedipus, in which the son takes his mother and kills his father, not by a Hebraic one like the Adam and Eve story. God was a totemic projection of one's fear, hate, and love for one's father. Sin was an explanation for one's paralyzing fear, because of one's helplessness, and the underside of one's need for psychic and cultural structure: if there were no sin, there would be no law and order within us or in society. But Freud wanted more than merely to criticize religion; he wanted people to grow up and away from the dependence he saw in religious people. He wanted people to grow into reality by what he called "education for reality." His whole critique of religion is to be found in simpler and more complete form in one of his last works, *The Future of an Illusion*, which he wrote in 1927.

Freud's Critique of Religion

> Religion would thus be the universal obsessional neurosis of humanity: like the obsessional neurosis of children, it arose out of the Oedipus complex, out of the relation to the father.[3]

In 1907, Freud published his first thoughts on religion in a paper he titled "Obsessive Actions and Religious Practices." There he saw the very roots of religion as pathological. It was a "universal obsessive neurosis." He was to repeat this formula again and again; in its most famous showcase, it would appear in *The Future of an Illusion*. In 1913 he published *Totem and Taboo* as a technical explanation for his psychological intuitions; he did not proceed inductively, slowly moving toward a conclusion. He knew what he knew immediately and later looked for scientific corroboration. Both *Totem and Taboo* and *The Future of an Illusion* are the results of intuition fused with latter-day attempts at scientific corroboration. *The Future of an Illusion* is a popular treatment of his serious, scientific ideas. It is a brief, well-written essay containing what he had to say about religion. Totemism and taboos (God and morality) were well taken care of by now. Next on the agenda was religion as such. His ideas on it had not changed since 1913, or even 1907: it was still a home for neurotics, for those who refused to grow up.

Freud ended his little book as he should have begun it, placing his thesis on the last page and in the last line: "No, our science is no illusion. But an illusion it would be to suppose that what science cannot give us we can get elsewhere" (i.e., in religion). (Illusion, 92) Freud the atheist, the nonpracticing Jew, the assimilated intellectual who would have humankind stand on its own two feet and face the dark of its loneliness without God in the light of its own human beauty and goodness; Freud, the humanist and the child of the Enlightenment, was never able to leave his roots. A Talmudic saying has it that "if there were no policemen we would eat one another." He began the book by saying that every individual is an enemy of civilization; each of us is antisocial and anticivilization. The engines of our psyches run on the fuel of our triplex desire to kill one another, eat one another, or lie with our sisters or mothers. Murder, cannibalism, and incest are the basic drives that society must legislate against; law is necessary for the domestication of our feisty breed. Without it, there would be chaos; our sexuality, our gluttonous compulsions, and our aggressions would destroy not only our neighbors, but ourselves as well. (Illusion, 3–12 passim)

So every society is a conspiracy of law against our drives. Civilization is built on coercion and the renunciation of one's instincts. The masses are lazy and unintelligent and must be led by a moral elite; this latter made possible only through education for excellence. (Illusion, 7) Virtue is possible, therefore, only if we educate the cream of the crop to be elite leaders of the masses. How much the child of Socrates he was, where knowledge is virtue! How much the descendant of Rousseau, who would see the best in us rise to the surface if only the obstacles to our goodness were removed. Nature is good. How truly Judeo-Christian was this optimistic insistence on the inherent goodness of men and women. It is ironic that as a moribund old man he should be shuffled out of his country by the underside of Germany in the name of the elitism of the Third Reich. Freud the visionary was ever the realist, however; he was too much the physician not to know the working variety of human imperfections. He concluded by stating that perhaps the best one could hope for was to curb the hostile majority through education and healing.

His whole healing method was bookish: like a book, we must be "read" by telling our story so that we might know the fear grinding our souls, and in that knowledge be turned back from our flights into that darkness, and in so doing free the long-repressed energies to move into healthy channels.

Freud possessed the vision of the Jewish mystic that we are good, of the practical Jew that we are less free than the Paradise myth would lead us to believe. He scotched out the myth of Paradise because he thought that it was unhistorical and in telling us of a primordial fall from preternatural heights to instinctual depths said nothing about our real condition. Freud said that we were born good (beloved of our primordial father) and yet were instinct with evil (burning to kill that Oedipal totem-father). It was a new way of explaining us to ourselves. His was a hermeneutics of suspicion because he knew that he must be wary of our killing and devouring instincts. His was also a hermeneutics of willingness to listen to our goodness, trusting that it was there by nature. More on this in my critique of Freud, but suffice it to say that his was a statement not only on human anthropology, but on theodicy as well. God had been brought to the bar of justice to answer why there was evil. Freud absolved God not only for creating evil—it is just there—but also even from living. God didn't exist any more; only men and women did; and they were a strange mix of good and evil in which there was no sin. Getting rid of Genesis rid us of neurotic guilt—Freud's intent from the beginning, since his patients hurt too much from self-inflicted theological wounds—and left men and women with the reality of an ambivalent nature on the move upward. There was a possibility of evolution; we are free but not as free as we wanted to be. Instinct saw to that, since it is a purpose not of our own design, running like engines, without our wills. Freud had the temerity to observe human nature without a Genesis lens and to tell us what he saw. This was an insult to the religious communities, since an observation becomes an insult when it tells an untimely truth.

He maintained that there was psychic energy that moved by mechanistic, biological laws. The law of conservation of energy was imperious in its demand that excitation be followed by tension and that it conclude in a displacement of energy. Man and woman are determined, and mental phenomena come under that rubric no less than do more obviously physical ones. So instinct in conflict with an external prohibition (law) cannot be satisfied by the frustration of its teleology. (Illusion, 12) In the New Testament, sin is missing the mark (*Hamartia* in Greek). Frustration is somewhat a sin against instinct, since it is not allowed to do what it was designed for. The prohibitions that civilization imposes on humankind have detached us from our primordial condition. It is this set of prohibitions that have made us hostile to civilization. The superego interiorizes these commandments and makes them a permanent member of its imperious cadre. But Freud says that this is a good thing in the moral development of a child; external coercion becomes part of one's psychic makeup. However, the grosser instincts—incest, cannibalism, and a killing lust—are so powerful that it is necessary to have enforcers of its laws just to keep the peace. One will indulge the lesser lusts, like aggression or avarice, or the lesser sexual adventures as long as one is not punished for them. The removal of morality would return us to the state of brutes in which no instinct is held back. (Illusion, 20) Nature would coldly destroy us if civilization did not perform its chief task: defending us against the inexorable destructions decreed by Fate. This makes the most important psychical item in a civilization the illusion provided by religion. Without it, Freud says, we would be bestial. With it, unfortunately, many neurotics have failed to internalize the kernel of morality contained in the commandments. (Illusion, 13) So here, in chapter two, Freud has begun his critique of religion. It is necessary for civilization and culture, but one grows beyond it as the child grows beyond its superego in the stages of moral development. Moral ontogeny recapitulates philogeny in the sense that each individual goes through its stages to maturity, as culture and civilization have gone through their stages from animism on up to religion and thence on to the apex, science. Hence, religion is both a cultural factor for good and an emotional retardant. He says all this in the third chapter, which could be titled "The Infantile Model of Religion."

He lines the human psyche with an irrefragable layer of terror. Men and women, at the very earliest times, needed consolations before their inner anxieties and outer fates, otherwise it would have been impossible to have the ego-strength to go on with things. Further, curiosity demanded explanations for the pains and baffles that life imposed on one's aspirations. The evil that destroyed our ancestors was senseless and forced them to their knees in postures of helplessness. This is the prime number of the religious equation for Schleiermacher, and it is not less so for Freud. (Illusion, 22) Thus, humanity genuflected, turned the inner anxieties into outer goals, and dealt with its feelings the way one would with a capricious brigand, a madman, or a shrewd bazaar hawker: depending on the god, our primitive ancestors used a farrago of methods, including appeasement and bribery, to rob the cosmic cruelties of their force. Since they could not use natural sciences to control Nature, primitives used psychology. Thus, psychology was the first level of religious life, and Freud would make his explanation of religion one of reducing the phenomenon to something he knew, like psychology. Religion was the primitive's salient against the irrational forces slavering beyond its pacific confines, lusting for innocent blood.

Freud describes the infancy of religion as a phenomenon coterminous with the infancy of the race; when the latter phase was over, so should the former have been, but it was not. Religion persisted not as something from our infancy, but as something intrinsically infantile, since it was a persistence beyond its time. Religion passed through three stages closely paralleling those of a child's growth. First, just as a child was somewhat helpless with fear before the awesomeness of its own father and the forces of Nature but knew that its father would protect it from them, so it is with religion: men and women pacified the mindless evils of Nature and the intelligent ones of their fathers by fashioning them into a father-god who would protect them. Freud maintains that this is a phylogenetic phenomenon ethnologically and an infantile one psychologically. The god's functions were simple but monumental: he would exorcize them of the terrors of Nature; he would reconcile men and women to the cruelty of the Fates; and he would compensate them for their suffering and privation. (Illusion, 24) So the first stage was the recognition of one's fear for one's father and for the terrors of history. The second stage was the creation of the gods, ordaining them to carry out functions that allowed their clients to live somewhat peacefully in the world.

The third stage in religious development occurred when men and women began to develop a knowledge of the laws of Nature and to contrive some tools with which to subdue it. The more this happened, the farther removed the gods became; their services were no longer required, since the very reason for their being was precisely to do what people could now do for themselves. The one function they could not perform was to keep the lid on human bestiality. So the gods, who had been so autochthonous and looked and deported themselves in so human a fashion, began to withdraw from their primordial closeness and to function from on high as moral gods. Freud accepts "the God of the gaps" hypothesis, in which God is where we humans are not; and where we come to be, God ceases to be. Thus, God became both the keeper of the moral code and its author; it was no longer remembered that it was authored on earth. God also acted as a heavenly watcher who aided us in avoiding evils and provided succor when they were unavoidable. Life had a purpose provided by divine Providence; an Intelligent Will guided all people and things. (Illusion, 25f.) The ultimate evil, death, became, not a human terminus, but a beginning that would see good rewarded and evil punished. Men and women contrived the concept of eternal life to defuse the radical terror of death of its potency. God's infinite goodness and justice fulfilled our fondest desires, but Freud said that it was these very wishes that had demanded and created God in the first place. Again, Voltaire's bon mot, "God made man to His image and likeness, and man returned the compliment," comes to mind. All that was best in man and woman was given to God. Feuerbacher lives on in Freud. It was at this stage of development that people recognized the kernel of truth in the whole god-contrivance: there was a God behind the gods. Now man and woman could return to the intimacy that they once had had with their Father and had lost, not in the lapse in Eden, but in an Oedipal totemic patricide. As time went on, people would create further fictions, such as being good would make a people God's people. Freud must not have known much of

103

the Old Testament history of his people to say that they were chosen because of high virtue; it was because of God's love, not their goodness. Freud said that America would even claim to be God's country; this was the supreme chutzpah, and folly in his eyes. (Illusion, 27) This is the pattern of what Freud called the "infantile prototype" of religious development and of religion per se.

Freud discerns three problems here. First, what are these religious ideas in the light of psychology? What do they mean and whence do they come? Second, he asked whence did religious ideas derive their esteem. Third, he wondered just what was the real worth of these religious ideas. First off, God arose from the primitives' need to protect themselves from Nature's depredations and from the desire to rectify the shortcomings of civilization, i.e., to make a just society of it. So humankind projects a god who looks quite like a human being to keep things under control. But Freud said that personifying Nature's forces in order to appease them is to follow an infantile model. He is more forthright here than he was in *Totem and Taboo* (1912–13). In 1927, Freud would essay that the religious person, childlike to the core, would both fear and long for his or her father and thereby create religion. But this longing *for* and need to be protected *from* God bespoke identical needs in humankind. (Illusion, Ch. 4, 30–35 passim) Thus, religious ideas are need-fulfillers, from a psychological perspective. They come from humankind's keen ability to create (project) on high what it cannot cope with here below. They are esteemed because they are reflections of oneself; they are images of self-love. Now Freud moves to the third query: Just what are religious ideas worth in the workaday world? This he answers in chapters five, six, and seven. In the fifth chapter, Freud begins to assign a value to religious ideas. His thesis is that they are assertions about "facts" that one has not discovered personally; hence, they demand belief, which is a weak word for Freud. He says that people believe because their primordial ancestors and successive generations have believed without interruption. Further, the traditional proofs offered for dogmas have come down to us without interruption. Religion forbids its devotees to demand what every scientist must have: authenticated facts. For Freud, this means that society is insecure in its claims. At best, religious proofs are weak and rooted in a past steeped in the ignorance of the ancients about things scientific. So if our forebears were ignorant about science, if their ideas were weak or incorrect, why should the same not obtain with religious ideas? Hence, he says that the proofs the ancients adduced for religion "bear every mark of untrustworthiness. They are full of contradictions, revisions and falsifications." (Illusion, 37–40 passim) Even bringing revelation into an argument is to hoist oneself on one's own petard; as proof, it is a *petitio principii* (begging the question), since one cannot prove the truth of revelation by appealing to its revealed roots. Religious truth, its adherents aver, must be true because it has the "feel" of truth about it; but that is certainly no proof for anyone else. So one is forced to believe *als ob* (as if) in the modern world. Freud complains that he and his generation know all this, but why, then, is religion still such a force? (Illusion, 40–43 passim) He answers his own question in his sixth chapter, which might have been entitled "The Psychological Value of Religions." His thesis is that religious ideas are not the end-product of a reasoning process, nor are they the precipitates of personal experiences; rather, they are illusions that humankind uses to fulfill its oldest and most profound wishes. The strength of religion lies in the strength of these wishes. Freud, therefore, appeals to a central mantra of the nineteenth century: religion as illusion. Marx and Nietzsche felt oppressed by this aspect of religion too. The finest minds of the century seem to be merely articulating the hubris of their compeers in this; that they knew more and better than anyone else, and that they knew it *nudo e crudo*. History had not been kind to what Robert Bellah has termed "this Enlightenment fundamentalism." Freud rehearses the three most cherished wishes in religion: Providence, which deals with human fear and the desire that a plenipotentiary offer us aid in times of danger; the wish for world justice and someone to superintend it, which has produced the illusion of a moral world order; last, the desire for eternal life gives people both the place and time in which to enjoy those oldest and fondest of their wishes. (Illusion, 47f.)

But, Freud hastens to add, an illusion is not necessarily an error; and to this praising with faint damns he appends his psychological hook. An illusion, though, is something derived from human wishes—which is healthy enough—but to live off them is to live off something akin to a psychotic delusion, since the object of an illusion does not occupy extramental space. Illusions are not false in the true/false sense, since one cannot prove them wrong, but they are not capable of realization and therefore contradict reality. Again we see secularization's tendency to accept the soul of Aristotle's concept of the real as the mind's grasping something that is "there." But with this "soul," modernity demands an empirical body: reality has to be measurable to be proved, and religion is impatient of such scientific proofs. Ergo, illusion is a belief in which wish-fulfillment looms large as a motivating force. So Freud concludes that one cannot take religious people seriously, since they do not place verification—the hallmark of all truth for the scientist—high on their hierarchy of values.

Freud then delivers himself of two axioms: First, all dogmas are illusions, since they cannot be proven. Second, only through science can one gain knowledge of the world outside the self. Intuition and introspection yield only knowledge of the self, not about the problems that religion treats—like Providence, justice, and eternal life. Dogma's conclusions are too facile for Freud, but he is quick to answer to obvious objections that he (Freud) had not refuted dogma. He asserts that one can neither prove nor disprove dogmas, since any and all are irrational, and he finds those adhering to them irresponsible in the light of modern science. One would not be so facile about other things, so why does one hold the unprobed-unproved-unprobable in a world demanding a more serious life posture?

The greatest dogma of them all is the concept God, which one might define, using the Freudian mind-set, as a confection of analogies stretched beyond belief to faith. Religious affect is injurious not just because of one's feeling helpless—that is entirely normal—but in doing nothing about it. That, for Freud, is truly irreligious. (Illusion, 49f.) How much Marx's notion of praxis and Nietzsche's barb to the effect that there was only one Christian and that we killed him on the cross go to the heart of what we claim is religion here in the West: a change of heart (*metanoia*, Greek for loving penance) that emerges in a change of circumstances in an unloving world, which in turn leads to a greater change of heart and so on. It would be nice to have a God, just as it would be nice if there were a changeless moral order and eternal life, but there just is not any for Freud. The very roots of these concepts are in the wish-life of our ignorant, "wretched" ancestors. (Illusion, 51–53) How sad to have read history in so backward a way. Within five years of writing this, Adolf Hitler would be making the "wretched refuse" of our ancestory look much better. This is the most empirical of facts, and for this Freud's system had no answer and could have none.

But what if one were to follow Freud's piping to a time without religious precepts. Would this not lead to chaos? Should one not behave "as if" religious dogmas were true in the name of societal and psychic order? Freud answers such gradualism with the assertion that more harm would come if one kept religious illusions than if one gives them up. (Illusion,

56f.) Further, religion has not made people happy, and that is its chief claim. Men and women are not more moral because of it, which is also one of its paramount claims. They use the sacrament of penance—a priest's concession to their baser instincts—as an excuse for not growing up. The scientific spirit has led to the discovery that primitive religious men and women basically had the same wishes as contemporary ones. Religious life, then, has not improved since the time of the savage. Therefore, it is incredible. Culture has been secularized, so that the more men and women come in contact with the spread of its scientific knowledge, the more will they fall away from religion. This must be so, says Freud, or else when people learn that there is no God—through the good offices of science—they will kill their neighbors, if they have not learned some basis in reason for not doing so before the scales fall from their eyes. (Illusion, 61–64) There are other illusions, but Freud thinks that religion is sufficient for his purposes, which were to teach us to grow up.

What does Freud propose to leave in God's empty Tabernacle? He offers a program for emotional growth based on rational truth. Morality deals with things that are proscribed because they are unreasonable, not because they are against God's will. Health demands that one renounce any moral base rooted in the God-concept and take on the onus of living with the risk entailed by a morality based on reason. One must rid culture of the infection of "sanctity," which has spread from the major proscriptions of religion to all moral and ethical law. One cures the infection by admitting that God is nowhere to be found in cultural and religious laws. Freud had become the beneficiary of so much demythologization of historical and culture-specific statute law in both secular society and religion, and he applied his knowledge with both verve and ideological fervor. And his critique has been well heard in the religious "discovery" that the dogma and morality enunciated in church *pronunciamenti* are historical and must be read in a human and limited context. This allows spiritual directors to come up with different sets of answers than their forebears and to be more merciful and healing in their ministry, especially with those suffering from sexual distresses.

Freud argues for a more reasoned and reasonable approach to human instinct; that we humans are not all reason, but happily fraught with instincts as well. Here, Freud thinks the God-concept is worthy of admiration for its mythological homily against the killing lust. The primal Father is the object of this love/hate instinct found in all humans but first in primitives. Oedipus' will to destroy is a splendid expression of humankind's displacement of the human will onto God. Oedipus is a tragic hero who kills a father standing in for God. So Freud says that dogma truly defines the proscription against murder; that it was not reason which gave us the law against killing, but a will. Religion says that it was God's will; Freud says that it was the human will achieving mythical dimensions in order to speak with immediacy and efficacy to our primordial level. One would think, therefore, that a myth, in this sense, is a larger-than-life statement that speaks immediately to our primordial level. Freud, on the one hand, is an iconoclast and, on the other, a fashioner of new icons. It is not that he is wrong, since he wants it both ways—indeed, all of us must have it both ways. Truth is not an either/or and a true/false brace of binary pairs, but a both/and thing where truth and falsity are concerned. Heresy is a truth too far, but it is first a truth. Freud, the pleader for rationality in an irrational world, is also an apologete for irrationality (instinct and its expression in myth) in an all too rational world made sterile at its source: the reasons of the heart. Freud knew this but had to lock himself in battle with both his colleagues and their religious allies and in so doing had to use only one set of arrows while his quiver bristled with missiles, not just those tipped with rationality. So dogma is, for Freud, *both* wish-fulfillment *and* the all important memory of past deeds: we remember the primal patricide. (Illusion, 67–69 passim) By seeing it in that light he hits directly on a major truth of religion. It is a memory (*anamnesis* in Greek) of past deeds; it is a remembering of who we are, passing through the past to the present so that we might have a future. This is hope, and Freud has stumbled onto it with his brilliant flashes of insight, unfortunately dimmed by the systematic reductionism of his articulation of those insights. Marx was right in his sociology of knowledge that one's roots create one, and Freud's roots were nineteenth-century German anti-religion.

Now Freud comes to his central and most devastating charge against religion. He is a therapist and interested in free and mature people—or free ones who are able to live with their inner and outer dreads, at the very least. Each of us must pass through a more or less neurotic stage on the way to growth and maturity. This is somewhat because of ignorance or intellectual weakness. One's instincts must be tamed: this is done by repressing them, and repression rests on a basis of anxiety. The normal person grows out of these fixations, though. Freud universalizes this schema for growth to say that all humanity passes through such a neurotic stage because of its ignorance of intellectual things, necessitating a renunciation of those instincts that would make civilization impossible.

The precipitates of this neurotic renunciation are still operative in religious men and women. Civilization runs, on an engine composed of repressive parts. Therefore, he concludes to the centerpiece of his critique: religion is the "universal obsessive neurosis of humanity" whose roots are Oedipal—religion rose out of humanity's relations with its father individually and thus created a "universal father" with no other basis in reality than the hope, and need, that there be one. Knowledge of this is bringing about the next stage in civilization: a turning away from religion, which Freud said was happening in his day.

His second conclusion is that religion is a system of wishful illusions that disavow reality; it is analogous to the hallucinatory confusion found in amentia. (Illusion, 67–69 passim) Religion has many good things to recommend it, but it has seen its day. Freud says that his conclusion was born from the "superior" vantage point afforded by science in his personal study of neurotic paralyses. He found that these morbid states were the way that men and women coped when there was no superior way available offering them an alternative either less neurotic or positively healthy. Now there is such an alternative, and Freud says that he offers it to us. He would not see religion destroyed; there are many healthy believers who are bound by sincere affection for religion. These should be in no danger of losing their faith because of his theory. But there are countless others who believe because of a self-inflicted or culture-imposed terror; these should break away from the threat of religion as soon as possible, since the very aim of religious education is to retard sexual development and make its influence for retardation felt at such an early age that the children are helpless to thwart its influence for unhealth. Religious consolation is a narcotic for the masses. Humanity has a chance to live with its helplessness and insignificance in the universe if religion would be removed; this would allow one to live in the lonely but healthy knowledge that one lives by one's powers, not overseen by Providence. Religious infantilism must be surmounted, since one cannot keep people children forever. Freud's "call" is to educate people with what he calls "education to reality." This is his sole purpose for writing the book: an evangelical cry, written with brilliant intuitions into the minds of the sick people he tended, that it is religion itself that is the evil bacillus, not man and woman. To educate his "elite" corps it is necessary to propose a program for doing so; this he had done in his book. Its first step is a liberation from the thralldom of illusions held since the dawn of time. "One should come down to earth and not waste time and energy on heaven's hope. One should leave heaven to the angels and sparrows" (taken from Heine's *"Deutschland."* (Illusion, 76–81 passim)

Freud's elite will be a race of men and women who will make life here on earth tolerable. Now he becomes the Socratic rationalist in advocating that if one but educate generations without religious doctrines the intellect with take primacy of place over the baser human instincts. (Illusion, 83) He replies to the objection that he wishes to replace a "proved and emotionally valuable illusion" with an unproved one without demonstrated emotional value that his "illusions" do not have the character of delusion about them that religous ones do. (Illusion, 86) Further, if his case be weak, that does not strengthen the case for religion. Intellect may be weak, but it will not be still until it is heard and succeeds. In place of Yahweh and Jesus, Freud offers a god of Necessity *(Ananke)* and a god of Reason *(Logos)*—the former deity to make us able to live in and with reality and the latter to offer, not the immortality of an unforseeable future, but a reasoned present; not a future perfect bliss, but a present of pain and human decisions to discard all unreality for the solidity of truth. Religion contradicts the most irrefutable of human facets: one's experience. Reason jibes with human experience, but it cannot withstand either. He and those he has educated have dropped their infantile wishes and are able, thereby, to bear the loss of some of their rational desires, which are, too, illusions. Therefore, one must live in the real world with modest expectations for both the world and for one's god *Logos*. He finishes by saying, "No, our science is no illusion. But an illusion it would be to suppose that what science cannot give us we can get elsewhere." (Illusion, 92)

CHAPTER 5

THE ONCE AND FUTURE ILLUSION: THE PAST-PERFECT OF FREUD'S CRITIQUE

Physics is only an interpretation and exegesis of the world . . . and not *a world-explanation; but insofar as it is based on belief in the senses, regarded . . . as an explanation.*

—Friedrich Nietzsche[1]

Hermeneutics as Healer? or Analysis as Religion!

In reading Freud's critique of religion one tends to be carried along by the sheer force of his personality, the verve of his zeal, the dynamisms of the superlative apologete; here there is something to thrill, there something to ponder again and again; here an outrage, there a brilliant insight fashioned into an unworthy reductionism. One tends to forget the most obvious things about Freud: First and foremost, that he was a healer. Second, that he had extruded from his extensive experience as physician a rather tightly reasoned hermeneutics. Life had revealed its meaning to him, and he intended to retail it to the world.

He was a healer and used his therapeutic technique in *The Future of an Illusion* to do for his nonbelieving readers—those who did not "believe" in either his thoughts on religion or his theory of therapy—what he did for his patients: to remove the masks of false consciousness (illusion) through an experience in which the neurotic illusion was evoked, became active, was seen by both therapist and patient, and was then translated from a symbol state into what it really was, a neurotic illusion. This enlightenment was intended to allow a reintegration of the personality to happen, because of Freud's belief in the ineradicable health of human nature. Let me dwell on this with you for a few moments, after allowing me to fill in just what his theory of healing was. Jurgen Habermas, in *Knowledge and Human Interests*, calls his first chapter on Freud "Self-reflection as Science: Freud's Psychoanalytic Critique of Meaning."[2] Both Freud's theory and his practice of psychiatry were a philosophy of meaning, a hermeneutics. It was one of self-interpretation; that is, he provided both the theory and the rules for its application in the interpretation of the symbolic structures that go to make up our personality. His theory of dream interpretation followed the hermeneutic model of philological research, but instead of exegeting books, he exegeted people by interpreting their dreams. (Habermas, 214) Interpretation no longer would deal with contraries such as truth/error and science/opinion, since the problem was no longer an epistemology dealing in the coinage of error or a problem of morality questing for lies to expose; rather, interpretation dealt with illusion, it became a tactic of suspicion intended to rip off one's masks. This subordinated the truth/error problem to the one of the will to power. So exegesis as interpretation is stretched to find out just what it is that one desires.[3] Nietzsche's theology, too, gave primacy of place to interpretation that sought out one's illusions. Nietzsche had borrowed the term interpretation *(Deutung)* from philology; he linked it with the problem of representation *(Vorstellung)*. To interpret, one dealt with meanings that were hidden within their symbolic representations. At bottom, psychoanalysis looks for one's will, for what one desires. Freud, Marx, and Nietzsche used the interpretation of symbols to get at meaning in order to overcome falsifications or illusions; both amount to the same thing for all three. Paul Ricoeur says, "A symbol exists . . . where linguistic expression lends itself by its double or multiple meanings to a work of interpretation." (Ricoeur, 18) Freud did both psychoanalysis and the phenomenology of religion. Both are interpretative disciplines, and both are arts demanding talents that many highly intelligent practitioners lack, thus rendering both the mind and the heart of religion quite opaque before their acute, but uncomprehending, gaze. Psychoanalysis works with symbols that have distorted elementary meanings; the symbol arises from either a dream or one's narration of one's history—both of which are distortions of the truth of one's personality, a truth hidden from the patient in the soft arms of a coping device. A neurosis, then, is a defense against one's truth, an illusion contrives, not to deceive as mischief, but to deceive as comfort, to allow one to be accepted and function in society.

Phenomenology works with symbols as manifestations of deeper meanings, i.e., as manifestations of the sacred. Freud found that one hides one's deeper meaning from oneself, that these symbols not only fool one's viewers, but also, above all, oneself—and were intended to do so. They have intentionality but are double-meaning linguistic expressions that demand interpretation; and interpretation is "a work of understanding that aims at deciphering symbols." (Ricoeur, 9) There are two ways of "listening to" these symbols in order to crack their code: the first way is a hermeneutics, which is a "manifestation and restoration of a meaning addressed to . . . [one] as . . . a kerygma"; i.e., as something akin to a gospel message freshly given. The second hermeneutics is a demystification, a reduction of illusions to their truth kernels. (Ricoeur, 27) Freud's phenomenology of religion lines up with the second type; his psychoanalysis lines up with the first one. He treats people as gospel and gospel as illusion. Thus, hermeneutics is both a "willingness to suspect" and a willingness to listen. Freud would listen to patients but not to religion. He would restore patients to sanity but willed not to restore—in the hermeneutical and therapeutic meaning of that word—religion to anything but its place on the back shelf of history. The willingness to suspect would be brought into play after a respectful and loving listening had brought out one's illusions, since extreme iconoclasm would often restore meaning to a symbol and thereby to a person's life; the idols had to be smashed in order to see the small, gathered truths that make us up. So, as therapist, Freud swung between the twin poles of hermeneutics—the one of demystification and the other of the restoration of meaning—in order to deal with the crisis of language that he encountered in both his patients and religion. He had to demystify their distortions of meaning, which were so often wrapped in packages of hysterical piety, in order to restore them to health through injections of truth against their delusive self-deceptions. Later, he would take out after the great mystifier, religion, to reduce it to its true meaning by applying his hermeneutics of suspicion to its neurotic symbol distortions. (Ibid.)

Ricoeur says that the contrary of suspicion is faith, as far as the restoration of meaning is concerned. This is not a simple faith, but faith

113

that has undergone the criticism that hermeneutics provides. Freud would subject his patients to analysis, which was hermeneutics as a dialectical therapy. Freud believed in his patients, in the goodness of persons and being. His was the faith of the positive secularist par excellence and not a religious faith. Ricoeur would have us move past the naivete of first faith through criticism to a mature appreciation of one's darknesses and lights to stand before our broken idols and integral, fragile self with relative peace and calm. Freud would give us this calm in a being stripped of any hint of God.

Psychoanalysis treats the flaws in the human text differently from the way the philologist treats the written text. In the latter the meaning of the text has an intentionality consciously meant by the author; in psychoanalysis, however, the symbolic intentionality is hidden from the patient who unconsciously intends the meaning. In the written text the corruptions of the symbols are external to the text itself. In the human text the corruptions are internal to the person undergoing analysis. Thus, the analyst unites the techniques of linguistic analysis with those of the psychological investigator in order to bring out the hidden meaning of the corrupted "text"; these meanings are the causal connections hidden by the distortions seen in the symbols. There is always a "biographical connection that has become inaccessible to the subject itself," but memory fails to raise the real meaning to view. This failure of memory becomes so central to the enterprise of analysis that hermeneutics is called onto the scene in order to discern the objective meaning structure of the symbols presented through the faulty offices of memory. Freud found that there were systematic memory disturbances and that these expressed meanings. (Habermas, 216f.) When the odd acts and expressions, brought about by these hidden causes, began to appear in one's life-flow, Freud contended that they have an intentionality all their own and are to be construed as being as much a part of one's history as anything with a consciously known and intended meaning; these odd epiphanies are just that: appearances from beneath—from far away—coming to us to reveal something having a meaning. They were, then, caused for a purpose, but it is a purpose hidden from the subject in which they appear. The subject deceives itself about the meaning of the phenomena, but they objectify the subject nonetheless. The subject, therefore, deceived itself about itself. Freud said, "We have treated as Holy Writ what previous writers have regarded as an arbitrary improvisation, hurriedly patched together in the embarrassment of the moment." (Habermas, 220, from Freud's *The*

Interpretation of Dreams, 5:514) Hermeneutics will give the meaning of the dream text but not of its distortion; that latter is provided by the healing artist serving as analyst. Freud says that there are patterns and systems here, but this first moment of pattern analysis, quasi-science that it is in its linguistic analysis and phenomenology, becomes an art in its second moment, namely that of the meaning of the meaning. Only a loving and talented listening can provide life-meaning to the hermeneutic meaning. There are two moments here: the hermeneutic moment and the analytic moment; both are analytic, but only the latter is the psychoanalytic, healing moment. The text is either the rehearsal of one's life through a narration of consciously known events or the more direct—but infinitely more subtle—telling of one's dreams. Freud calls the dream "the royal road to the unconscious." This affords the analyst an immediacy that the conscious level cannot provide. Freud had tried hypnosis to get at this level but gave it up as not useful; the dream would provide access to this great data bank. (Habermas, 224) What would come out would be what one desired, what one intended: in a word, what one's life meant. This would be one's truth; it was not provided by an extrinsic meaning, but it was part and parcel of one's very self.

The distortions of the dream occur as omissions and displacements of content; these are the defense mechanism that one uses to protect oneself. This obscures the repressed material from the subject. The distortions come, as well, from the condensation of material; images are compressed into a symbol system that is not easily recognizable. It is the "degrammatized" logic of the infant that the analyst sees when "the nocturnal regression of psychic life to the infantile stage renders understandable the peculiarly timeless character of unconscious motives." (Habermas, 223f.) Dreams, then, produce condensed versions of conflict situations from one's childhood. One's deepest wishes stem from repressions that happened at a relatively early age. The analysis of dreams hopes to overcome the amnesia that suffers from these early repressions. Analysis is an *anamnesis* (a remembering) working on the repressed material, which is directed against oneself in disguised form, which is often projected beyond oneself to the outside world. (Habermas, 224f.) It always works on a level that Freud thought was infantile. When he was working with hysterical patients, it would always be an easy conclusion to make to see not only their religious fixations as infantile, but also religion as its cause; an infantile religion caused infantile reactions in his patients. In reality, this logic worked both ways for Freud; he brought a bias against religion to

115

his work, saw its deleterious effects on his patients, and so concluded that it was neurotic and obsessive of its very nature.

Freud said that one must translate the unconscious to the conscious level to rid oneself of repression. Thus, the task of analysis was one of translation, a hermeneutics, or a healing through reflection. This reflection process works on resistances to the revelation of what one's desires actually are, of what one has hidden one's pain away from one by more or less subtle self-delusion. This allows us to cope by use of the defense mechanism we have contrived with more or less success. The analyst begins by working on these sets of resistances, which are blocking forces keeping us from overcoming our infantile state. (Habermas, 229) His is a therapy for the repressed. He healed through a critique of the repressed symbolic content. This he applied to religion as well. He criticized it as he would a sick patient, since he saw it as holding down an infantile— sick—place in human evolution. It had a place in world development, when humankind was a child. It dealt with the terror by creating gods and rules to keep it at bay. Now, however, science has replaced the gods in their tabernacles with ciboria filled with hypotheses; these would free us, if only we would let them. But Freud was too wise and canny to fall completely for the Socratic fallacy that knowledge is virtue. If he would fall, it would take a subtler snare to catch him. False consciousness (illusion) was not only a cognitive, but also affective, affair for Freud. Merely communicating cognitive content would not heal one:

> It is a long superseded idea, and one derived from superficial appearances, that the patient suffers from a sort of ignorance, and that if one removes this ignorance by giving him information (about the causal connection of his illness with his life, about his experiences in childhood, and so on) he is bound to recover. The pathological factor is not his ignorance in itself, but the root of this ignorance in his inner resistances; it was they that first called this ignorance into being, and they still maintain it now. The task of the treatment lies in combating these resistances. Informing the patient of what he does not know because he has repressed it is only one of the necessary preliminaries to the treatment. If knowledge about the unconscious were as important for the patient as people inexperienced in psychoanalysis imagine, listening to lectures or reading books would be enough to cure him. Such measures, however, have as much influence on the symptoms of nervous illness as a distribution of menu-cards in a time of famine has upon hunger. The analogy goes even further than its immediate application; for informing the patient of his unconscious regularly results in an intensification of the conflict in him and an exacerbation of his troubles. (Habermas, 229f., from Freud's "Wild Psychoanalyses," 11:225)

116

One of the chief ends of phenomenology is the naming of the things that have revealed themselves. This is not enough in therapy. Naming is one thing, but owning what is named is another. The name is intrinsic to the self, not an import or an accretion. One must say, "This is myself; this is me" to be on the road to healing. This turns the false-consciousness into more than something notionally true; it becomes a step toward healing. But false consciousness is normally inaccessible. Further, the illusion is not only a distortion of vision, but it also freezes one's affectivity into a system of habitual attitudes. These latter are also part of the sickness. Healing begins with a remembering *anamnesis*-as-enlightenment. (Habermas, 230)

The remembering process is much like that of an archeologist putting together the whole of one's history on various strata and at a variety of sites. The patients and the therapist delve into the *disjecta membra* (bits and pieces) of their lives in order to bring about a recollection in the present of their past. This restores them to their lost life history. It is a process of self-reflection. Both patient and therapist begin in ignorance of what the distorted text means. Little by little the therapist comes to translate the meaning of the text and hopes that his or her knowledge becomes appropriated by the patient as the patient's knowledge. As would be expected when anyone treads on our most sensitive areas, the patient throws up a series of resistances to the doctor's knowing what it all means and to the self-appropriation of the therapist's insights. The therapist seeks to alter the repression's function in such a way that resistance may be dissolved, not stabilized. (Habermas, 231) Enlightenment comes through the therapist's induction of a little neurotic crisis, not in a peaceful heuristic process. Freud says: "This struggle between the doctor and the patient, between intellect and instinctual life, between understanding and seeking to act, is played out almost exclusively in the phenomena of transference." (Habermas, ibid., from Freud's "The Dynamics of Transference," 12 : 108) The analytic process is composed of two components: the first is the weakening of one's defenses by ridding one of conscious controls. This is brought about by relaxing the patients, or putting them in neutral, through free association, which allows them to go on and on about anything and everything concerning themselves. Second, this opens one up to the need to act out what one is freeing up from the unconscious level. The therapeutic situation does put one's psychic motor into neutral, but the dynamics of repression run one's unconscious all by themselves, continuously. One has only to "get down" there to see and experience them. The therapist brings this about by taking all life's pressures off, thus allowing patients to "let go," free of the moral and cultural constraints that normally hem them in. This allows the therapist to induce a transference neurosis wherein the patients act out their compulsions so that what they wish to "discharge in action is disposed of through the work of remembering." (Habermas, 232, from Freud's "Remembering, Repeating, Working-Through," 12) This repeats the repressed material in a controlled situation to give the therapist an opportunity to translate it, i.e., give it a new meaning, and begin treatment at the same time. It is not merely a process of hermeneutics, but hermeneutics-cum-sanation. The original scene of the repression is reconstructed so that the old action that so twisted a young life that it had to hide the hurt from itself is transformed into reflection. Analytic techniques turn the symbols that tell of a primordial disintegration into something integrating. The old repression forced publicly accepted symbols into a language so private that even—and especially—patients could not understand them.

Neurosis is a compromise with the split-off portion of one's personality; that is, the repressed portion splits off, becomes autonomous, and forces on the unconscious compulsions and linguistic games that deceive the subject as to its true state. This is illusion, and this is why Freud was so hard on religion: it was an illusion forcing one to hide from one's true state, to compromise with a harsh, but good, reality; to play self-deceptive symbolic games transforming publicly accepted reality into a set of arcane religious symbols. The dynamics of the neurotic were those of religion. It was a gross overstatement on Freud's part, but one with a basis in fact. Many religious people use religion to hide from their truth; many turn a manifest truth about themselves into some arcane religious mystery in order to function. They repress themselves and, by the alchemy of repression and neurosis, turn it into something religious in order to hide the hurt, in order to cope with an acceptable but truncated reality. Analysis reduces neurotic complexes to their simples; this decomposition is not to be put together again in a poesis that creates us all over again. Freud denounces this notion. Rather, the very decomposition is synthetic and causes reintegration. Freud does not have to do it and, indeed, cannot do it. He believes in the intrinsic goodness of things, that they will put themselves in order, given the chance. His is not a psychosynthetic process. It is a decomposition through analysis; it is to cause—in a context of a therapist who loves and accepts the patient—a minor crisis from which health emerges autonomously. The formative process is once again taken up, traveling from autonomous repression to autonomous health. He says:

> In actual fact, indeed, the neurotic patient presents us with a torn mind, divided by resistances. As we analyze it and remove the resistances, it grows together; the great unity which we call his ego fits into itself all the instinctual impulses which before had been split off and held apart from it. (Habermas, 233, from Freud's "Lines of Advance in Psychoanalytic Therapy," 17:161)

Analysis is a reflective critique possessing the power to dissolve the frozen, dogmatic attitudes of mind (the cognitive sphere) and of affectivity, which are the roots of one's motivation, of one's will. Critique transforms this will when the patient passionately believes in the power of critical analysis to heal: one must believe in psychoanalysis with a passion, or it will not work. This holds not only for Freud's and Jung's systems, but for every therapy technique as well. As the patient begins to heal, the instinctual force, which is the root of the patient's compulsive activity, begins to lose its power. Freud says that this instinct is the source of healing, so it must be kept running at full spate. Thus, he induces another crisis to keep the patient in pain, this to allow the cure to come to completion, not to die of inanition in a half-cure. Second, the patient must be made to see, and to accede to, the truth that this malformation is part of one's makeup, not a symptom or something extrinsic, but part of oneself. The patient must take responsibility for the illness. (Habermas, 234f.) Freud would have the patient struggle, not with secondary defenses—symptoms—but with one's darkness itself. He would destroy illusion in the light of one's painful truth. Health and reintegration could come only in one's truth translated and self-appropriated:

> For the mental process which has been turned into a symptom owing to repression now maintains its existence outside the organization of the ego and independently of it. Indeed, it is not that process alone but all its derivatives which enjoy, as it were, this same privilege of extra-territoriality; and whenever they come into associative contact with a part of the ego-organization, it is not at all certain that they will now draw that part over to themselves and thus enlarge themselves at the expense of the ego. An analogy with which we have long been familiar compared a symptom to a foreign body which was keeping up a constant succession of stimuli and reactions in the tissue in which it was embedded. It does sometimes happen that the defensive struggle against an unwelcome instinctual im-

119

pulse is brought to an end with the formation of a symptom. As far as can be seen, this is most often possible in hysterical conversion. But usually the outcome is different. The initial act of repression is followed by a tedious or interminable sequel in which the struggle against the instinctual impulse is prolonged into a struggle against the symptom. (Habermas, 240, from Freud's "Inhibitions, Symptoms and Anxiety," 20:145)

Like Marx before him, Freud said that the most religion could deal with was with symptoms, never with the reality at hand. Religion, for Marx and Freud, dealt with illusion, not reality, and certainly not the truth. Neurotics suffered the consequences of infantile traumas, which kept them in thralldom until they were freed by a truth that could free them cognitively and affectively. Only truth could free one, and Freud could not see any religious truths in the enlightenment that he led his clients to in psychoanalysis, since religion was the cause of many of the neuroses his clients suffered. Religion itself was an obsessive neurosis whose strictures were rooted in primitive taboo and whose gods were rooted in the theophagous rites of the totem. These were universal. All religious law was fathered by taboo, and the love/hate for father impelled people to create gods of their wants and fears. God was a laboratory product concocted by the alchemy of the human capacity to want law, a Provider and Lawgiver, a just society and a supernal Cop to see to its maintenance, and an afterlife providing us with the time to enjoy it all. Thus, the philosopher's stone was a product of wishing and fear; these are the roots of religion, and they are primitive at best, infantile at worst. This is the origin of religion offered us by Freud's hermeneutics, which used the history of religions, ethnology, and anthropology to rip away the masks of both his neurotic patients and their neurotofacient religion. Religion was neurotic because neurotic people were sick in the same way as it was, and science proved it. He saw it and science proved it; but did it?

Freud's Healing Hypothesis Lacks a Basis in Ethnology, History, and Anthropology

That there should be patterns akin to the Christian religion in the ancient religions that Freud studied should not cause consternation, nor should it necessarily be used as an argument against religion, as it was with him. It offers, instead, a strong argument for religion. Otherwise, it would be to argue for incredibility from commonality. Such commonality provided a basis for continuity, from which the Christ arose as theme and historical person. He appeared on a higher level, but his patterns fit quite neatly into many of those seen in the "old religions." A religion is not untrue, therefore, because its categories fit older and cruder patterns; such argumentation is both naive and arrogant. The new is not always the best or the most correct. The religion of Jesus is not true because it fits old patterns, nor is it false because of it. Age is a somewhat, but not totally, neutral characteristic that, if it leans at all, tilts rather favorably toward religion.

Freud, in *Totem and Taboo*,[4] offers us humankind's ambivalent attitudes toward the totem father in killing/mourning, hating/loving him as proof of religion's origin. The enormous tenderness that one manifests in offering propitiatory sacrifices to the god is obviously a Christian theme. The historians of religion whom Freud uses as authoritative sources for his hypothesis against religion are not taken seriously today, although they were all but gospel in the past century. Today we view Frazer as a learned and perceptive dilettante. Robertson Smith's Kantian bias made him automatically antipathetic toward any religion that smacked of magic (read "Roman Catholic" here, the sacramental system of which he deplored). Wundt lies unused in the great libraries of the world. Spencer and Taylor, too, have gone into scholarly oblivion. They had their day and luxuriated in the kudos bestowed by both colleague and an awed lay society. But their evolutionary theory does not fit religions in the light of later evidence adduced by the respective disciplines they represented. Freud could have used the work of a much more accurate and learned historian, Boas, who was his own contemporary and whose work still carries weight; but he did not. And because he did not, Freud is far from credible as a historian of religions and as an anthropologist and less weighty as a theorist of psychoanalysis. In a word: his sources are dated and *simpliste*. Evolutionary theories of religion's origins are no longer tenable because the evidence at hand either does not corroborate them or points in other, less definitive directions. Further, since he used themes so patently Christian, and since the prelapsarian primitives he writes of (with no personal experience of them, nor did the historians of religion who wrote of contemporary totemism and animism and its devotees as if they were the first religions and Adam, Eve, Cain, and Abel *redivivi*) look so familiar, it is more than possible that he is projecting his own religious notions on those of another, less complex period and *using* the work taken from other fields to bolster a mind already made up.

Freud's idea of the primal crime as root of the ambivalence of our feelings in religion, morals, society, and art is an attempt to interpret what Jews and Christians mean by Original Sin. However, the Oedipus complex and its primal archetypical patricide is not a demythologization, but a displacement. Freud cannot abide Judeo-Christian religion. The vapid ritualism of the one and the mindless bigotries and magical prayer rituals of the other, plus the memories of almost daily personal beatings and harassment visited on him by Catholic schoolboys, drove him to avoid at all cost any hint of Jewish prayer and ritual in his own life. But he retained with something akin to passion his love of things Jewish, such as food, humor, and cultural attitudes, and had a personal inner circle consisting almost exclusively of Jewish members to whom he was both devoted friend and joyous companion. Consequently, he takes the Adamic myth and makes it Greek instead. Where there had been a divine father looking for his masterpieces in the cool of an oasis evening, now there was a regal father, a son, and a wife and mother beloved of both. It is a translation of one set of religious categories into another one. Now it becomes Greek, tragic, and elegant instead of Semitic, Christian, and irrelevant to the educated upper class, the members of which were his constituents. It makes an interesting, but not very cogent, argument. But what is important is not his rejection of his own Jewish tradition—his own "father"—but his tenderness toward it in retaining it and depicting the human psyche individually and collectively as a patricide/patrophile. In *Totem and Taboo*, Freud works from an Original Sin model. He drops this in *The Future of an Illusion*, in which latter book he is quite rationalistic but less believable as a scientist. He had become more the apologete—it was an age of apologetics—rather than laboratory scientist.

Freud ventured out of his field into those of ethnology, history of religions, anthropology, and philosophical hermeneutics. Today's academics in those fields have adopted a rather critical attitude toward the usefulness, truth, or falsity of Freud's work. Alfred Kroeber, a recognized expert in historical anthropology, as well as a practicing psychoanalyst, wrote two criticisms of *Totem and Taboo* several years apart. He says that Freud drew his theory concerning early humankind from Darwin and Atkinson. It ran thus: primitive people lived in small communities presided over by an adult male and allowing a few immature males to stay on until puberty forced them to seek their own herd. To this, Freud adds Robertson Smith's hypothesis that sacrifice is essential in all ancient cults. Kroeber says: "The Oedipus complex directed upon these two hypotheses welds them into a mechanism with which it is possible to explain most of the essentials of human civilization."[5] Freud explains himself by applying the patricide of the primal horde to all races. All shared in the ambivalent feelings of guilt, the need to sacrifice, and the love/hate feelings for the "father." Kroeber criticizes Freud on these points: first, Darwin and Atkinson only guessed about the composition of the primal human grouping—whether it resembled that of the gorilla or the monkey. Second, Robertson Smith's assertion that blood sacrifice is a universal phenomenon and essential to all cults holds good only for the Mediterranean cultures of the last two thousand years *B.C.* and subsequently. Kroeber asserts that "it is at best problematical whether blood sacrifice goes back to a totemic observance. It is not established that totemism is an original possession of Semitic culture." Further, it is a conjecture that the sons would kill and eat the father. Freud makes this assertion on his own, not backed by any scientific or historical evidence. Because children displace hatred of the father onto an animal is not proof that totemic man and woman did so. And then, "if they 'displaced,' would they retain enough of the original hate impulse to slay the father; and if so, would the slaying not resolve and evaporate the displacements? Psychoanalysis may affirm both questions." Even granting a strong remorse on the part of the sons not to kill again, it is doubtful whether it was a resolve powerful enough to enforce their refraining from sexual commerce. If the brothers allowed strangers to have access to their women, where would they find an outlet short of celibacy or homosexuality?

Most damaging is Kroeber's charge that it is not only not established, but far from it, that exogamy and totem abstinence are the twin prohibitions of totemism. (Kroeber, 50) That the roots of all totemic taboos are in the taboos against patricide and incest is, he says, "pure assertion." Freud never proved it. Moreover, "social psychologists assume a 'continuity in the psychic life of succeeding generations' without in general concerning themselves much with the manner in which this continuity is established." Freud's method "substitutes a plan for multiplying into one another . . . fractional certainties—that is, more or less remote possibilities—without recognition that the multiplicity of factors must successively decrease the probability of their product." Last, Kroeber levels the charge of insidiousness at Freud's method of stating the main thesis of *The Future of an Illusion* at the end of the book, thus not giving the idea much of a testing. This was due to the haste with which the book was written, which was due, in part, to Freud's propensity to be a propagandist rather than a scientist. But, Kroeber insists,

123

the consequence of this is that this book is keen without orderliness, intricately rather than closely reasoned, and endowed with an unsubstantiated convincingness . . . [which] the critical reader will ascertain . . . but the book will fall into the hands of many who are lacking either in care or independence of judgment . . . who, under the influence of a great name and in the presence of a bewilderingly fertile imagination, will be carried into an illusory belief. (Kroeber, 51)

Kroeber closes with the judgment that the book is an "important and valuable contribution." Its solid contributions are (1) that he has set up a correspondence between taboo customs and compulsion neuroses. (2) He has outlined the parallelism between the love/hate ambivalence in totemism and in neurotic behavior. (3) He has highlighted, if not explained, the combination of mourning for and fearing the dead. (4) He has thrown light on the striking similarities between magic, taboo, animism, primitive religion, and neurotic behavior. He ends with: "However precipitate his entry into anthropology and however flimsy some of his synthesis, he brings to bear keen insight, a fecund imagination, and above all a point of view which henceforth can never be ignored without stultification." He thinks that Frazer occupies so great a place in Freud's theory since the former knows nothing of psychoanalysis, "and with all acumen his [Freud's] efforts are prevailingly a dilettantish playing; but in the last anaylsis they are psychology, and as history only a pleasing fabrication." (Kroeber, 52f.)

In 1948, Kroeber again appraised Freud's *Totem and Taboo*. There was little change in his outlook. In fact, his opinions grew even stronger: "The psychoanalytic explanation of culture is intuitive, dogmatic and wholly unhistorical." (Kroeber, in Lessa and Vogt, 53) He thinks that the book contains many a profound psychological truth, that, unfortunately, will not stand up before the evidence given to back it up. He goes on to say: "It is difficult to say how far he realized his vacillation between historic truth and abstract truth expressed through intuitive imagination. A historic finding calls for some specification of place and time and order; instead of which, he offers a finding of unique cardinality, such as history feels it cannot deal with." Later, confronted by just this criticism, Freud said that his primitive historical "event" is to be construed as "type." Kroeber counters with:

A typical event, historically speaking, is a recurrent one. This can hardly be admitted for the father-slaying, eating, and guilt sense. . . .His argu-

124

ment is evidently ambiguous as being between historical thinking and psychological thinking. If we omit the fatal concept of event, of an act as it happens in history, we have left over the concept of the psychologically potential.

Kroeber goes on to say that Freud should have confined himself to psychological insight, which he had in abundance, instead of history, which he used so poorly. Reduced to the psychological truths contained in the book, Kroeber accepts these: certain psychological dynamisms are of universal value: the incest taboo and filial ambivalence, i.e., the "Oedipus situation." (Kroeber, 54) Further, science has accepted into its lexicon the terms "repression, infantile persistences, dream symbolism and overdetermination, guilt sense, the effects towards members of the family." Terms that have not been accepted by the scientific community are "the censor, the superego, the castration complex." (Kroeber, 56)

It might well be argued that the shape of Freud's psychoanalysis is that of a surrogate for religion—better, that its use is that of a "secular religion" and its shape is that of a mysticism. David C. McLelland defends the thesis in *The Roots of Consciousness* that Freud draws heavily on the Hasidic mystical tradition in his attempt to counter the legalism of the Orthodox Judaism in which he grew up. McLelland asserts that its shape is religious. He substantiates this by saying that the leading practitioners of psychoanalysis have had charisma. [6]

Further, Freud's theory gives meaning to life, as does religion, and philosophers take the metaphysics of psychoanalysis seriously. And last, "above all it heals." It has many of the characteristics of a religious movement: the zeal of its practitioners, its healing potentiality, its emotionalism, and its techniques are religious. Thomas Mann, in *The Magic Mountain*, outlined his feelings and intuitions concerning psychoanalysis, a movement that he encountered around World War I. Dr. Krokowski, a resident psychoanalyst, says in the book that "the symptoms of disease are nothing but a disguised manifestation of the power of love; and all disease is only love transformed." (McLelland, 120f.)

> Dr. Krokowski had raised his voice and so drawn attention once more upon himself. He was standing there behind his table with his arms outstretched and his head on one side—almost despite the frock coat, he looked like Christ on the Cross!
>
> It seemed at the end of the lecture Dr. Krokowski was making propaganda for psychoanalysis; with open arms he summoned all and sundry to come unto him. "Come unto me," he was saying, though not in those

words. . . .And he left no doubt of his conviction that all those present were weary and heavy laden. He spoke of secret suffering, of shame and sorrow, of the redeeming power of the analytic. (McLelland, 121)

Some say that psychoanalysts have mysticism to thank for their healing technique and power. David Bakan, in his *Sigmund Freud and the Jewish Mystical Tradition*,[7] offers us such a thesis. He states that the roots of psychoanalysis are in Hasidic mysticism. Even though the leaders of psychoanalysis are antireligious Jews, Bakan holds that they borrowed unconsciously and heavily from the mysticism of the area in which they grew up. Central Europe was a stronghold of Hasidism—Jewish enthusiastic mysticism led by such Zadiks (the leader, a living Torah in himself) as Baal Shem Tov. An older, legalistic orthodoxy led Jews to believe that punishment came as a result of backsliding from the Law. The more the punishment, and there was no paucity of Jewish suffering in central Europe, the greater the pressure to follow the Law. Freud, representing many of his contemporaries, felt that this was out and out incorrect. He left religion as a result. The Hasidim sought direct contact with God in their joyous effusions of prayer and dance.

> The goal of psychoanalysis is practically identical with that of Jewish mysticism—to release and fulfill the individual by contact with emotional, irrational forces. Freud's image of man is hemmed in by conflicts and anxieties arising primarily out of the thwarting of natural impulses by society. The central problem for neurosis is the need for freedom, for release from guilt, from an oppressive superego representing the demands that society makes on the individual. (McLelland, 122f.)

McLelland's second point is that the techniques that psychoanalysts use are like those of the Jewish mystical tradition. The Hasidim used allegory in their mystical book, *The Zohar*. Jewish religion is one of the Book. Exegesis looms large in any religion of a Book, and Judaism is no exception. Theology and spirituality are an elaboration of the text. *The Zohar* translated this to us: we became a text to be interpreted. The root of the religious experience was knowledge (*yada* in Hebrew), which word constantly connects with sexuality in the scriptures: "Adam knew his wife." The modern era reflects this in its expression "carnal knowledge." In its exegesis, *The Zohar* did not use the slow, rational method of moving from point to labored point. Rather, the Hasids joyously skipped about the text using allegory and allusion to bring light from the word. The use of imagination was geared to free one's emotions for an immediacy with

God—one had an affective union of joy with God. It is a special knowledge that heals and frees. This is precisely where "Freud stands at the center of the Jewish Mystical tradition." *The Zohar* is couched, as mentioned, in sexual terms. Israel is "the female part of God, the Shekinah, which is cast aside and then redeemed by God in a mystical union described in sexual terms." (McLelland, 125f.)

Freud and the orthodox analysts of his school adopted this sexual hypothesis rigidly. In fact, "there is evidence that Freud felt in his psychoanalytic work that he was entering into a pact with the Devil, that by exploring the underworld of the mind he could gain control over the evil forces within it." (McLelland, 127) Goethe's *Faust* drew on a cabalistic source in his depiction of Faust's dealing with Mephistopheles. The cabal has a strong "pact motif." Freud saw that sexual instincts are rooted in evil. In its instinctual life, a babe is capable of any heinous act—incest, murder, and so on. Therefore, "psychoanalysis was religious in its origin, a secular outgrowth of the Jewish mystical tradition in its continuing struggle with Mosaic orthodoxy." Further, "the leading analysts both in Europe and the United States were for a long time nearly all Jews." Freud may not have realized that he was drawing his material from religious sources, but if he did, he had ample reason to conceal it. (McLelland, 129) McLelland closes by saying that the subjects undergoing psychoanalysis are put into direct emotional touch with a power beyond themselves, called libido by some, positive growth force by others, and God by those in a mystical tradition. (McLelland, 132–43 passim) Last, Freud's antireligious feelings are close to those of liberal Christianity in its effort to rationalize its religion. But Freud's intuition of humankind is of an existential condition that is deeply wounded. Liberal Christians see the problem as one of "knowledge"; Freud sees it as one of being. Freud seems to be more on the side of the angels here than are the theologians.

In her fine book on Freud, *Freud and Original Sin*, Sharon MacIsaac deals with the application that Freudian analytic techniques have for those whose lives depend on an Original Sin model. She shows that his insights fit in well with the existential—the situation of man and woman in the world is one of persons in need of great healing; that humankind is a victim not only of its environment, but also of its unknown, radical, impulses. Freud works from a dynamic of guilt-transmission. Guilt from a primal sin is passed on from father to child almost like an infestation of the genes. We began in awful evil. For him, our ancestors tried to become

127

gods, as they did in Genesis. Even in rejecting the name Original Sin, Freud enriches the reality of religion, adding to it the basis for a healing in medicine and honest prayer that is in touch with one's full life—the ambivalence of love/hate, conscious/unconscious, mourning/joy, and so on. This is really a new birth for religion, since it kills off its neurotic counterfeits.

Freud, in rejecting the Judeo-Christian God as referent for human acts, accepts the framework of religion. The cataclysm that we call Adam's sin and the contagion that we all fall heir to as his children, Freud sees as a primal sin of patricide and incest. He translates Christianity, he doesn't fully reject it, but he does reduce it. There is a sin, a Father, a magical tradition that passes on the tradition. As far as the history of religions is concerned, the tradition of sacrifice, sacrament, and prayer falls under the rubric of mantra, a short, uttered prayer (or phrase that may be meaningless, more or less) that evokes the presence of the god and places one in communion with that deity. There is prayer and ritual to assuage and alleviate the human condition. Whether it is scientific or not doesn't really matter. The greatest mystery of religion is that God can have anything to do with us at all. All the rest flows rather easily after one accepts the first premise. Freud, in dealing with religion as its critic, deals with it in its own framework. He translates its symbols into something secular and feels that that is telling criticism. He is not radical enough, however. Eschatology is the dimension of the Christian religion that did in the sacred/secular dichotomy. All is in touch with spirit-divine material or demonic-spiritual material; we are not dichotomized, but homogenized. Profane is a neutral category that religion has made otiose. The history of religions has brought back the profane in its hermeneutics, but is quite unhistorical in doing so, to say nothing of its sometime irreligiousness. Christ's coming is the event that homogenized creature and Creator, sacred and profane, a fact that we have rarely lived up to and even less frequently understood. Christ's coming has made it necessary to discern dominations, either by the Holy Spirit or by the demonic one. Freud is a nineteenth-century man in translating the sacred into the "profane"; romanticism had done it before him in naturalizing the supernatural. All well and good; our home is here. All there is is a here. Hope is in the here—not only in the here and now, but also in the here and later. Freud, Matthew Arnold, and Darwin, to name a few, domesticated and naturalized humankind. The natural is a Christian category. Freud goes as far as he can go. But his criticism also tries to domesticate the Holy

Spirit. That is not an error; it is an irrelevance. Science does not speak of a Holy Spirit because it cannot. Human symbols, scientific or religious, point, no more. Religion, to a scientist, is a system of pointers. Freud used Jewish and Christian pointers in indicating the contents of the soul. He took good pictures. The album he put them in makes little sense, however. Science, in pointing out the truth, makes sense to a religious man. In pointing out the truth, and then saying to one who has undergone a "true experience of religion" that the pointer does not point to God, he becomes unscientific; he utters nonsense.

Freud, therefore, in his role as intuitive wisdom figure, is eminently useful to a religious person. As history, his work is nonhistorical guesswork. As anthropology, it was dated in his own time and antique in ours. As philosopher, he offers a real option—what spirit one wished to follow, secular or religious humanism. As healer, he is without peer. As teacher, he revivifies Jewish Hasidism and Christian mysticism as well—the prayer life is always a question of becoming real to the self. His first step—placing one in immediate contact with one's libido—really allows one to experience oneself as the imago dei. One becomes a god in doing this. One experiences the roots of one's being—roots that are not only in God, but also growing out of oneself as analogous to god. The libido, however, is ambivalent. One is in touch not only with the divinity, but with the demonic in one's nature as well. Perfect love casts out all fear, which easily becomes libido. The experience of one's roots is at once a healing experience and one that can easily be destructive, so that the wounded healer becomes the healed wounder. The experience of one's godness is always healing at first; it is only later that it can become filled with demonic hubris. In Prometheus, it was man at his best whom the gods hated. Freud makes us real to ourselves. What greater service could one ask? It takes a God to make God real to us; so it really doesn't matter if Freud believed or not. What does matter is that his criticism cleansed the Temple. If bad money drives out good money in economics, then bad religion drives out the good. Freud helped to drive out the bad in criticizing it and helped to bring in the good in placing us in a position of being capable of "first mysticism." As a Christian, I believe that all noble things, all good human endeavors, are inspired with hope by a merciful God. All religion, insofar as it is good, is divinely revealed and the organon of Christ's grace. In experiencing oneself, whether one be Jew, Christian, Hindu, or Buddhist—or atheist—one is in the first throes of mysticism. Any system that puts one in touch with oneself on such a deep level is a step toward religion. Because it puts us in touch with our nature with no intermediary, it is natural and therefore good.

Scripture scholars tell us that much of the Wisdom literature in the Old Testament has its roots in "pagan" oriental literature. Its insights are wise and healing. So are Freud's. Religious people are looking for a way to tell their story today. Freud used old myths, couched them in "historical language," inspired them with healing truth, and became a writer of *Helisgeschichte* in so doing. The fact that he believed his "history" does not matter. What does is that his wisdom does not dim with age, but burnishes with use.

Freud is, therefore, is to be understood against a gestalt of Wisdom literature and salvation history. He has aided in divinizing us by making us free—but has also put us in touch with our demonic side, if Bakan is to be believed. I am not "baptizing" Freud in order to win an argument. I am merely approaching him in my roles as a historian of religion and as a Christian theologian. As a historian, his work is one that reveals religious patterns and, if followed, "sets off" religious experiences. As a theologian, I think his work heals—and I call nothing evil that does lasting good for people. I realize that his criticism is trenchant; so was Quoheleth's and Amos'. Who can forget the bucolic Amos preaching to the first women of the northern kingdom and calling them "O you fat cows of Bashan"? The greatness of Freud is in criticizing, and thereby freeing, religion. His danger is in his genius. He discovered and hymned the ambivalence of humankind. The other root of our divine nature is the demonic one. The other side of the God of mysticism is the Mephistopheles of analyst-playing-god. The dynamic is mystical; the effects can be disastrous over the long haul, the more so since the process can begin so well. The strength of analysis is its use of mystical techniques, playing to the inner levels of the client to touch and free the self within the ego. But if that is its strength, then it is also its weakness. The sins of the just are usually their virtues; the virtues of the wicked are frequently their sins.

In giving us a set of ambivalences like love/hate and attraction/repulsion toward our parents and religion, Freud erected a new set of categories. Gone are the natural/supernatural, sacred/profane, body/soul, for example, of so much religious literature over the past few centuries. Freud unified humankind; he integrated it, which is no small achievement. If we look to both the Old Testament and the New Testament, we will see that man and woman are not dichotomized, but unified—homogenized. To speak of body and soul did not compute until Neoplatonism and its apologetes Augustine and the monk who wrote under the name Denis (Dionysus) modernized Christianity in an early stab at relevance. What was relevance in one age, however, became irrelevant in Luther's age and mischievous as it persisted in Roman Catholicism before Vatican Council II. Freud helped to force out these no longer useful theological categories. He threw out the gods in doing so, but the god he feared is not like the God whom I (and my contemporaries) have gotten to know—a God of utter humanity, appearing in the muck of my manhood like a Buddhist lotus, beautiful in the midst of the dark ooze in which I would not tread. Freud aided us in descending, not into a hell of our making, but into the hell of our makeup and in facing the loss of our illusions, in discovering the imago dei (God's image) in the prismatic effect that pain has on us. We know we are good by going through our evils. There is a joy at the center of our griefs. Freud's healing technique is an engine to take us to the courageous enjoyment of our joy in passing through our griefs. His reductionism consisted in explaining too much. He explained religion in terms of its origin: totemism and taboos are rites and rubrics fashioned out of our need to face the pain of life. But to explain any complex phenomenon, such as religion, in terms of its origin is to reduce it. Further, he did not locate the origins of religion. His proofs were and are not taken seriously by either historians of religion or ethnologists, and certainly cannot be taken so by theologians. To explain religion as a function of a neurotic urge to create gods against the frights of the night is both correct and a slander: correct, since so much of religious experience and religious expectations among peoples' lives is infantile and neurotic, a dodge away from one's truth; a slander, since religion at its best is not such a dodge. The cross is not an escape, but a gentle and forceful reminder that we must find peace only in the painful truths of our collective and personal histories. Freud took the best of his theory, applied it to the sickest people in religion, and concluded to religion's intrinsic and irremediable illness. That is not only a slander, but what is most damning, it is also unscientific. His practice was with the rich and neurotic, with the females of his time who had no one to "listen" to their hearts. He damned not only religion, but women along with it. Reductionism was almost a must in Freud's day, but today it is the ugliest of nineteenth-century masks and the greatest of all their illusions: they thought they thought without illusion, which is the greatest illusion of all. All thought is a tincture of both truth and illusion; pushed too far, it becomes an ideological myth, i.e., one not pointing to our realities and allowing their healing in the revelation, but pointing only to fragmented truth as if it were the whole thing. Such a myth is destructive, especially in the hands of the gifted and brilliant. Freud was both.

Freud became an ideologue in ridding religion of its ideology. He succeeded. Now religion must criticize its healer and demand that the physician heal himself of the mote in his own critical eye. Freud explained religion away, so his hermeneutics are not the meaning of religion, but the meaning of neurotic symbols in the makeup of people who happen to espouse a religion. There is the difference. Freud has become a staple in the diet of religious formation today; the college student, the novice in convent and monastery, the seminarian in his or her seminary, all descend into their private hells to find their salvific truths; and all are escorted by a wise wisdom figure (professor, novice-master, spiritual director, or pastor) as they make this frightening descent to the joy that all religions know exists at the bottom of the well.

In summary, Freud's intuitions about human nature are correct: we are good but live off batteries of illusions. His healing method still heals. His hermeneutics of personal illusions works in casting down the idols of our fears. His hermeneutics of humanity's collective life—that all religion is intrinsically ill—does not tell us much about religion that is true or helpful. It tells us more about Freud and his patients. His scientific proofs about the origins of religion are false—illusions.

Freud, Marx, and Nietzsche offered us hermeneutic systems to get at the meaning of human life and, in so doing, overcame falsifications. (Ricoeur, 17) As psychoanalyst, Freud demanded that we take a view of human nature that was developmental, on the way to growth, rather than the more static anthropology deriving from Augustine's Neoplatonic view. This evolutionary view is in line with Irenaeus' evolutionary point of view, in which Adam and Eve never had the perfections of Paradise, but only the beginnings of perfection and beatitude. This means that they were not created with all the preternatural gifts that the Augustinian "high view" demands, for example, infused knowledge, infused virtues, freedom from death. Augustine's view is that Adam and Eve were created humanly perfect and fell from a great height. Sin is human responsibility and guilt is its partner. Irenaeus' view is that Paradise meant that man and woman were created to begin the long trek toward perfection; but they were created in an immature state, not a perfect one. They were children. This would partially jibe with Freud's view of our ancestors as primitive in the beginning stages of life, such as infants would be. But it corrects Freud's errors that religion is always primitive and thus today, infantile. If Freud were to have put his thought in the way that coincided with the Irenaean view, he could have seen how healthy religion demands growth, human responsibility, a moral life constantly in fear that one is alone in choosing the good and rational, and the one is the other. The fact that he was not open to healthy views of religion was a red herring to many of us. We looked more to what he denied—God, sin, guilt—than to what he affirmed—our goodness, our responsibility for our desires, our need to grow in and through truth to intellectual and emotional perfection. Freud's phenomenology of religion was a failure, since it told more about sick religious people than about religious origins and religion per se. His psychoanalytic theory incorporated a growth principle that accords well with Christian theology. Men and women were created in a lower state than they were ultimately intended, by their nature—Christians and Jews would say "by their Creator"—to reach. Thus, evil is to be found in the rejection of the maturity—the healthy relationships with father, mother, and peers—that one's evolutionary stage demands. Both religion and Freud concur here.

Freud rejected the concept of Original Sin, since "guilt," as he had found it in his patients, was not rooted in some prelapsarian failure, but in the dialectics of one's psychosexual makeup. Something inside one exists—something that wants healing, wants to come to the light and be dealt with—but one represses it as a way of protecting oneself from the necessity of accepting it and thereby growing. The ego defends itself against this intense self-reproach quite frequently by projection. Freud extrapolated from his practice to his hermeneutics unscientifically because he did not have laboratory verification of his assertion and because it was going from the particular to the general, which is always without warrant. His anthropology, deriving from his practice, was one demanding that we see man and woman as good and in a developmental posture. His phenomenology of religion—which was his concept of religious anthropology—was crude and a mistranslation of the symbols he rightly interpreted to put men and women in touch with their reality. His mistranslation is not the patrimony he left us; his theory of therapy and his anthropology derived from this practice are his bequest to us all. This healthy view of man and woman does not answer where they came from or where the roots of morality and human ambivalence are to be found; religion will do this when it finds the proper exegetical and psychological tools and weds them. Rather, this salutary view of humankind is just that: a view of us that rests on a belief in the goodness of things and persons, although not missing for a moment the admixture of illness and wickedness that people are capable of. His developmental view is eschatological: it looks at humankind with hope, demanding of our fragility that we both acknowledge it and do something with it that is constructive.

Thus, Freud's psychoanalytic theory lines up with both Irenaeus' anthropology and his theological interpretation of the Genesis story of the creation and the fall. Rejection of one's human, knowing and loving nature is *the* paramount human evil. Man and woman were created in an infant stage and were meant to make mistakes; but they were meant to acknowledge them, to make redress and get on with it. Covering them over with a lot of religious symbols leads religious people, especially Catholic ones, to the neurosis called scrupulosity, in which one feels totally constricted by one's sensuality or one's life of piety to such an extent that peace with God, others, and the self eludes one. This is a "ruse" contrived by the repression dynamism by which one sets up a "phoney" sin that one subconsciously knows a priest or a minister will say is not a sin at all, or at least not a serious one, to keep both the priest or the minister and oneself from the real problem, which frequently is rooted in either the fear of death or an infancy-stage trauma. Freud knew us Christians, especially the Catholic ones, and had the effrontery to publish our ruses to the world; he was an atheist, a Jew, and a foreigner to most of the world, and this, in itself, was enough to convict him. Furthermore, he made the mistake of contriving a cosmic interpretation of all religion. This hung him before he could get out of the courtroom. He translated the symbols of the soul quite well, those of the book of religion not at all. But in telling us who men and women are, he did something central to all religion: he made us "remember" *(anamnesis)* who we are. Jesus came not only to be a human, but also to call us to humanity. In humanity we are to find divinity; this is the message of the incarnation and of our religion in its practical implications. Freud's anthropology was superb in demanding that we acknowledge the terrible intimacy we have with matter and its laws in human physiology and psychology. He helped to put a schizoid humanity back together by giving us a way to interpret ourselves as rational animals. He put us back in touch with our instincts in a way that could find health and affirmation in religion. Religion would find its own hermeneutics, but it could not have done so without someone pointing out just what was going on in men and women. There is, after all, no such thing as religion; there are only people. God is a person; we are persons. Religion, as a noun, is a distillate, a reification of the loving relationship between God and God's creation. It easily becomes an idol interfering with our loving relations with God and one another. We can be religious but never religions. Both Barth and Bonhoeffer were correct in asserting that religion, as presently construed, was a theological aberration. Freud, the great intuitor, knew this. He explained it sufficiently well within his field but badly when he ventured into philosophical and theological territory demanding both scientific proof and religious faith. He had neither. His lack of faith freed him to see us as we are, partially at least; but he did see us. His lack of proof held up his use as therapist by religious people for a generation or two. We do not fear Freud's interpretation of religion anymore, and we rather applaud his healing theory. Freud, the atheist Jew, has become one of the fathers of modern Catholic and Protestant theological anthropology. Freud, the materialist, has returned us to our mother: Matter.

Chaste Queries for Christmas '80

Chaste matter, what entropy
frails you to subject us so
totally to your busy final thrall?

Chaste, innocent stuff,
what have we done to you
to object to you
so religiously?

Chaste matter,
                    whose heart is God,

can we not live
at peace with you,
and flow gently
in your arms
innocent of sin?

Chaste matter, whose laws
flout our discounted religion,
cheapening the fleshed God,
sucking out his greed
for love at your virginal nipples;

is not your entropy
flown over by his more
than human investiture?

135

Have you not jelled
to permanency by Mary's
ligamented love forcing
our catechised noses away
from easy answers
to the query:

> Nonne Mater Filiusque
> materia?*

—William Lloyd Newell

*Are not Mother and Son matter?

Part III

~

NIETZSCHE'S CRITIQUE OF RELIGION

CHAPTER 6

The Wrongdoing of God

You lack innocence in desire; and therefore you now slander desiring!

—Zarathustra

What Freud did was separate guilt from sin; he then interpreted guilt to free so many from the illusion of sin to deal with the reality of their situation. Obviously, this would open men and women to deal with their real sins, not their putative ones, to deal with the whole gestalt of humanity, not with its parts in isolation. So often theologians had taken those parts, blown them up for closer inspection, and forgotten their original size and their place in the original hierarchy of things. Marx, too, saw that sins in the Judeo-Christian religions were too often seen as only "below the belt," when they were really things of the heart. Men and women could macerate each other and go to church or temple with good conscience as long as they had not broken some smaller law, frequently sexual. Marx saw that religious people often dealt with reality at one or two removes—at best. But from his early study of theology he knew that religion was taking care of widows and orphans (James' Epistle and most of the Prophets). Marx knew this, and so did Nietzsche. The reason the latter criticized Christianity so sharply was because it had taken men and women away from their instincts, and this had brought ruin to the best in Europe: the intellectual and artistic elite. This Lutheran pastor's son had seen Protestantism at its best in his excellent parents' lives, but it had not been enough to redeem the religion. It had been successful in crushing the growth potential of so many of his peers, and he would not let it happen to him. He would sound the clarion call that Christianity was a fraud because it ruined the human in us. In *The Twilight of the Idols* he says:

> All passions have a phase when they drag down their victims with the weight of folly—and later, very much later, a phase when they wed the spirit, when they spiritualize themselves. Formerly one made war on passion itself on account of the folly inherent in it: one conspired for its extermination—all the old moral monsters are unanimous that *"il faut tuer les passions."* The most famous formula for doing this is contained in the New Testament, in the Sermon on the Mount . . . [where] it is said, with reference to sexuality, "if thine eye offend thee, pluck it out"; fortunately, Christians do not follow this prescription. To exterminate the passions and desires merely in order to do away with their folly and its unpleasant consequences—this itself seems to us today merely an acute form of folly. . . . The church combats the passions with excision in every sense of the word: its "cure" is castration. It never asks: "How can one spiritualize, beautify, deify a desire?"—it has at all times laid the emphasis of its discipline on extirpation. But to attack the passions at their roots means to attack life at its roots: the method of the church is hostile to life.[1]

Earlier on, in the same essay, he said that passion is the soil from which a fruitful humanity grows. Morality and its categorization of humanity has beclouded man and woman. In Nietzsche's eyes, it is the very concept of the good and evil that has ruined people. Virtue is so often either the fear of desire or the fact that no opportunity arises for its pursuit. In *Thus Spake Zarathustra* (II, "Of Immaculate Perception") he says, "You lack innocence in desire: and therefore you now slander desiring!" In his practice, Freud saw those who were hurt by the mindless imposition of moral labels; his own rejection of his orthodox Jewish roots decried the same rejection of knee jerk morality. Freud's senior, Nietzsche, too, rejected the Kantian model of humanity, the apotheosis of which was the civil servant doing his or her duty. As such, the civil servant is "a thing in itself," and Kant's philosophy was set over humanity to judge only what is an appearance of a civil servant and not a true human at all. (Idols, "Expeditions of an Untimely Man," 29). Philosophy applied to revelation yields theology, and this further yields morality and spirituality, each at a further remove from the man and woman who were subjects of the revelation in the first place. Thus, Nietzsche says, "it is by being 'natural' that one best recovers from one's unnaturalness, from one's spirituality." (Idols, "Maxims and Arrows," 6)

Nietzsche's philosophy was an exercise in anthropological and theological retrieval: to retrieve men and women he would have to go beyond what had lost them to themselves: morality. He transcended categories by negating them and found human beings beneath the verbiage. To retrieve the transcendent itself he would have to go beyond the concept of God that came down to him from Judaism and Christianity. He would end by finding divinity in all things; he divinized creatures by creating divinity in us all. This is his work in a nutshell: the retrieval of humanity and of one's personal divinity by denying categories like "the sacred," the "supernatural," even the "natural," at times; and finally, he had to scotch out God to get at divinity.

Any category that denied either humanity or one's divinity—the imago dei—went by the boards. His view of things was that life was tragic. Jesus did not redeem men and women. They were divine to begin with. He faced up to reality without giving any ultimacy to things beyond this world. Hence, he did not solve the problem of evil, philosophically; he found a way to live both with the evil and with the good he found once again in humankind: will all that happens; if it becomes necessary, will it. Many pastors would, eventually, come to the same conclusion by the third quarter of the next century, so far advanced was he. There is a goodness in us all. Nietzsche knew it and said we must be Promethean and steal back the fire a misused Christianity purloined from us, but we will have to face the tragedy at the end of the saga. Nietzsche made the divine comedy into a human tragedy, but a good and noble tragedy worth living. He took things as they were, tightened his belt, and tried to live generously and nobly in his straitened circumstances, sans bell, sans book, sans all religious candles, to find—like the Buddha—human beings within the cowering thing that the gods and revelation had made of us. His reformation was as radical, almost, as the Gautama's, except that he stopped short at ridding us of humanity and divinity, whereas the Indian sage said that they would only cause us pain. Nietzsche said that one should will the pain to find the joy within; the Buddha said that there was no man or woman there at all, that anthropology was a nonsense imposed by the illusion of permanency; and that God was an irrelevancy called down to soothe us in our pain. Nietzsche cauterized the pain without a god but demanded that anthropology take the place of Christology and that we find the divine spark within. Like Freud after him, and Marx before him, Nietzsche's corpus yields us an anthropology; his very reason for writing was to put sensuality, feeling, and will back together, to bind up the trifurcated people that he saw in the pew in nineteenth-century Germany.[2]

141

In sum, Nietzsche's critique of religion was based on his perception that it was opposed to love (action, praxis) and to reason. Walter Kaufmann, in his magisterial work on Nietzsche, *Nietzsche, Philosopher, Psychologist, Anti-Christ,* says that Nietzsche's view of his critique is different from that of most of his commentators: the latter think that his criticism of morality is the centerpiece, but Nietzsche says that his views on religion, not morality, are the essence of his thought.[3] Kaufmann accedes to this view, wrongly, I think. (Kaufmann, 342) Praxis in Christianity is love in action. Nietzsche says that Christian praxis is, however, anything but loving; in this he is, in large measure, correct. But to split off morality from love, moral theology from Christian living (religion), indicates either that Kaufmann misunderstood Nietzsche or that Nietzsche misunderstood our religion. Kaufmann blunts Nietzsche's religious critique to so bifurcate religion. Christian praxis, the Christian religious life, is to be loving. Moral theology tells Christians what the loving thing to do is and what it is not. For Nietzsche, to criticize the religion for splitting things off and to accept it in its split-off state, to desire to put us back together again, and to fall into so deep a trap conceptually is the greatest flaw in his critique. He could have done so much more for Christians if he had put theology together again for us. I propose to put both his critique of morality and religion together and see what it looks like.

Faith Is Against Action (Love)

In his best moral treatise, *Beyond Good and Evil,* Nietzsche says that some Puritan fanatics prefer a certain nothing to an uncertain something so that they can have ample reason for giving up the struggle.[4] Nietzsche gives people no such leeway. He says, "You want to live according to nature? . . . live according to life. . . . Why make a principle of what you yourselves are and must be?" (Beyond, I, 9) The moral person is "the free spirit." (Beyond, Part II) This free person wears many outrageous masks fashioned by Nietzsche, the master mask-maker. These facades so frequently put off honest inquirers into his work. But they were meant to do so; he meant to offend, to prick sensitivities and so teach, not so much by what he said, as by what they themselves knew to be true. He had no need to teach them the truths of the gospel; what he intended to teach was that they were not living up to them. The fact that he rebelled against them did not mean that he was against God, good, or Jesus; he was against God's religion because it had robbed him and his age's best of their best instincts—all in the name of religion, flag, and commerce.

Nietzsche was himself a free spirit; he could stand little of the cant and pomposity that passed for religion in his day. So he offered a principle of exegesis to those sensitive souls who were scandalized by his "depomping" devices: "Whatever is profound loves masks; what is most profound even hates image and parable. . . . Every profound spirit needs a mask: even more, around every profound spirit a mask is growing continually, owing to the constantly false, namely *shallow,* interpretation of every word, every step, every sign of life he gives." (Beyond, II, 40)

Thus, when Nietzsche uses code words such as "beyond good and evil," "the will to power," "master morality," "hardness," and "cruelty"—as he does in his other works—one is to interpret them in exactly the opposite way as they appear. He is "masking" his intent with hyperbole, sarcasm, and humor. No one who does not understand the preacher's hyperbole, no one who cannot laugh, should read Nietzsche; the evil in Nietzsche is, in large part, in the eye of the beholder. He is a philosopher who writes in poetic style—so well that the philosophers rejected him as a "poet" and the poets scanted him as a "philosopher." He wishes to tear away masks, which is often the supreme mask and illusion; he himself says that we must mask our deepest selves. Thus, to the philosophers he says, *Adventavit asinus/Pulcher et fortissimus"* (The ass came/ Beautiful and very brave). (Beyond, I, 8) The ass in question is the philosopher with a bag of a priori judgments, the categories into which the philosopher would put reality, which is the supreme irony for Nietzsche, since reality is people. So he calls this a prioristic faculty *niaiserie allemande* (the German foolishness). (Beyond, I, 11) He continued his criticism with a *reductio ad absurdum:* "All the young theologians of the Tübingen seminary went into the bushes—all looking for 'faculties.'" Kant and those who use his concept of the transcendent "horizon" (the *Vorbegriffe,* so in vogue now with H. G. Gadamer, K. Rahner, and B. Longergan) wish to rid us of the sensuous. Theirs is a *"sensus assoupire"* (it puts the senses to sleep); it is, as such, antihuman. (Beyond, I, 11) Too much emphasis on the a priori is procrustean. For Nietzsche, it leaves love at the door of one's ready-made categories. He wanted, therefore, to tear away the masks of hypocrisy and prefabricated categories and leave the masks—since the mysterious must be masked—of naturalism and humanity.

Nietzsche says that morality derives, not from what we intend—as we have been taught classically—since intentions are only symptoms, but from the unintentional. The intentional is the skin of the deed; it shows something but conceals more. So "intention is merely a sign and symptom that still requires interpretation." Intention is a sign that means too much and therefore almost nothing, in Nietzsche's estimation. If one were to get at the deeper meaning of things, the meaning beyond the cages of conventional philosophical and theological morality, one would have to overcome traditional morality. Like Freud, Nietzsche says that only the "finest and most honest" can do this, though. There is esotericism here, as there would be in Freud; only the elite can follow Nietzsche's *Philosophenweg* (Philosopher's Path). The esoteric person beholds things from above; the exoteric (the mediocre outsider) person views them from below. Nietzsche says that he is basing this on both Greek and Indian philosophy. (Beyond, II, 30, 32) His method of human (anthropological) retrieval is what Paul Ricoeur calls "a hermeneutics of suspicion." Nietzsche says that philosophers have such bad reputations because they have a right to their bad character. Their perfidy derives from the necessity of doubting everything; it is a philosopher's duty to "squint maliciously out of every abyss of suspicion." His suspicion seems to have authored not only that hermeneutical rubric in Ricoeur, but also the latter's "second naivete," which, in the Nietzschean schema, is a return to faith through suspicion and criticism. It is a naivete arrived at by methodological doubt. Ricoeur uses the same words and gives them much the same meaning, even though his faith is in Jesus as Lord, not in Man-as-Lord, as Nietzsche would have it.[5] Nietzsche's philosophical method, his organ of liberation to free him to be a man, is to be free to see what is both "out there" and "in here." Anything denying one the possibility of seeing is to be ruthlessly overthrown—like the Christian's duty to pluck and maim himself or herself if organs become instruments of sin. Thus, convictions are prisons,[6] and so is every person, every attachment, every virtue, even pity. The philosopher must be detached even from detachment in order to be free to work as philosopher. (Beyond, I, 42)

Nietzsche could not abide the dogmatism of Christian theology and its theologians; his esotericism was linked with this antipathy for dogmatism. Dogma is what is held by the herd; it is common, and whatever is common should be shunned by the philosopher, since "whatever is common always has little value." Hence, "great things remain for the great, abysses for the profound, nuances and shudders for the refined, and in brief, all that is rare for the rare." (Beyond, I, 43) Like Hegel, Nietzsche refuses to accept an isolated proposition as truth; its truth depends on its context, its overall meaning, the significance of its terms; truth is to be found in systems, in interconnections with life, with other—isomorphic—concepts. (Beyond, I, 53, n. 27) He also eschewed the liberalism and egalitarianism of his day. He called such liberals "slaves to egalitarianism"; he railed at their foolishness in trying to abolish all suffering. He did away with the concept of salvation and redemption. Thus, his way of facing up to the problem of the evils that liberalism tried to expunge was to opt for the value in whatever was odd, strange, different, or evil. He is something of a modern Pythagorean; Pythagoreans would go down to the town dumps and meditate on the offal of the city to free themselves from the appearances of optimism. Nietzsche sees just as much good accruing to human advancement from "hardness, forcefulness, slavery, danger in the alley and the heart, life in hiding, stoicism, the art of experiment and devilry of every kind, that everything evil, terrible, tyrannical in man, everything in him that is kin to beasts of prey and serpents serves the enhancement of the species 'man' as much as its opposite does." (Beyond, II, 43) He considers himself not a free-thinker in the sense that those in the nineteenth century understood that term; he was, rather, a "free-spirited philosopher" who, unlike the free-thinkers, went beyond the categories of good and evil. He knew this to be a dangerous formula to follow in philosophy, but if it would keep others from thinking him a free-thinker, it was worth it. He preferred to look for the good everywhere, especially where one would think it was not. Hence, he found value in "God, devil, sheep, and the worm in us." (Beyond, II, 44)

Like Freud, Nietzsche went to the classics to find his heroes. Freud used a Greek myth (Oedipus) to do away with both sin and guilt and to explain the origin of evil and the ambivalence of human emotions. Nietzsche, the trained doctor of philology, also went to the Greek classics to find his categories and models. His criticism of Christian morality was rooted in Aristotle's *Nichomachean Ethics*. Of the good man, Aristotle says that "he ought to be a lover of self, since he will then act nobly, and so both benefit himself and aid his fellows; but the bad man ought not to be a lover of self, since he will follow his base passions, and so injure both himself and his neighbors." (Kaufmann, 382; Ethics, 1169a) Nietzsche is not against morals; he is for Aristotle's greatness of soul *(megalopsychia)*, in which decency and morality are beyond question. But there is more, much more, to be expected of a "great-souled one." He claims much and deserves much; he does not falsely claim less than he is or vainly more than he deserves because of what he has not produced. (Kaufmann, 384) When Nietzsche speaks of the Superman *(Ubermensch)* and the "will to power," he is not talking the wicked nonsense of the Nazis, who co-opted these terms for their own perfidies, but he is calling for men and women to transcend mediocrity. Nietzsche is not against weakness per se, although his rhetoric would have him appear to despise it, but against a brand of Christian humility and compassion done out of egotism, the egotism of those who do not use their talents for love, beauty, and art, but hide behind the Savior in a way that he felt incapacitated them for happiness. Hence, only the strong can be happy in Nietzsche's sense; it means a peace that comes from facing up to, not only one's talents, but the tragedy of one's evil and the evils of the world around one. The great-souled one backs off from neither his truth nor that of the world surrounding him. This is the meaning of his aphorism, "for the mediocre, being mediocre is happiness." (Kaufmann, 385; *Anti-Christ,* 57)

It was not morality that Nietzsche desired, and not hedonistic license. He wanted nobility, generosity in a world created divine and, tragically, never redeemed. He wanted a joy and nobility in the face of all that. Christianity stopped the talented, the noble, and the great from being so.

> To be ashamed of one's immorality—that is a step on the staircase at whose end one is also ashamed of one's morality. (Beyond, "Epigrams and Interludes," 95)

> Sensuality often hastens the growth of love so much that the roots remain weak and are easily torn up. (Ibid., "Epigram," 120)

> Even concubinage has been corrupted—by marriage. (Ibid., "Epigram," 123)

> What a time experiences as evil is usually an untimely echo of what was formerly experienced as good—the atavism of a more ancient ideal. (Ibid., "Epigram," 149)

> Jesus said to his Jews: "The Law was for servants—love God as I love him, as his son! What are morals to us sons of God!" (Ibid., "Epigram," 164)

> Whatever is done from love always occurs beyond good and evil. (Ibid., "Epigram," 153)

> Having a talent is not enough; one also requires your permission for it— right, my friends? (Ibid., "Epigram," 151)

Categories triumphed over praxis (love) in Christianity; theologians took revenge on their fellows with the power of their paradigms. Hence,

Nietzsche sought a pagan spirituality in which "the spiritualization of sensuality is called *love:* it is a great triumph over Christianity." (Idols, "Morality as the Enemy of Nature," 3) For him, faith is against love. To be Christian, it became necessary not only to live a life in dialectical opposition to so much of what his old religion had called both evil and good, but also to invert everything—in a Marxist way—to find a good person at the bottom of the categorical heap. The kingdom of heaven had to be stormed by the ruthless, just as Jesus had said. Hence, to rediscover the good in religion, it became necessary for Nietzsche to deny the mainflow of Christian praxis.

Religion in General: His Critique

In *Beyond Good and Evil,* Friedrich Nietzsche fashions a rather tight-knit critique of religion in general. Of course, he is speaking about Christianity, but he saves his most mordant critique of that specific religion for *Thus Spake Zarathustra,* written between 1883 and 1885, a work that many had difficulty understanding. He published his most understandable and tersest critique of religion, *The Anti-Christ,* in 1888. Sanity was to remain with him only a little while longer, until 1889. He slipped into hopeless insanity then and died in 1900 at age fifty-six.

In *Beyond Good and Evil,* in a section he titles "What Is Religious," Nietzsche says that the very stuff *(Wesen)* of religion is neurosis. (Beyond, III, 47) At its very roots, the Christian faith—which was the foil for his religion *in genere*—demands a sacrifice of all freedom, pride, self-confidence of the spirit, which in turn involves slavery, self-mockery, and self-mutilation. Religion (Christianity) is, therefore, antihuman. This can be both said and defended, if one forgets Christianity at its best—as the defender of the weak, the teacher of the ignorant, the founder of the great universities, and the patron of the arts and all things humanistic. But Christianity has another side with a sad record of bestial Crusades against Islam; of venality and greed in the South American missions and in Hawaii; of bigotry and terror imposed by legalistic minds heedless of the healthy demands of the religion that we love with obedience, not with a spirit of mindlessness that can so easily become ruthlessness in the pursuit of goals utterly irreligious. But Nietzsche delivers himself of his own classicist's cry of the heart in *Beyond Good and Evil* (III, 46–52) when he says that the cross inverted the values of ancient Rome; there, no faith was demanded. The new, lower class (slave) converts to Christianity

147

wreaked their vengeance on their masters by demanding that they believe, when their culture demanded just the opposite. This slavery has continued in Christianity in the demands it expects to be obeyed slavishly, which demands are rooted, not in love, but in an unseemly rage and hatred of all enlightenment that frees. Slaves understand only the tyrannical in morals; they demand only the unconditional in ethics; and they batten on the pain and suffering imposed by faith with a relish beyond belief, whereas the Roman spirit was a "noble taste that [seemed] to *deny* suffering." (Beyond, III, 46)

The religious neurosis everywhere demanded a change in the Roman-disciplined sensuality, a change that negated its humaneness. Fasting, solitude, and sexual abstinence were the instruments of this neutering of our humanity. The continence of the Roman gave way to enormous swings, in both the savage and the civilized, from extreme indulgence to "spasms" of penitence, something Nietzsche's refined German taste looked on as decidedly Latin in temperament, not German. One could argue with him on this. Luther was the quintessential German, and his pre-Lutheran days were ones of extreme scrupulosity, which called forth his theology of grace, allowing him to scotch out the need for penitential practices as he had done them in the Roman Church. Nietzsche defends himself against Christian penances by asserting that sainthood is a denial of one's very essence; one's will is the stuff of humanity. It is good, although unruly, and will ultimately opt for the good, more or less. The saint swings from one opposite—the evil person—to the other—the holy person. Nietzsche sees this as a neurotic swing, a power piety. In the main the religious meaning of sainthood is that men and women are awed by the power of the saints' wills—that such fragile facades should mask such steely souls. Religious people, therefore, do not honor the saints with devotions, but themselves. As Freud and Marx, so Nietzsche indicted religion of projecting its best (and worst) on God and the holy ones. (Beyond, III, 51)

As for the passion for God manifested by the mystical and devotional tradition of the church, it was no more than the lusts of young women and the hysteria of old maids "ignorantly and bashfully translated from puberty into an *unio mystica*." He cites the lascivious behavior of the Quietist mystics as examples of pious people sitting prayerfully on a volcano of sneakily expressed lust. (Beyond, III, 50)

Besides, he says with Teutonic archness, the mother of all this penitence, Catholicism, is more for Latins than for Teutons and northern Europeans. The Reformation has turned this section of Europe back to its natural state: one of unbelief. With the exception of the Celts, he says, northerners are barbarians and have little talent for religion. The ancient Greek religion was life-affirming, but the rabble ultimately instilled it with a type of fear that made it quite ready for Christianity. (Beyond, III, 47f.) The faithlessness of the modern European is not a bad thing, however. The Romans were faithless and they were human—much more so than Christians. Nietzsche concludes that in Europe theism is declining, but religion is growing. Theism's god is Father, Judge, Rewarder and full of Free Will, but God cannot hear or help humanity. Hence, the decline. God cannot communicate clearly, so people have sworn off God and given allegiance to atheism. But, for Nietzsche, the religious instinct is alive and growing in Europe. (Beyond, III, 53) Modern philosophy is anti-Christian, but not antireligious. It disbelieves the Christian soul in which people believed as they did in grammar and the subject "I" synthesizing the predicate. Nietzsche says that the predicate synthesizes the "I" or "me." So the "I" is a product of thought. Hence, thought thinks me rather than I thinking the thought. Soul is a product of thinking about ego; because the ego is a product of thought, and not vice versa, so the soul is a product of one's ratiocinations. Modern philosophy, therefore, cannot abide the concept "soul." Kant thought the subject "I" only apparently existed, somewhat as Hindu Vedantists think the ego is a fictive thing created out of desire that it be. (Beyond, III, 54) If there is not "I," then there is no ego; nor is there any soul. Philosophers have gotten rid of the one by grammar and the other (the soul) with their epistemological skepticism.

Religion is cruel and has moved through three stages of harsh impositions on humankind: First, it demanded human sacrifice on us—the preferred *oblatum* was the most beloved of the family, the firstborn. Next, religion demanded a more intimate, and therefore more cruel, sacrifice: that one offer up one's very nature by sacrificing one's strongest instincts to the deity as an act of asceticism, which, together with enthusiasm, was anti-natural to Nietzsche. Last, religion demanded the sacrifice of God, or of whatever was holy, comforting, healing, hopeful, and held out to its clients the possibility of future happiness. Thus, even faith was demanded by religion, not as virtue, but as sacrifice. When religion demanded the sacrifice of God, however, humankind obtained nothing in return. This is the age that Nietzsche saw coming: a religion demanding all and offering nihilism in return. (Beyond, III, 55)

But Nietzsche would not succumb to the nihilism of the coming age. He who was thought to be the sickest of the sick thinkers, the nihilist of nihilists, was a believer. This is his belief, the point of all his writings: he intends to run right at the evils of his day and not flee from them as religious people tell him to do. He is going through pessimism to optimism. He will do this by thinking through all the half-Christian theologies of demi-German simplicity, such as Schopenhauer's. He will become as world-denying as any Asiatic, especially the Buddhists, deluded by their morality; and by turning things upside down he hopes to come out the other end affirming the world, people, and things by descending into the hell of the nihilism of his age. His ideal is

> the ideal of the most high-spirited, alive, and world-affirming human being who has not only come to terms and learned to get along with whatever was and is, but who wants to have *what was and is* repeated into all eternity, shouting insatiably *da capo* (from the beginning)—not only to himself but to the whole play and spectacle, and not only to a spectacle but at bottom to him who needs precisely this spectacle—and who makes it necessary because again and again he needs himself—and makes himself necessary—What? And this wouldn't be—*circulus vitiosus deus?* [a god made out of a vicious circle?] (Beyond, III, 56)

This is just about the whole of his system of religion. He will, like Rimbaud after him, go to his divinity, to his heaven, by passing through hell. The means he will use is to hope for an inversion of all the nonsense and mischief, both pious and philosophical, of his age by undergoing all of it with a vulnerability to it that will convert him to it and flip him into innocence, joy, and eternity. The theme of the eternal recurrence, so predominant in *Thus Spake Zarathustra* (especially sections 10 and 11), is his belief in the goodness and eternity of all things, in particular that of men and women. He believes in all of it and them and would have them back again and again as would a Hindu, whose belief is that, at bottom, one is the Ultimate and that all shall return over and over again. He installs a "blunder factor" in his philosophical equation by stating that he might not happen on the good of things intentionally, but any way he arrives will be satisfactory to him.

Thus, philosophical pessimism (Nietzsche's "going through evil") ends by affirming all that is. By performing this reconciliation of opposites he becomes a bit of a nature mystic in the sense that I outlined in *Struggle and Submission*, in which one becomes one with all things in a return to one's materiality. It is an intuition of one's unity with matter, but it is an undifferentiated form of matter, and hence a throwback to an earlier stage of development.[7] In its homogeneous state it affirms all that is. Good and evil are thoroughly commingled and reconciled because they have not been philosophically distinguished. This phenomenon is to be found in the Early Upanishads and in the ravings of manic-depressives and those under the influence of such drugs as mescaline or LSD. Matter seems innocently commingled with a joy in all that is: rejoicing in sun, moon, stars, sea, in good as well as evil, without the necessity of space and time. One feels immortal, since time is gone, and omnipotent, since space is warped almost to uselessness. Hence, morality, the rims of which are the space/time continuum, can be no more. It is a euphoric experience in this expansive phase—one called *bast* (expansion in Arabic) by Sufi mystics. But its twin is an experience called *qabz* (contraction in Arabic) by the Sufi masters. The first phase is one of happiness in the feeling that all one's sins have been forgiven. One exults in the body and finds nothing loathsome in it. One is not only united with the all, one has become the All. There is no God in the experience. The other side of the experience (qabz) is one in which one loathes the body and everything to do with it. One is locked into one's ego with one's sins, and there is no way out. This experience some medievals called "diabolical possession."

Nature Mysticism is never attended by the need for others, so one's humanism is usually self-centered and thing-centered; the ego is expanded happily and one is united with things and is intuitively aware of both one's materiality and one's goodness. It is a powerful experience and can be quite healing. It can be either the first step in, or toward, religion on a rather primitive level or the step away from it that many who have been burned by religion (especially by Christianity) take in compensation. Nietzsche's philosophy was such a step, I submit. As such, it is a surrogate for religion for many of its afficionados. Aldous Huxley was high in its praise, but on his deathbed he told his wife that he had not touched the divinity at all, as he had claimed his mescaline experience had done for him, but only his expanded ego. Rimbaud, Proust, and William James, as well as R. C. Zaehner and a host of sixties drug users, have altered their consciousness in the same way. So many have done it in order to do for themselves what their Christianity—half-used or unused—had not: they wanted to procure happiness. Nietzsche wanted the same thing, but he used philosophy, not chemicals, to alter his consciousness. The religion presented to him by his forebears proved unfaithful to him, so he made one for himself—not one for the weak liberals who were "soft" on evil or one that avoided all the truth. His was a religion that included all the hard truths he thought Christians and free-thinking liberals avoided.

The two most troublesome concepts in the "old religion" were God and sin; these he scotched out of his own, since they imposed more suffering on people than any others in human history. God had to go, since God imposed law and its concomitant, sin. Sin had to go because it mantled us with guilt. His religion would be ethical but based on the naturalness found sensuousness, not in a "Nature" devised of prefabricated categories, such as he found in Christian-Greek morality. Of the Incarnation and Redemption, Nietzsche says, "A god who would come to earth must not *do* anything except wrong: not to take the punishment upon oneself but the *guilt,* would be divine." (Ecce Homo, I, 5) Further, "one is best punished for one's virtues." (Beyond, "Epigram," 132) Both sin and virtue are impositions on one's naturalness, causing guilt on the one hand and hubris on the other. He would have neither. Hence, his naked intent on the existential rather than on the conceptual. He hoped that humankind would outgrow God and sin, in much the same way that Freud would. (Beyond, III, 57)

But if Nietzsche excoriated Christianity for its failings, he was no lover of modernity either. He harkened back to Renaissance man as his model. He needed a leisure class in which to flourish, and free-thinking egalitarians so bruited about industriousness as an ideal that it "dissolved the religious instinct"; the latter was not a faith in ideas made by theologians, but a trust in things not made by us at all: it was a trust in being's goodness and a tolerance for its innate evils as well. Egalitarianism and modernity—the one was the other for Nietzsche— offered one future only: hubris in excelsis. He said that free-thinkers in Germany had forgotten what religions are for. This had prepared the people for nothing but unbelief. Most of these middle-class German Protestant free-thinkers, and this includes especially the intellectual class—for whom he cherished a particular scorn—had become so busy that they had left no time for religion and its pursuits; so they stood dumb and amazed at the presence of religion's very existence in society, especially in their own preferred sanctuary: the German university in which theologians were confounding them, not with their reasoning, to be sure, but solely by their presence. They stood mildly amused by religion, mixing cocktails of superiority toward religion to which they added ironic dashers of bitters and disdain, for the unclean lines of religion offended the neatness of their empirical Teutonic minds. So the modern burgher and intellectual shunned religion as a Pariah. To be human and tolerant demanded that one avoid the pain of tolerating the ancient religion. Nietzsche could not abide the superior attitude of the Enlightenment scholar, who viewed religion as a naivete and religious people as an inferior type that had been outgrown. For Nietzsche, there was only scorn for modern enlightenment. The German leadership class was composed of "presumptuous little dwarfs"; and these people are, individually, a "rabble man." (Beyond, III, 58)

Just when the religious reader settles in for a comfortable time of viewing unbridled secularity getting its proper "licks," Nietzsche, ever the scold, turns back to inflict his heaviest damage on religion. In a nutshell, his critique of religion, or what really bothers him about religion and religious people—and the two are the same thing for Nietzsche—is that religion *in se* is a result of people having been burnt by reality. It is an effective bomb shelter forcing religious people to make shallow interpretations of the real to avoid being burnt again. Thus, religious men and women have to be "flighty, light and false" in order to preserve themselves. The lack of Salvation and Redemption in Nietzsche's own religion forced a tragic interpretation on the whole of human existence, the parts of which were joyful—human and painful, but peaceful in knowing the evil and willing it as one of life's necessaries. Religion created Redemption and Salvation to rid itself of the real, and in doing so got rid of the joy along with the pain. He found that religious men and women were incurably pessimistic at heart, their optimism being the thinnest veneer. Implicitly, Nietzsche demanded that a religion be what it was intended to be: an optimism demanding an openness (vulnerability) before the full panoply of reality—both its weals and woes. Therefore, Nietzsche—ever the philosopher—concludes his critique of religion by saying that piety, or life in God, is the "subtlest and final offspring of the fear of truth." Religion is the "will to the inversion of truth, to untruth at any price." Until now, religion has been our best cosmetic, beautifying us only on the surface so we would not have to face up to the ugliness below and its attendant pain. The religious love of people for God's sake is the highest attainment of religion, even though it is off the mark. To love someone for no ulterior motive would be "brutish" and "stupid." Thus,

whoever the human being may have been who first felt and "experienced" this, however much his tongue may have stumbled as it tried to express

153

such delicatesse, let him remain holy and vulnerable for us for all time as the human being who has flown highest yet and gone astray most beautifully! (Beyond, III, 60)

Nietzsche concludes his critique of religion *in genere*—the models of which are Christianity and Buddhism—by stating that religion is a useful tool but must never be taken as an end in itself. The philosopher finds religion useful as an instrument with which to educate and refine humankind. Religion serves to educate future rulers by offering them high paths of spirituality. These same rulers will find religion useful in governing their fractious subjects. When the ruling class itself becomes insufferable, religious contemplation offers one shelter from both crude forms of government and the rough and tumble of dirty politics. As for asceticism and even Puritanism, Nietzsche finds them useful and even necessary as tools for "educating and ennobling a race that wishes to become master over its origins among the rabble and that works its way up toward future rule." To the ordinary, religion offers peace of heart, contentment with their state and lot in life, and a way of ennobling the obedience imposed on them by rulers. Religion refreshes, refines, makes the best of suffering, and even, in the end, sanctifies and justifies people in their lives. Of all religions, Christianity and Buddhism receive the highest marks from Nietzsche for teaching both high and low born to put all things in the hands of a higher order, thus rendering people somewhat content with their experience of a harsh reality. (Beyond, III, 61)

Then Nietzsche begins to shift gears and name names in his critique. Religion must be a tool for the philosopher and never an end *in se*. It is an inversion to make religion one's master. For a philosopher, to make religion into anything but what it is—a means for the cultivation and education of a philosophical mind—will cost dearly in the end, an end that he portrays in detail in *Thus Spake Zarathustra* and *The Anti-Christ*, as we shall see momentarily. There are many means one uses for the education of the philosophical mind; religion is merely one of them. There seems to be some "law of absurdity in the whole economy of mankind" that inflicts its heaviest damage on the best types of people. To these best of people, the best religions—Christianity and Buddhism—have offered the wisdom that life is to be suffered "like a sickness." Religions, sadly, demand that all feelings about life are to be considered false and impossible, this in order to preserve and succour humankind, which Nietzsche says will suffer anyway. This pastoral care for the suffering forces religion to act in a sovereign way, keeping the best human types "on a lower rung" because there is something in religion that impels it to preserve too much that must perish.

Religion has been of inestimable value to Europe in producing the great spiritual men and women of Christianity; but in comforting the savaged and ravaged of the continent, by taking them into monasteries and convents, the church preserved not only the sick and suffering people of its day, but too much that was sick in culture as well. In Nietzsche's estimation, this had a disastrous effect on European history. The church's penchant for preservation stood values on their heads so that it could give the sick, hope. What resulted was that the strong were broken by mediocrity; the church even cast suspicion on beauty and enjoyment. This caused the church to bring down everything earthly, which means all that was humankind's best instincts, such as "manliness," *hauteur,* and whatever allowed one to domineer or conquer—by which Nietzsche means "face up" to one's full reality, the bad with the good. The result was a person of "unsureness, agony of conscience, self-destruction" who inverted "all love of the earthly and of dominion over the earth into hatred of the earth and the earthly—that is the task the church posed for itself and had to pose, until in its estimation 'becoming unworldly,' 'unsensual,' and 'higher men' were fused into a single feeling." (Beyond, III, 62) Thus, the church's will was, for eighteen centuries, "to turn man into a *sublime miscarriage.*" Christianity has been calamitous and has consummate arrogance because Christians were not "high and hard enough" to form people as artists; nor was it strong and far-sighted enough to let necessary calamities happen on the way to human progress. It produced a race of men and women who were unable to see that there are higher and lower types of people; they are ranked by nature. The church has ruled Europe with its ideology of equality before God, and this produced a "smaller, almost ridiculous type, a herd animal, something eager to please, sickly, and mediocre has been bred, the European of today." (Ibid.) This leads him to undertake his major religious critique, the one against Christianity.

Nietzsche on Christianity

I have often laughed at the weaklings who thought themselves good because they have no claws.

—Zarathustra

In the final section of *The Anti-Christ*, Nietzsche delivers his verdict on religion: it is to convict Christianity.

> With that I have done and pronounce judgment. I *condemn* Christianity, I bring against the Christian Church the most terrible charge any prosecutor has ever uttered. To me it is the extremest thinkable form of corruption, it has had the will to the ultimate corruption conceivably possible. The Christian Church has left nothing untouched by its depravity, it has made of every value a disvalue, of every truth a lie, of every kind of integrity a vileness of soul. People still dare to talk to me of its "humanitarian" blessings! . . . The worm of sin, for example: it was only the Church which enriched mankind with this state of distress! "Equality of souls before God," this falsehood . . . finally became revolution. . . . To cultivate out of *humanitas* a self-contradiction, and art of self-violation, a will to falsehood at any price, an antipathy, a contempt for every good and honest instinct! These are the blessings of Christianity!—Parasitism as the *sole* practice of the Church; with its ideal of green-sickness, of "holiness" draining away all blood, all love, all hope for life; the Beyond as the will to deny reality of every kind . . . the Cross . . . a conspiracy against health, beauty, well-constitutedness, bravery, intellect, benevolence of soul, *against life itself* . . . I call Christianity the *one* great curse, the *one* great intrinsic depravity, the *one* great instinct for revenge for which no expedient is sufficiently poisonous, secret, subterranean, petty . . . Revaluation of all values! (Anti-Christ, 62)

Christianity, in a word, is to be condemned because faith is opposed to both praxis (love) (Anti-Christ, 10) and reason (Anti-Christ, 47).

Faith Is Opposed to Praxis (Love)

Christianity is not a religion of good news and it certainly is not a religion as was the early church, but it is something else. Nietzsche is not against Christ or the early church, but he opposes what the church and theologians have made of both Jesus and the good news. "In truth, there was only *one* Christian, and he died on a Cross." (Anti-Christ, 10) Nietzsche had respect for Jesus, so his criticism was intended to shock his Christian readers; and in this he was the consummate artist. It is not that he accepted the gospel, but that it was never lived up to by the church. This galls him. Christians have made of the Evangel a "disangel" because of their loveless praxes. (Anti-Christ, 39) Jesus was against the established religion (Anti-Christ, 27) and was blithely unaware of how anarchic and shocking his actions and preachings were to his listeners. Nietzsche says, "One has to regret that no Dostoyevsky lived in the neighborhood of this most interesting *decadent;* I mean someone who could feel the thrilling fascination of such a combination of the sublime, the sick and the childish [as Jesus was]." (Anti-Christ, 3)

This sympathy for the weak is worse than any vice. The Christian is a herd animal bred out of fear. The values of the present society—values bred by both Christianity and the culture it gave rise to—are merely decadence to Nietzsche. "I consider life itself instinct for growth, for continence, for accumulation of forces, for power: where the will to power is lacking there is decline." (Anti-Christ, 6) Again, he thinks it nihilism to fail to see humankind as the supreme value. To hold God as the supreme value is an inversion caused by Christianity. His whole point of view is a humanism, and his philosophy is an anthropology. His bête noir, his very antithesis, is "theologians and all that has theologian blood" because their idealism is the supreme arrogance, and this becomes a theological arrogance because it takes one away from the sensual, from the existential to the ideal. The idealist and priest have stood truth on its head, since their holiness has harmed life itself with its humility, chastity, and poverty. "Pure spirit is pure lie." Nietzsche, the son of a Lutheran clergyman, whom he revered, takes out after clerics next: "So long as the priest, that denier, calumniator and poisoner of life by *profession,* still counts as a *higher* kind of human being, there can be no answer to the question: What is truth." (Anti-Christ, 8) Theologians have a false consciousness because what they call faith is not a vision of life, but an ocular occlusion precluding the very possibility of seeing life and things as they are. No part of reality is good to a theologian. Faith is a pose; it offers falsity as truth. Only that has real value for Nietzsche which affirms life, enhances or justifies it and causes it to triumph. Theologians call this disvalue, so Nietzsche is unalterably opposed to them. He is no friend of either Catholicism or Protestantism; he calls the latter the half-sided paralysis of Christianity. He despises the Protestant Kant's concept of universal duty as morality; this is not it at all. Any act that is joyfully performed by one of life's instincts is his idea of a right act; and Nietzsche says that Christians object to this joy. (Anti-Christ, 11)

Further, Christians have forgotten that we are rooted in the animal, not in the divine. Things have been totally inverted by Christianity and its philosophy. The real philosophy, the philosopher of truth, sees things in this way: we are not the crown of creation, but the sickliest of creatures

157

because we have strayed from our instincts. We are machines, and will is not a cause, but an effect; it is a result of physical stimuli. Thus, consciousness is not a sign of divinity, but a pulling into oneself and away from the outer earth, where men and women were created to be in the first place. Therefore, spirit is an imperfection of the organism and "pure spirit" is pure stupidity. (Anti-Christ, 14) The causes of Christianity are God, soul, ego, spirit, and free will, and these are as imaginary as its effects, which are sin, redemption, and grace. God, spirit, and souls are imaginary beings; and religion is the interaction of chimeras, not realities. Teleology is as imaginary as natural science; there is no Last Judgment. The church has made natural things reprehensible and hateful. The actual is not loved at all. Religion is caused by a moral feeling, and Nietzsche—as did Marx before him—could not stomach the emotions playing about in such a serious enterprise as philosophy. (Anti-Christ, 15)

The Christian God is a projection of one's needs. Men and women offer thanks to God when things are going well and offer God admiration when they are going bad. Further, when a people wills to have power, then God becomes someone triumphant as the representative of an aggressive and powerful people. When the people are not in their ascendancy, God is depicted as poor, weak, and lowly. The God of the weak becomes weak but is called "good," just like the weak who call themselves "the good." The weak strip God of evil and God becomes the "good in itself." These same weak people revenge themselves on their masters by changing the God of their conquerors into a devil. But both gods produce nothing but decadence. When the God of Israel was stripped of his manliness and became a Savior for the weak, God became a retrograde concept. This made of religion a hospital; and it made of its God, not a proud pagan god, but a Jew. The very concept God became weaker and pale stuff to behold the more God became an ideal, a spirit, and an absolute. God became reified—a thing—and this is the "decay of God." (Anti-Christ, 15–18 passim) Thus, "God degenerated to the contradiction of life, instead of being its transfiguration and eternal Yes!" God is, therefore, "nothingness deified, the will to nothingness sanctified!" So, Christianity's concept of God is corrupt, since it denies life when it was designed by Jesus to affirm it. Even if it were true—and Nietzsche thinks it is not—something happened to Christianity; and whatever happened to it turned it about in the opposite direction. (Anti-Christ, 19)

Next, Nietzsche launches into a long panegyric on Buddhism. He praises it for abolishing the god concept. It is, for him, the world's only positivistic religion—it struggles against suffering, not sin. It has no concept of morality—it is "beyond good and evil." It is a phenomenological religion based on (1) human overexcitability, which leads to pain, and (2) overintellectuality, which dwells too much on logic and conceptualizations—all of which erode person in favor of un-person. Bodily conditions lead one to depression. Hence, the Buddha enjoins a life of open-air wandering and moderation in food, drink, and emotions. He holds out ideas that produce cheerfulness, kindness, and health. Prayer and asceticism are gone from Buddhism, as are categorical imperatives and any compulsion at all (one can leave the order). He misreads Buddhism badly by stressing what he calls "egoism" as one of its chief values. The central "dogma" of the Buddha is that there is no self (the teaching of *anatta*, or no self). Nietzsche sees ridding oneself of suffering as egoism; "in the teaching of Buddha egoism becomes a duty." (Anti-Christ, 20)

Nietzsche is fond of Buddhism's mild passivity before power and its upper-class style; he seems to know nothing of Mahayana Buddhism, which broke the elitist model of the earlier Theravada. He is against Christianity because it is a haven for the lower classes and because of its doctrine of sin; he calls conscience a "specific against boredom." He inveighs against Christianity for positing the possibility of an affective relation with God through prayer and for making perfection unattainable except through grace. He is against it for despising the body, for masochism, for "hatred of mind, of pride, of courage, freedom, libertinage of mind is Christian; hatred of the senses, of the joy of the senses, of joy in general is Christian." (Anti-Christ, 21)

He is attracted to Buddhism because it is a religion for cultivated people, whereas Christianity is for the barbarous, with its blood drinking and contempt for both culture and intellect. Christianity overpowered the brute by making him sick. "Buddhism is a religion for the end and fatigue of a civilization. Christianity does not even find civilization in existence—it establishes civilization if need be." Further, Buddhism is colder, more objective than Christianity. It "says what it feels: I suffer. Christianity makes suffering into sin." Christianity denies the suffering and says that it is from the devil. Next, Nietzsche describes his feelings about the theological virtues, faith, hope, and charity. Faith sees truth as unimportant. It values only the intensity of belief. Hence, inquiry must be forbidden by the church. Hope stimulates life more than does actual

159

happiness; the future is more important than the present. Greeks considered hope *the* evil. (Anti-Christ, 23) Love demands that God be person. Further, God must be young to satisfy the baser instincts; saints must be pretty women for the men and handsome men for the women. Chastity renders a cult more enthusiastic, since men and women must invest more of their affective lives in it. "Love is the state in which man sees things most of all as they are not." Love tolerates more than a normal state would. These three are, therefore, the three Christian "shrewdnesses," in Nietzsche's estimation. (Anti-Christ, 24)

In inverting value, Judaism and Christianity killed the world. Christianity is not a counter-Judaism, as some thought, but a continuation of Judaism. Judaism-Christianity is antithetic to nature; it is "the radical falsification of all nature, all naturalness, all reality, the entire inner world as well as the outer." Further, "they inverted religion, religious worship, morality, history, psychology, one after the other in an irreparable way into the contradiction of their natural values." The "they" is the Jews. Christians merely copy Judaism. In order to deny this world, religion invented another one. It rejected all in life that ascended, "well-constitutedness, power, beauty, self-affirmation on earth." The Jews inverted good and evil, true and false to "calumniate" the world. Judaism, therefore, denaturalized natural values. Inversion killed the world. Like Marx, he would reinvert the world and its values. In the beginning, with Israel, God was Nature. "Yahweh was the expression of their consciousness of power, their delight in themselves, their hopes of themselves." God saved them through military victory and by providing rain. (Anti-Christ, 25) But when God didn't deliver the natural goods, they changed God into a "moral god"—one who rewards good and punishes evil. Thus, the priests stood cause and effect on their heads. God became a demanding god, not a helping god. Morality should be "an expression of the conditions under which a nation lives and grows, . . . a nation's deepest instinct of life." (Anti-Christ, 25) Morality became, instead, abstract and anti-life. Nietzsche feels that this "new morality" robbed us of imagination and put the evil eye on things. "What is Jewish, what is Christian morality? Chance robbed of its innocence; misfortune dirtied by the concept 'sin'; well-being as a danger, as a 'temptation'; physiological indisposition poisoned by the worm of conscience." (Ibid.)

The Jews translated all their past "into religious terms," thus falsifying history. Nature was gone and a moral order of things became the criterion for one's acts—God's will emerged, so did Providence. (Anti-Christ, 26)

History, to have any punch at all, had to become a Revelation. Hence, religion forged one. History became a sacred book—a Book. The priest denatured all human events, like birth, meals, deaths, by sanctifying them. Therefore, to sacralize is to denature is to desacralize. In reading this, Bonhoeffer and Harvey Cox come immediately to mind, epitomizing as they did—Cox has since changed—the secularizing of Christian categories to get the religion back on an even keel.

Nietzsche scores religion for being against the profoundest instincts of the ruling class—which instincts are Nature. For Nietzsche, the holy is the natural. Life is holy. (Anti-Christ, 26) Jesus was guilty of stirring up the lower classes of Palestine against the natural instincts of the upper classes. Hence, Jesus died for his own sins, as a political criminal. It is wrong to make a hero of Jesus, whose evangel demanded passivity before struggle. (Anti-Christ, 29) Christianity's fear of pain forces it to become a religion of love, to hate the real (which is painful). These two feelings are the psychological basis for the doctrine of redemption. As such, the Christian religion is an Epicureanism, a hedonism, a paganism. Christianity is an escape to pleasure—the ersatz pleasure of escape, not the healthy pagan tragedy that Nietzsche wanted. Christians created their god according to these two requirements: fear of pain and hatred of the real. (Anti-Christ, 31) It has also incorporated the type "fanatic" into the type "redeemer." Redemption's heaven is for children, certainly not for adults. Further, the kingdom of God has no sword, it leaves its people defenseless. "It is precisely on condition that nothing he says is taken literally that this anti-realist can speak at all." (Anti-Christ, 32) Nobody, therefore, in his or her right mind, nobody with a desire to live in the real world, can take the Christian message literally or seriously.

Nietzsche blasts Christianity for making only inner realities "the real" and for making God a person. He demythologizes God the Son by making him into a theme: the transfiguration of the world. God the Father becomes the very feeling of perfection and of eternity. Jesus' death redeemed life, not sin. Christ's religion is a praxis, not a forgiveness. (Anti-Christ, 34) Christianity's history is one of misunderstanding of an original symbol, one that Christians vulgarized and barbarized by absorbing the morbid customs of the Roman Empire. (Anti-Christ, 37) Earlier on he says that the world is beyond good and evil. He has no concept with which to deal with evil in the world. This forces him to put it into a rational mold—a mold that would frequently be procrustean. He cannot deal with the avowed object of Jesus' death, stated by Nietzsche's unbeloved Paul, in which Jesus died for our sins and rose for our resurrection. He deals with a new man and woman, a superman and superwoman, a resurrected man and woman; but he cannot deal with a fallen humanity, since it makes no sense in his system. He did not feed into his scheme the possibility of there being any sin; evil certainly, sin never. Thus, Christianity becomes a life, but the life went through a suffering to become what it is. Christianity is a doing, not a belief. And belief has become a disangel for Nietzsche. The real evangel is the way that Jesus lived. "States of consciousness, beliefs of any kind . . . are a matter of complete indifference . . . compared with the value of instincts." Faith (belief) has never ruled Christians; instinct has. (Anti-Christ, 39)

Furthermore, Christians invented doctrines that obviated the necessity of having to practice Christianity. Paul's doctrine of faith was an invention; in fact, Nietzsche says that Paul invented the Christian religion and was its first devotee. (Nietzsche's *The Dawn*, 68, 75; Kaufmann, 343) Paul could not follow the Law so he invented the concept faith, which was taken up by Luther; the latter's *sola fide* (people are saved by *faith alone*, i.e., God's power covers over all their sins; works are unnecessary, but show to oneself and others that one has received God's grace) inverts Christ's gospel. (Anti-Christ, 39) Nietzsche detests the doctrine of faith alone but says that Christianity is possible for some and even necessary for others in order to live their lives. So Christians invented their doctrines.

Nietzsche moves on to condemn Christians for their hardness of heart. When Jesus died on the cross, his followers never forgave the Jews for their complicity in the crime. They invented a logic of hatred that made them the judges of their enemies. Christians would have their revenge *(ressentiment)* on their enemies. (Anti-Christ, 40) They had to invent a resurrection to make their doctrine of retribution plausible. (Anti-Christ, 45) In fact, redemption itself is an invention of Christians because Christ did away with the very concept of guilt. In looking to do away with the guilt heaped on him and his generation by overzealous preachers, he has to scotch out not only Jesus' words on the necessity of repentance, but also the meaning that the non-Pauline evangelists attach to his death: it is redemptive. So, for Nietzsche, there was no chasm separating God and humanity, ever. Christ lived the unity that existed between the deity and humanity. That is the good news. Hence, sacrifice was not necessary to rid us of guilt; we were not guilty in the first place. Christian logic invented doctrine after doctrine predicated on a pagan sacrifice: for them,

Christ's death was a sacrifice for sin. Hence, Christ was the Redeemer and he will come again; so the logic goes. Thus, human blessedness in the present was thrown out by Christians for one in the future. The gospel became a homily on personal immortality, a promise that Nietzsche says is unfulfilled and unfulfillable. It is an impudent and contemptible promise. (Anti-Christ, 41) Faith in Luther's theology is merely a screen behind which the personal inability of Luther to love and the collective inability of the whole Reformation to love, hid. Praxis was thrown over for faith. Luther could not live like Dostoyevsky's prince Mishkin, with his simple love; neither could Calvin nor John Knox. (Kaufmann, 349) Nietzsche does a serious disservice to himself by seeming to be against pity and love of neighbor; he is not. He attacks both, however, when not done in a real Christian spirit. His self-image is one of being a philosopher whose role in life is to uncover cant and hypocrisy. (Beyond, VI, 212)

He despises Christians for their *ressentiment*, which is a perduring rage and vengefulness. It is one of Nietzsche's key points of criticism. This *ressentiment* is a slave's virtue, in which one appears gentle because one is fearful of saying or doing the truth and suffering its consequences; but one is, in reality, seething with rage and not mild and good at all. Kindness done out of this spirit is a weakness; and humility and an obliging attitude emanate from fear. Nietzsche certainly knew a good deal about Christian foibles. This *ressentiment* is, for him, a slave's virtue making holiness out of the necessity of being servile and nice in a world that had dominance over one's life; this is the essence of *ressentiment*. To have power and refrain from its use out of kindness is to be above *ressentiment*. This is the mark of real power: forbearance. (Anti-Christ, 40) To this craven fear masking itself as kindness, love, and humility, Nietzsche opposes the superman and superwoman who had "Dionysian faith." Nietzsche hated the romanticism of the nineteenth century in general and the romantic "pessimism" of Christianity in particular. In *The Gay Science* he said that there were two types of sufferers. The one suffers from a personal "impoverishment of life and seeks redemption from [oneself] through art and knowledge, or intoxication, convulsion, anaesthesia, and frenzy." This is the romantic—Christian—sufferer. The other suffers from a fullness of life; this is the Dionysian type. Romanticism is rooted in poverty; . this is typified by Wagner and Schopenhauer. The Christian suffers *in* his or her own poverty and *from* that poverty. As such, the Christian needs "mildness, peacefulness, and goodness . . . and if possible, also a god who would really be a god for the sick, a 'savior.' " The Christian is rooted

163

in an impoverishment of spirit that is manifested by its meanness of spirit *(ressentiment)*. It is the art of the "misdeveloped, needy, underprivileged who destroys . . . because . . . all existence . . . outrages and provokes him." Romanticism is a pessimism, and Nietzsche would have none of this because it is not done out of love and joy, as the Dionysian would and the Christian says he or she should but does not, but out of impoverishment. *(The Gay Science*, 370; Kaufmann, 375)

The Christian's soul is impotent before the real, and the Dionysiac is potent before it. Hence, Christian morality and faith are rooted in revenge and hatred *(ressentiment)*, as are romantic philosophy and art; and Nietzsche finds the roots of modern anti-Semitism in this meanness of spirit and its romantic manifestations. (Kaufmann, 376) Romanticism is an "egoism coupled with weakness"; this is Goethe's formula, which Nietzsche took as a model, just as he took Goethe himself as a modern representative of Aristotle's "great-souled man." Goethe said that classicism is healthy but romanticism is sick. Hence, Nietzsche's criticism of both art and Christian morality was rooted in an appreciation of the Dionysian, which was in turn rooted in Goethe's classic ideal, not in the popular romanticism of the day. (Ibid.) Again, it is greatness of soul, not immorality and license, that Nietzsche desires. Greatness means facing up to one's talents and to the fullness of one's reality—good and bad, pleasurable and painful—and comes out as "power." It is not the power of the shallow and wicked Nazi mode of construing that word in Nietzsche, but the power that comes of living without Savior, Redemption, or the need to put one's faith in a power beyond one's humanity. This is a power that comes of trusting in one's humanity; the power of being human means that life is both a "doing" (praxis) and a "being" that makes one a human being. Faith not only weakens this humanity, this power, but destroys it at its roots. Nietzsche's belief is in one's ability to be a man or woman in the world. It is living out one's imago dei in a way that makes a statement that one is not an imago (God's image), but divinity itself. This is a very Indian mode. Nietzsche's language is Greek; his hero—Goethe—is in the Greek mode; but the substance of his anthropology—a statement that one is divine in a world that is a commingling of both good and evil—is Hindu. It is the *Philosophia Perennis* of Aldous Huxley and, especially, of the contemporary Sufi Frithjof Schuon; it is also the world view of Christopher Isherwood and Radhakrishnan that one is divine and need only let loose that divinity by any means decently available to become what one is.

Hence, Nietzsche's first point of criticism is that Christianity gets in the way of its own gospel: faith subverts praxis because the faithful are filled with *ressentiment*, which is the antithesis of the gospel. Again, Nietzsche knew us Christians well. How accurately he, Freud, and Marx outlined our pious hypocrisies; how infallibly did they see God become a god for the neurotic and the exploitative, instead of an infinite and loving being demanding maturity and love of God's images. One had only to name the three in older church circles to hear "Communist," "atheist," "lascivious Jew," and "madman" come down on the heads of these feisty critics and the invoker of their names.

Faith Is Against Reason

In *The Anti-Christ* (47), Nietzsche states it *nudo e crudo* that faith is a "veto against science." He cannot abide the saw *credo quia absurdum est* (I believe because it is absurd). (Nietzsche's *The Dawn*, 417; Kaufmann, 351f.) Nietzsche indicts Christian scholars for keeping two sets of theological books: they have one standard for exegeting their sacred books and another for doing so-called secular books. One cannot have truths and two standards for their verification.

Belief is scorned as much as systematizations of truth—both become prisons; both are procrustean. Of belief, Nietzsche says, "convictions are prisons." The great intellects are skeptical; this alone affords one the freedom to see the truth. (Anti-Christ, 54) Belief occludes the vision that one should have to see the values and disvalues of those things above and below one's values and one's vision. But the fanaticism of belief comforts one's soul; "fanatics are picturesque, mankind would rather see gestures than listen to reasons." (Anti-Christ, 54) The greatest force of one's being is a "grand passion," which moves one into truth and reality. Convictions are not what one is called to; they are but means. Nietzsche knew so well that Christians use their beliefs as ends in themselves; the moral convictions—both the laws and the vows that one takes before God—and intellectual convictions that one holds as dogmas are means, not ends. One is called to god, not to laws or dogmas; Christians confuse means with ends, and Nietzsche had the courage to say so. The engine that runs men and women is this "grand passion." It endows them with the base of courage to use any means to arrive at truth, even unholy means if need be. Freedom is Nietzsche's despot; it demands that one be free. With believers, convictions are not based on courage, not founded on grand passion, but on moral weakness. The need for conviction, "for belief, for some

165

unconditional Yes and No, Carlylism . . . is a requirement of weakness—the believer is necessarily a dependent man." The strong person derives ends from within the self; one belongs to oneself and knows one is not a thing in itself, a person in oneself, but a means. Here, Nietzsche rightly recalls Christians to the standard theological notion that *proxima regula fidei conscientia est* (the proximate guide for faith is one's conscience). Along with this old Catholic axiom, written in the fine print of the old theology manuals that trained so many pastors—many of whom never read the fine print—he recalls us to the fact that we are created in God's image and likeness. We are the image by nature and the icon (the very Trinitarian life shared) by grace. This makes us an ultimate and an absolute by nature—like God, not fully, but in the things that matter. Hence, any principle of moral and intellectual life should be able to come from within. The hyperconservative Vatican Council I was quite bullish on the unaided intellect's ability to find and prove the existence of God. Nietzsche recalled Christians to their age-old optimism in human nature's powers, which make us an absolute, although not an infinity, people who can stand by themselves and know what good and evil are and what truth is.

His hyperbole on the matter of conscience was merely a poet's and preacher's license—a conceit to get our attention so that he could recall us (*anamnesis* = a remembering) to ourselves. Secularity in Nietzsche's sense was a healthy belief in the Judeo-Christian and Islamic doctrine of creation: that God is creator and we are like God. So Nietzsche concludes that Christians have no conscience—to say that it was misplaced or lost would have been kinder and more accurate—because Christians are not free to have one where the truth or falsity of its claims is concerned; for Nietzsche, the philosopher, this is the damnation of the Christian theological enterprise. Christians have no backbones because they take them from externally manifested and imposed convictions; they aren't something derived from within. (Anti-Christ, 54) One might say that this is the heart of existentialist ethics, whether religious or atheist.

Had Nietzsche been able to move into the experiential as the arena for not only one's conscience, but also for one's consciousness of God, he might have been able to help Christians move positively into accepting their own humanity—their secularity as created state—as hierophany and the arena of any theophany that can be. If God exists at all, God will come in a way that we can see and hear and so perceive sensuously what God wants to communicate. Nietzsche wanted to retrieve the sensuous and put us back together affectively and volitionally as well as intellectually. His criticism hit home; but he gave us only an existential leap to humanity, with no valuation of affectivity as a cognitive organ. He had seen so many affective phoneys, heard so much pious blather uttered as if it had come down from Sinai that it seemed beyond him to take anything but pure intellect seriously. Yet he wanted to put us together again. However, his first step was beneficial: he helped us to discover our passion for truth in the very way things are, in the "Is"—the existential.

The preexistentialists Kierkegaard and Schelling, as well as Pascal and William James, felt that what makes one happy is also useful and true. Nietzsche opposed that. He said that truth might also be found in what was obnoxious and dangerous. (Kaufmann, 355; *Beyond Good and Evil*, 39) His hatred for romanticism colored his judgment on affectivity; weakness and helplessness are *the* premiere religious emotions for Schopenhauer. Nietzsche could not abide the concept of limitedness as it was construed in his time by Christians, both in the pews and on university rostra. He felt that this limited one's ability to think, to judge between right and wrong, between truth and falsity. He said that Christians wrongly believed that reason does not have the right to decide the rightness or wrongness of a thing. (Beyond, 10)

For Nietzsche, Christianity and Judaism began in hatred of knowledge and science. Eve was the door through which evil came into the world, but so was science the door of evil. To know the difference between good and evil was sin for our patriarch and matriarch, Adam and Eve. Hence, science was the first sin: "This alone constitutes morality: 'Thou shalt not know.'" Humankind needs leisure in order to think, and Paradise afforded it just that luxury. So God cast Adam and Eve out so that they could not think. The distress caused by our exit from Paradise was perpetuated by the priestly class, which invented new distresses to militate against thought; but thought cannot be held back permanently, so God intervenes by inventing war to divide and confuse the creatures. When people achieved a perfection of thought perilously close to real knowledge, God sent down the great flood to drown the thinking brood. (Anti-Christ, 48) God would not have us think, but it is the priestly class that Nietzsche indicts as inventing religion as a toxin against thought. "The priest knows only one great danger: that is science—the sound conception of cause and effect." People need peaceful surroundings in order to achieve something scientifically; so priests invent sin, guilt, and punishment to flagellate the thought out of us. Grace, redemption, and forgiveness are the means that

167

priests use to soothe away the possibilities of thought by destroying the causal sense in us. The need for a Savior extirpates the possibility of science. This is "an outrage of the priest! An outrage of the parasite." (Anti-Christ, 49)

Nietzsche excoriates religion further by saying that the very preconditions of knowledge are destroyed by doing away with cause and effect (here he wanders over into the necessity of having a priori categories, contradicting his previous rage against them). This does away with the "natural" as concept because the only way "cause" may be introduced into one's life is by the invention of a surrogate category, which is why the "supernatural" as agent in our lives was created by theologians. The supernatural as category destroys the natural as category. Nietzsche's rather silly anticlericalism throws off the casual reader with either mirth or pique, and one is often not too impressed by his broadside against the "supernatural." I incline toward accepting his thoughts on the supernatural. If there is no natural base left for the agent, the supernatural is only otiose, it is impossible; and the necessity and excesses of the supernatural as category have, in effect, been the cause of so much passivity among religious folk. The supernatural is no substitute for an aggressive inner life, and Nietzsche knew it. (Anti-Christ, 49)

The supernatural demands a "super" language and a set of "super" categories, which we tend to use—with its wholesale introduction by Thomas Aquinas and its later acceptance by Protestant theology—instead of standing on our own two feet and just trying to be human. The human arena is the arena of God. To approach it from on high, as one has to do when one sets such great store in "seeing" through super categories, seems to denigrate human nature the more it is used—and grace is built on nature, it doesn't supersede it. People depend on God when God wants them to be themselves in order to be open to divine graceful irruptions and eruptions. There seems to be an inverse proportion here: to the degree that one emphasizes the supernatural as the vehicle, or agent, for the divine in one's life, to that degree does human self-reliance shrink toward a vanishing point. Obviously, one does not rely on oneself ultimately, but one must rely on oneself as an ultimate. That is the human dilemma that false supernaturalism not only diminishes, but also infantilizes.

Anyone who has done the least bit of pastoral work knows how much otherwise intelligent and reliable people throw away their creatureliness—read their humanity—when they switch to God's frequency.

Natural does not demand supernatural to explain either God or humanity. The incarnation says that God "pitched his tent among us" (John's prologue), which means that God is like us in all things, save sin (Paul). Real faith, therefore, demands that we believe in ourselves, love ourselves, before we can believe in and love God and our neighbor. Nietzsche is correct when he scores our theological and pastoral use of "sin," if he means the all-too-frequent equation of sin and sinfulness; by the latter I mean what Paul Ricoeur means by "fragility." Our weakness is not a sin; it shows that we were created on the move toward growth, not in a state of perfection. Nietzsche implicitly repudiates the Augustinian theological construct that demanded that Adam and Eve were created on a high level of perfection, endowed with gifts that theologians were forced into calling "preternatural," and fell from that dizzy height into sin. Preternatural, again, works against the simpler interpretation of both our "nature" and origin and the problem of evil and its origin when it demands something "beyond," although not above, nature. Why is it necessary? If, as Irenaeus held, men and women were created on a low, childlike level of perfection and were intended to grow into greater things, then these "gimcrack" categories like supernatural and preternatural would not be so necessary to explain us. The simpler the better when interpreting the way that God works in the world. If God is intelligent, and God is, then to create once is enough; God is the divine economist (which word means "good housekeeping" in Greek), according to the church fathers. Once done, one works realistically through what is there without necessitating other creations—notice that I say "creations," not realities, even if grace is a "created participation in God's life." Grace is created analogously; it works through our nature naturally, following its laws. That is why instant conversions are so suspect in pastoral care. Thus, God is the simple economist, using what God has created as our way. No superlanguage is necessary when interpreting the Incarnation, nor is it necessary when interpreting divine Providence. Sin there is, but it is neither to be equated with our limits nor with our concupiscences. I do not think concupiscence is to be interpreted as an effect of our postlapsarian state; they were there before the fall but not in so deadly a way. Thus, we were a bit "unglued" from the start, created for an eschatological integration, not an initial one. We were children on the way to growth. Evolution demands that we view things as being on the way, as being pilgrims. This is precisely the way in which contemporary Protestant and Catholic theology has defined us Christians. Sin there is, and that aplenty, but it is not where theological hacks would have us believe that it is. They would oppress us, by their very mediocrity, into reversing things and seeing sin where there is only weakness and merely politics where there is a direct attack on human dignity effective enough to destroy not only people's self-evaluation for generations, but also their very lives—I am speaking of our recent history with both Jews and blacks. There are sins, and there are sins. And sin is a means for telling us who and where God is, not who we are essentially, but who we are relationally, i.e., as loved sinners. Hack theology has reversed the process, and Nietzsche rightly walked out on that sermon.

The happiness that religious truths hold out is not a proved verity, but only a promise. Dogmas prove nothing; they only promise. In that, Nietzsche is correct. But dogmas do instruct within the belief structure. He goes on to say that belief itself makes people happy in the very thought of future bliss; but belief proves nothing. "The proof by 'pleasure' is a proof of pleasure—that is all." But truth's service brings one unhappiness and pain; so Nietzsche says that only the great-souled can really be philosophers. One must despise one's feelings and be stern to one's heart to serve one's conscience. (Anti-Christ, 50)

Nietzsche concludes that Christianity needs sickness of mind and heart in order to flourish; hence, it causes this sickness in its creation of the salvation process. Catholicism is a "mad-house" because of it, but then, so is the earth a madhouse. (Anti-Christ, 51). The church has demanded that the religious state be a neurotic one. Normalcy for religious people is neurosis. The highest religious states are forms of epilepsy; and the church canonizes only lunatics *in majorem dei honorem* (for the greater honor of God). Hence, one cannot really be converted to Christianity; "one must be sufficiently sick for it." He says that it takes courage and health to have contempt for a religion that "teaches misunderstanding of the body," teaches the superstition that a soul exists, makes a virtue out of eating too little, sees a morbid state as holiness, "holiness itself [being] merely a symptom of the impoverished, enervated, incurably corrupted body!" (Anti-Christ, 51) In opposition to all this is Hellenism; it needs health, whereas Christianity is predicated on sickness. Classical antiquity was noble. It did not cause Christianity; the inference was that Judaism, an alien ideology, did. Besides, Nietzsche cannot abide democracy, and Christianity is just that; and it is a decadence to have a majority ruling the better types of people, who are maturer and nobler than any Christians. Christianity rejected all that was "well-constituted, proud, high-spirited." The cross, in making all sufferers divine, thereby killed classical nobility and its nobles with it.

170

Does faith want to know anything? Nietzsche answers in the negative. He scorches priests of "both sexes" for keeping out the truth. Besides, theologians have a compulsion to lie; they cannot read a text without falsifying it. The pietists and "other cows of Swabia dress up the pathetic commonplace and stuffiness of their existence with the 'finger of God' into a miracle of 'grace' . . . of the 'experience of salvation!' " (Anti-Christ, 52) Therefore, Christian hermeneutics is childish when it comes to construing God's Providence:

> A God who cures a headcold at the right moment or tells us to get into a church just as a downpour is about to start is so absurd a God he would have to be abolished even if he existed. God is not a servant, postman or almanac-maker. The beliefs of many cultured Germans are very strong arguments against God's existence and also a strong argument against Germans. (Anti-Christ, 52) This needs no comment; healthy Christianity laughs at that god and those kinds of Germans, English, Americans, and so on too.

Thus, priests do not lie about things, since lying means that one has the capacity for knowing the difference between truth and untruth, and revelation does not permit this liberty, since priests are only God's mouthpieces. God knows, but they do not. Hence, "Law," "will of God," "sacred book," "inspiration," and so on are just means that priests use to come to power. All priests, of every religion, use "holy lies" to come to power. So whenever the man or woman of religion says, "The truth exists," he or she is lying. (Anti-Christ, 55) One cannot find the truth in Christianity; faith is not truth. Where is it to be found? In the great-souled person of classical culture who lives by a Dionysiac faith, as did Goethe, his hero, the founder of much of contemporary German culture.

Again, it is Christianity's spirituality with which Nietzsche has the most difficulty: it denied life in trying to affirm God. One need not affirm God; God can take care of that. There is divinity in men and women, and Nietzsche's own religion will take care of that truth, which is central to his thought; more on that in chapter 7. Nietzsche's anthropology uses this as its linchpin; it becomes, in his affirmation of human nature, a Dionysiac faith, which is to say a faith in the goodness of life. To effect this transition to his Zoontology—his philosophical affirmation of life—he must move away from Christianity's thanatology—its doctrine of death that pervaded life at its best, especially where it should have been its most joyous: where men and women could use their powers to love, to create and find a joy in the most human of endeavors and bodily functions. He found this joy in both classical paganism—that of Greece and Rome—and in Hinduism's empirical knowledge of a divine core in human nature, which knowledge was gained through yoga, a technique geared to descend to one's center and, therefore, exult in what Christianity calls one's imago dei and Hinduism calls atman, the divine core of humankind perceived only when one has shucked off the illusion of ego as a snake shucks off its skin.

He concludes that Christianity has no good ends, its chief goal being the denial of life, which is an evil: "denying of life, contempt for the body, the denigration and self-violation of man through the concept of sin— therefore its means too are bad." (Anti-Christ, 56) In Hinduism's Laws of Manu he found another corroboration from his classism and elitism. These laws are radically different from "any sort of Bible: it is the means by which the noble order, the philosophers and the warriors, keep the mob under control; noble values everywhere, a feeling of perfection, an affirmation of life, a triumphant feeling of well-being in oneself and of goodwill towards life—the *sun* shines on the entire book." (Anti-Christ, 56) The whole principle of his Dionysiac faith is to be found also in these laws: it is a complaisance, a peace, in the self. Nietzsche's anthropology was a naturalism, which is a triumph of human nature and of all created things in their created perfection. The naturalism of the Laws of Manu bespeak an evolution in people and things; they are on the move from a lesser perfection to a greater one. This evolution is reflected in Manu, but Nietzsche says that for one to say that there is a type of revelation is pure mendacity. For some strange reason, Nietzsche finds it scandalous for anyone to think that God would work through evolution; I say it is strange because this is precisely the conclusion—and the use we contemporary theologians have made based on Marx's, Freud's, and his use of evolutionary theory—one takes from his critique of Christianity: God works through the natural, and corrupted Christian theology has denigrated nature by its use of the category "supernatural." But Nietzsche's use of the category "natural" is no less scandalous to our generation, which has seen the use to which Nazism put his classism.

For Nietzsche, caste is the natural order; there are human types, and these modes of humanity brook no mixing. (This caste mentality is well defined in the Indo-European cultures by the classic divisions of sacerdotium, imperium, the burghers, and the lumpen proletariat and peasant; L. Dumont's *Homo Hierarchicus* throws into high relief the Western analogue of India's castes. To North Americans, such classism is a blot and a scandal. But it is a brute historical fact that one must take into account in understanding Europeans in general and Nietzsche and his

Nazi interpreters in particular. What once worked had become a wickedness.) Nietzsche's first type is the spiritual person. In India this would be
the Brahmin; in the West it would be the person who is sensitive to the
higher things in life. But for Nietzsche, it is nature, not Manu, that
separates the highest type from the rest of humanity. All the types are
what Christians would call "holy." Manu and its devotees "have a way of
being polite to woman which has perhaps never been surpassed. 'A
woman's mouth'—it says in one place—'a girl's breast, a child's prayer, the
smoke of a sacrifice are always pure.' . . . 'There is nothing purer than
. . . a girl's breath.' 'All the openings of the body above the navel are
pure, all below impure. Only in the case of a girl is the whole body
pure.'" Nietzsche, ever the ironic sexist, appends to this encomium of
nature and woman that what he says is "perhaps a lie," meaning what he
says of woman. (Anti-Christ, 56).

But to return to his caste system, Nietzsche says that this highest,
spiritual caste represents happiness, beauty, and benevolence on earth.
Further, "only the most spiritual beings are permitted beauty, beautiful
things . . . , the good is a privilege. On the other hand, nothing is more
strictly forbidden them than ugly manners or a pessimistic outlook." The
lower classes, the Chandala, are permitted indignation and pessimism but
never the spiritual class. For the latter, "the *world is perfect*, [this is] the
affirmative instinct." There is a great distance between them and the
Chandala person, and Nietzsche says that this distance is the pathos and
perfection of the Chandala. The latter traffic in the lesser perfections; the
former, in both the highest asceticisms, and even in the highest of the
high: namely, the reconciliation of opposites when not only do they exult
in the most arduous of tasks, but even consider it a privilege "to play with
vices which overwhelm others . . . [for them this is a] recreation." (Anti-
Christ, 57) The center of the spiritual person's life lies in asceticism, not
in license, however. These types of human beings are "the strongest . . .
[and] find their happiness where others would find their destruction . . .
their joy lies in self-constraint. . . . Asceticism becomes [their] nature,
need, instinct. . . . [And] they rule not because they want to but because
they *are*; they are not free to become second in rank." (Ibid.) This is, in
my estimation, the basis of his moral theory, left us in his *Beyond Good
and Evil*. Hinduism, especially the Hinduism of the early Upanishads,
had not arrived at the distinction between being and either the good or the
evil. All being was good, and evil was subsumed under this goodness.
This allowed them to make a reconciliation of opposites, which all

religions seek to do. Luther had his *simul justus et peccator*, in which one is both holy and sinful at the same time; and Augustine had his "love God and do what you want." The latter is taken out of the context of Augustine's demand that the "love" be a following of the moral laws; but nevertheless, it is a pastoral praxis of many today who construe this as a finding of the divinity in one's life where one would appear ecclesiastically unworthy otherwise. Origen devised a strategy allowing the lesser of two evils if they are done lovingly. And in Graham Greene's early novels—such as *The Power and the Glory* and *The End of the Affair*—he seeks an answer to the conundrum: can one be justified by God's grace and yet sinful at the same time? None of them came up with the answers of such devotees of the *Philosophia Perennis* as Aldous Huxley, Frithjof Schuon, Christopher Isherwood, Radhakrishnan, and Huston Smith. Classically, one does not reconcile sin and the good; God forgives sin but knows it for the evil it is, totally irreconcilable with God; the thing is, we are God and yet we are other. Thereby hangs the tale; we are a congeries of good and evil, sin and virtue. Religions have struggled with the reconciliation of good and evil for centuries with mixed, and sometimes disastrous, results.

Nietzsche has found that there are ethics for the highest types that allow such a reconciliation; for the others, he does not provide any solace. Theologians today, and I am one of them, use this reconciliation to distinguish for all classes between the presence of God in one's life and both ecclesiastical and divine law. For instance, in Galatians 5:19–26, Paul distinguishes between the deeds of the flesh and those done in the Spirit, i.e., those done by one's unloving inclinations and those done in love (in the Spirit). This is not "flesh" in the sense of a physical thing, but what is done under the influence of any passion that takes one into an unloving situation over against self, neighbor, and God. Thus, what is done in love, i.e., in the Spirit, produces "love, joy, peace, patience, kindness, goodness, faithfulness, gentleness, self-control; against such there is no law" [Gal. 5:22–23]. Paul has reconciled the law of God with the presence of the Spirit. He calls for a crucifixion of the passions in verses 24f., but he has given pastoral and moral theologians the means with which to reconcile situations in which one is in contravention to a law of either the church or even of God, but where one's life appears to be "in God" nonetheless. One has one's ethics, and one has the highest law: love. Life, at times, forces one into corners not of one's making, and Paul would not paint us into that corner, firm but merciful pastor that he is.

174

God leaves one a way out, and that way is love. Love covers a multitude of sins (1 Peter 4:8); this demands that we love one another and assert that such love reconciles us to one another in the church and to God, even though we may seem to be in violation of a church law or even one of God. God has priorities too.

The second caste, or type, for Nietzsche are the muscular warriors and keepers of the law, i.e., those who maintain order in society. These are the kings, nobles, and lawyers, as well as soldiers, who sit at the feet of the first caste to be taught what is good, right, and noble to do in society. These second types do all that is too coarse for the first types to do, thus relieving their betters of the burden of becoming sullied with the "nuts and bolts" that executives care for in any society. The upper class must be separate from the lower classes because the supreme law of life demands this separation for the very maintenance of civilization itself. Therefore, "*inequality* of rights is the condition for the existence of rights at all. A right is a privilege. The privilege of each is determined by the nature of his being." (Anti-Christ, 57) Society is firmly established on a pyramid's lines, the "very first prerequisite [of which] is a strongly and soundly consolidated mediocrity." The happiness of these stolid mediocrities is their vocation to serve. "For the mediocre it is happiness to be mediocre; mastery in one thing, specialization, is for them a natural instinct." It is the duty of the upper caste to handle the mediocrities surrounding them with gentleness. Nietzsche despised what he called the "Socialist rabble" because they took the joy out of work for the working class. (Anti-Christ, 57)

This working class is the base of the pyramid; they are the third of the classes and the lowest. They are not the executive class, nor can they be. They become good at one thing: their trade. The executives become adept at their one skill, as well: to rule as the upper classes have taught them to. The warriors are good at doing what they are told. But the whole thing is based on the irremediably mediocre under class, whose privilege it is to be mediocre at all but its trade. At this it is to excel, and at this alone. Equality is an evil, therefore. It destroys the way things are; and the way they are is the very law of the universe. Nietzsche despised the social justice reforms that flowed from the sons and daughters of the Enlightenment and the French and American revolutions. These "rights" are bad because they proceed from "weakness, from envy, from *revengefulness* (ressentiment). The anarchist and the Christian have a common origin."

175

(Anti-Christ, 57) Christianity was constituted to destroy this eternal societal structure, since it is an egalitarian society. (Anti-Christ, 58)

Now Nietzsche switches to his central theme; after having used Hinduism to corroborate his intuitions of what constitutes man, woman, and society, he trumpets the happy nobility of Greek and Roman culture. Its "nobility in instinct, taste, methodical investigation, genius for organization and government, the faith or the *will* to a future for mankind, the great Yes to all things . . . present . . . as the *Imperium Romanum* . . . no longer merely art but become reality, truth, life" recommend it to him as the way things are meant to be in life and society. Christianity debases all this with its petty, vile, low vengefulness. Nietzsche says that Christian leaders are shrewd but dirty. They are devoid of the "cleanly instincts" that he discerns in classic nobles. Christians are not human; their soul is the "ghetto soul" suddenly on top, superseding the nobility of soul that he found in classical antiquity. (Anti-Christ, 59)

The Renaissance had done what Nietzsche tried to do in all his work: to revalue all things and thereby overthrow Christianity. But Luther came along and ruined the effort of the Renaissance by reaffirming Christian values with his Pauline theology. The Renaissance attempted to instill nobility in values and in instincts, needs, and desires; and the Renaissance popes were men in the classic mold. Luther demanded their removal; he saw this as corruption. So he restored Christians to their values, to their church; and Nietzsche despised him for this.

> Christianity *no* longer sat on the Papal throne! Life sat there instead! the triumph of life! the great Yes to all lofty beautiful, daring things! . . . And Luther restored the *Church:* he attacked it . . . Oh these Germans, what they have already cost us! . . . They are my enemies, I confess it, these Germans: I despise in them every kind of uncleanliness of concept and value, of *cowardice* in the face of every honest Yes and No . . . they have also on their conscience the uncleanest kind of Christianity there is, the most incurable kind, the kind hardest to refute, Protestantism. . . . If we never get rid of Christianity, the *Germans* will be to blame. (Anti-Christ, 61)

Therefore, Nietzsche pronounced his judgment on Christianity: he condemned it for imposing distress by its false humanitarianism instead of removing that distress. He condemned it for violating the self; for a "*will* to falsehood*"; for being antipathetic to all good instincts. It was "a conspiracy against health, beauty, well-constitutedness, bravery, intel-

176

lect, benevolence of soul, against life itself." (Anti-Christ, 62) Christianity is, therefore, not only opposed to love (praxis), but also to reason (theory). And Nietzsche repudiated it as it stood. But what would he put in its place?

CHAPTER 7

Nietzsche's Religion

Like so much contemporary theology, Nietzsche rejected the effect Neo-platonism had on religion and its concept of man and woman. Its effect on Christianity was to place the spiritual immeasurably higher than the material, which split humankind into two unequal parts: body and spirit. Nietzsche's program was to do away with this Platonic dualism. To do this he would have to deal with the twin categories natural and supernatural. He ended by abolishing the transcendent category and realm, which he found had devalued our life on earth, reducing it to a mere stage on the way to our eternal home in heaven. For Nietzsche, the sacred is life on earth. He would do away with the category "supernatural" as one that opposed and destroyed this life because of its emphasis on the "higher" life after death. This, therefore, is his religion: there is a creative, immanent principle in human nature and not transcendent to it at all. This principle is in men, women, nature, and God.[1]

Nietzsche based his view of God, world, people, and things on Goethe's view of the same. Their vision was a unified one and not the dualistic one they mistakenly thought was the quintessential Judeo-Christian way of construing things by dichotomizing them into the categories natural and supernatural, body and spirit. For both, God was immanent to their nature. Their God was neither person, nor will, nor intellect, but all things in sum. It was pantheism that they held, in which God and world are identical and not cause and effect. They thought that since the creative principle is immanent to the world, the effect is not different from the cause; in fact, it reveals the nature of the cause. So God is both *natura naturans* and *natura naturata*, i.e., nature both expressing itself and nature expressed by itself. This is definitely a view heavily influenced by Spinoza. (Pfeffer, 299f.) The world is God and is not created, ex nihilo (from nothing).

Nietzsche's atheism was not a denial of God, however, but a methodological tool he used to free himself from the guilt caused by the Christian interpretation of God. This is what he means in his *Genealogy of Morals* when he says that atheism is a "second innocence." (Pfeffer, 234, from Nietzsche's *Genealogy of Morals*, VII, 388, German ed.) He means this in the way that Paul Ricoeur means his "second naivete"—as I mentioned earlier—which means the faith that one arrives at when one has used criticism to clarify one's categories. Nietzsche finds atheism both useful and necessary as an enabler of human life, speaking psychologically and philosophically. In *The Gay Science* he says that God's death gives us a new horizon of freedom. (Pfeffer, 234; Nietzsche, V, 272, German ed.) Man (and woman) is the thing; one cannot prove that God exists, even if one could, one could not understand God.

Nietzsche's atheism is a retrieval system in which, by doing away with God, one finds human nature once again in all its freshness. He enthrones us in God's place in order to find innocence once again. To do this, he had to make a decision to become a god; to bring that about he had to kill God, since faith in God demanded transcendence and that brought with it a patrimony of sin and guilt that he could bear no longer. Thus, Nietzsche installed an innocence of becoming in the place once held by God's being. Men and women have created reason, freedom, and immortality, not God. In murdering the God-concept, men and women would be freed to flow into themselves, into full flowering instead of having to inhabit a God category in order to become themselves. His is a "man becoming," a developmental view of man and woman. It is not grace, but one's own powers that conquer existence's tragedies.

So Nietzsche created a new anthropology for us that moved us past the Godless humanism of Marx before him and Freud after him to a divine humanism. We are divine; to become so, God had to give way to the creatures. Again, when Nietzsche says that he "murdered" God, one should read this as hyperbole meant to bring one up short. He is to be interpreted in all these outrageous utterances—as I have said before—as meaning the opposite of what he asserts. He did not mean so much that God was dead, but that we are alive and on our own as human beings. He hated a religion that preached happiness on the plain and opted for one that preached it on the mountaintop for those who were willing to be

179

creative geniuses, when nature has determined them to be so; this rather than peaceful mediocrities, which Nietzsche thought was all one could attain following the Christianity of his day. (Pfeffer, 235)

Nietzsche's person is neither the religious person of Christianity nor the Enlightenment man and woman mulled in reason and seasoned by Natural Law. I recall Gregory Baum telling us that Therese of Lisieux was the saint for modern times. Her experience was one of darkness and emptiness, and she was declared a great saint of the Catholic Church. Her way was to be little and to take life as she found it—which is not as easy as it sounds, especially when one is as psychologically fragile as she was. Nietzsche, too, was a man of his time. He had suffered all the emptiness that pervaded the human experience of his day. Men and women were on the move, searching for their meaning, looking for a faith that would not destroy them as creative beings. Nietzsche's person is alone with the self facing reality without the necessity of there being a God, facing one's own nothingness. This is central not only to an undertanding of Nietzsche, who holds a place of importance in our history, but it is important for our own self-understanding as well. Nietzsche's "honest atheism" means precisely this facing up to one's own emptiness or nothingness. One's void drives the mediocre to resignation, pessimism, and nihilism, but for Nietzsche and his "noble breed," nothingness is a loss that leads one to ultimate liberation. The loss of God as structure and religious "sop" for all the tendencies that niggle us into "nothings" as persons is a positive thing for Nietzsche.

His nothingness does not bespeak a negative thing depriving one of his humanity, but it is the very center of human affectivity. One's deepest feeling is of being a responsible human being, and that gives one the feeling of nakedness that creativity demands of its clients. To be human is to *be* and *feel* naked; to be on the edge of one's limits; to know neither where one is going nor what is right or wrong in a given situation. It means that one generates morality from one's center, which is divine. Nietzsche is working from the imago dei model insofar as he does this. Morality and creativity are like philosophy in this regard: they do not demand a revelation from outside to meet their ends. Rather, they look within to find their truths. This puts one "beyond good and evil" morally, in the sense that one must look for oneself by oneself in one's deepest recesses. That one would not murder is not because of a revelation, therefore, but because of what one is; that one might kill or go to bed with a person not one's wife, for example, might be a morally acceptable act because of one's unique situation; that one creates literature or paints in a way never done before is due to one's facing up to one's uniqueness, to one's nakedness before the truths of art, which are the same as those of one's deepest being, and following out those truths as both one's own truth and the truth of one's art. This is not nihilism, but humanism and the invention (in the sense of a "finding") of the divinity at one's human core. And this is not, as Nietzsche says, for nervous types, but for those who wish to be human. This is its difficulty; like Freud's elite educated to moral maturity (rationality), it is only for the courageous few who are capable of wandering out onto the thin ice, alone, facing into the wind and dark. Nietzsche found reality good and said that one could trust it, even if one were to fall in and drown; one expected tragedy, but being was good nonetheless. One accepts the first part of his thesis: being is good and one must trust it to reveal not only itself, but oneself as well. But the second part, tragedy as the certain end of us all, noble or not—is being that good? He brought us to ourselves, which is to a good divinity at our core. But he failed to open us up to the God out of which our divinity flows, the same God existing at our core's ends. Nietzsche's theory, as such, is only for the few who have the grace to go that preternaturally lonely way.

Thus, Nietzsche accorded this status to far too few of us. Only the gifted, facing up to their naked talents could create beyond the limits of their mediocre brothers and sisters. He overlooked the fact that all are called to face up to their truths in the experience of their nothingness, limitedness, emptiness, or whatever one chooses to call the "human estate," which is the confluence point of two doctrines; the doctrine of creation—wherein one is an unconditional and unlimited being made in the image and likeness of one's Maker, albeit not an infinite creation—and the doctrine that one is limited also by some form of the import to our nature, which we call, for want of a better term, Original Sin.

Nothingness is a positive category for Nietzsche, not his ontological hermeneutics of evil. In the Augustinian interpretation, evil is a *privatio boni* (a lack of good), but that is not what we are dealing with here. This nothingness is not an evil, but a good willed by Nietzsche, who also willed content into it as well. Nothingness is an affirmation about being; as such, it is an ontological category for him. If he is to accept the meaninglessness and nothingness of his Godless world, then he must affirm that world. It means that one must have an unremitting will to face the world without God, without grace, and without salvation. It is to face up to it all . . . alone. (Pfeffer, 236f.) One wills not only the cosmic nothingness—the loneliness without God—but one wills one's personal nothingness or emptiness, the painful experience of one's limits. Later, Hiedegger and Sartre would root their own philosophies in Nietzsche's nothingness. This is the meaning of their *Das Nichts* and *le néant*, respectively. The existentialist categories we know so well in contemporary philosophy appeared first here, when Nietzsche bruited about his feeling of absurdity and his despair in having to live "thrown into a world" in which there were no a priori essences or norms. Nietzsche's thought is a dialectic in which one wills to be what one is—lonely, normless, and homeless—and in this way wills to become something positive. His is a willed supersession in which one feels one's nothingness impinging most painfully on one's consciousness and turns it to good by making this "Is" a positive thing by willing it to be one's truth. This superseded a tragic truth, which would have ultimately destroyed him, with a willed tragedy that turned it into something quasi-salvific by the transubstantiation of positively facing up to himself and the reality of his situation and by taking responsibility for it. One creates both one's values and the meaning in one's life because one must; otherwise, there would be nothing but "canned" values brought in by religion's imported, catechizing bell, book, and candle—and these are not one's truth, but an imposed truth, an imposture—and meaningless meanings, which would be both cruel and lead to madness.

Nietzsche's willing it turned tragedy into something positive. By doing so, he and anyone who chose to follow him could make something of the mess of their lives and world by following a call, not from above, but from within oneself—the kingdom was within. Nietzsche's religion affirms all life and sees it as holy. To will meaninglessness—which is the very center of contemporary, postmodern science, since no one can assign any causal finality to things generically or specifically—is the only way to give the pain meaning, and this latter is the heart of all religion, as I see it.

Nietzsche has made men's and women's essence their existence. One's essence is not determined by God or by the imposition of absolute norms, not by reason's ideas and laws, but by what one makes of oneself. Goethe's Faustian man is the same as Nietzsche's; the former turns from learning revelation and magic to wander through actual existence. His faith, his religion, was to be faithful to the earth. He does not look for otherworldly hopes. Hence, both Nietzsche's and Goethe's thought is a humanistic pantheism. (Pfeffer, 238–40 passim) This ensured that both humanity and divinity would be there, as well as divinity. In monotheistic systems the deity tends to overwhelm humankind almost to the vanishing point. Thus,

Goethe and Nietzsche made everything God—humankind attained its divinity as long as it became itself: a human being.

But if the essence of religion is to face up to strife, how do Goethe and Nietzsche accomplish this central task? Suffering and strife mean that one is dealing with the problem of evil, the Scylla and Charybdis of all theologians. Is human nature good? Are creatures that are less than human, good? Is the divinity principle good? If so, then whence comes evil? Both Nietzsche's *Zarathustra* and Goethe's Faustian man wish to view truth in the raw. They do and find reality utterly repulsive. This sends them into despair in their terror before what is. What they see, at first blush, is the destructiveness of Nature and humankind; but the process is irreversible. Things and people come back; they return eternally. So both Nietzsche and Goethe deliver themselves of an act of faith in the goodness of things and people. The move through the first stage—which is one of horror before the evils of reality—gives way to a Yes! to life in all its good and all its evil. Beneath the tragedy that evil exists and seems to dominate all people and things is a good in all things, binding them into one. Nature is, if given enough time to rise from its farrago of tragedies, redemptively one and good.

This is the faith of Goethe and Nietzsche; it is a faith in Nature and the unity of all things. Both believe in becoming one with Nature. They strip their faith of the Christian cross with its idea of sin and redemption in order to face up to the ugliness and wickedness of people and the mindless tragedies of Nature. They accept a heaven replete with all things, including the devil. All things—even evil—are necessary, and so all are accepted as holy because they are necessary. What is is holy, be it good or evil, diabolic or angelic. Faith for both means a heroic will to overcome all tragedy; and this implies that self-acceptance, often the most tragic of acts, is the way to peace. It is an affirmation and celebration of existence that they both demand of themselves and of their readers. In Nietzsche's *Ecce Homo* the devil is simply God's movement toward idleness on the seventh day. God made all things too beautiful and needed a respite from being God, so God became a serpent and coiled at the foot of the tree of knowledge. (Pfeffer, 241–43 passim) Again, both Goethe and Nietzsche retreat to a philosophic time contemporary with that of the Early Upanishads, when being was the primary category and neither good nor evil had been differentiated. It was a time for the interconnectedness of all things, a time when one's unity with Nature was not only contemplated, but also lived. It was a time when there was no time. It was the *in illo tempore* of Mircea Eliade, when the gods and heroes walked the earth. It was no time at all; that is the problem. The essence of the Judeo-Christian faith is that God came to make time out of the timeless nothings of previous mythologies; and having done so, one cannot go home to the *aevum* (a timeless time), since that would take away human responsibility, which is our being like God, who is Supreme Responsibility. Goethe, and especially Nietzsche, wanted to reconcile good and evil, as did Engels. It unifies things but disallows any human interaction; Nature Mysticism, and this is what it is, in part, absolves of guilt by taking us away from people to make them into things: matter, joy, unity; all stuff and ideas but no people; and Nietzsche's fondest desire was to remake people. Freud, too, wanted to absolve us of guilt (he did not distinguish between the neurotic kind, which kills, and the theological kind, which points to a loving and forgiving God) and raise us up to adult responsibility past religious and other infantilisms, among which he numbered Marxist dogma, for its utopianism. But both he and Nietzsche failed; the one because human history demands that we be responsible to more than just our neighbor and ourselves; the other because good and evil, once reconciled, become the mad downward transcendence warned of by Aldous Huxley in which the supremely wicked becomes a virtue and vice versa. Time is the thing. To absolve one of it, as do Nietzsche and Engels, creates a world in which one is responsible, ultimately, to no one, not even the self. To say other has been merely words in the recent history of our breed; the deeds of those desiring justice in Cambodia would make the young humanistic Marx of these pages blanche at the carnage.

Therefore, what Nietzsche and Goethe had accomplished was a form of Nature Mysticism in which the first pinches of pain turned the euphoric expansion in which one became one with, indeed became, the All into something religious. Nature Mysticism, as I have defined it, is not a religious phenomenon per se, since it does not face up to the human condition. It becomes religious when it admits of evil and suffering. Its essence is the warp of time and the waffling of space to become *utopia* (Greek for nowhere) and eternity (*aevum* in Latin). As such, one becomes one's god, since morality is done in time only; and one becomes omnipotent, since the feeling of being one with all places one everywhere. The first steps of this religious Nature Mysticism make one feel instinct with divinity. [2] Nature Mysticism itself admits of no God and no relations with anyone else. In Nietzsche's and Goethe's faith, one is the divinity, and that allows one to admit of evil but not of guilt and sin. So the tragedy is not that one is damned, but that there is evil at all, since all is affirmed as holy because necessary—holy, but not necessarily painless. This is the tragedy: That what is so good is also so painful and, ultimately, vanishes. The good in it all is that it returns eternally. Nietzsche rid himself of sin and guilt and God but not of pain. He turned it into something good in the heroic will to accept it, not passively, but actively to make something heroic and ascetic of its very acceptance. In becoming one with all things, Nietzsche's philosophy was a Nature Mysticism. In admitting of evil and facing up to it as the dark side of the human situation, he made of it a religious Nature Mysticism. In rediscovering human nature he had divinized man and woman in the process.

The heroic struggle to overcome one's fate—and this is the meaning of his *Ubermensch* (superman)—means that one is to realize oneself and vanquish the entropy that vectors one off to mediocrity. The struggle to become a man or a woman makes his philosophy dialectical. Finding life's meaning in the struggle ended by seeing the divinity in people and all things. His hermeneutics ended with the conclusion that all was divine. So it was a dialectical philosophy and a pantheistic faith. Religion meant struggle before the forces that would destroy one; religion was the force of one's heroic self-acceptance, not heaven's contemplative peace. (Pfeffer, 268f.) The creative principle is the kingdom within us, and that is a divine principle. But the masses cannot bear this burden of will, so the bearer of culture will be only the heroic individual destined by Nature to be spiritual. This is the *philosophia perennis* of Frithjof Schuon, Aldous Huxley, and others, who hold that there is an esoteric religion beyond the religions and that only the elite can know it and live it.

The way out of the dark hole of despair is to struggle out of it by using one's potential for heroism. The heroic type for both Nietzsche and Goethe is Prometheus, who defied the gods and became both the creator and the lawgiver by using his own inner powers. The Superman concept was rarely used by Nietzsche, but when it was (*Zarathustra*, Part I, "On Self-overcoming") it referred to stealing the gods' fire by overcoming mediocrity. It was not the vapid and wicked will bruited about by the Nazis, who derived their Superman from Nietzsche's writings, but the healthy will to be oneself and make use of one's talents. (Pfeffer, 245)

Nietzsche's faith was in human nature, and it was a deep and abiding faith. Virtue consisted in conforming, not to external laws, but to one's own truth. Creativity consisted also in being oneself; this was the divine element in human nature. Aristotle's great-souled person released the creativity and virtue locked away in his own nature. This is the Dionysian element in Nietzsche's faith: it consists in celebrating the dialectical whorls of our lives. To find good in the clash of good and evil, in the tragic consequences of one's patrimony as an individual or as a member of a culture, is to be religious. To find good in all things is the essence of Nietzsche's thought. This takes courage in launching out onto the ice when most have fallen through, at the very least, or lost themselves, at most. It is a courage to be, a courage to fail, a courage to believe in the goodness of things and of oneself. It is a salvation *within* tragedy, not from *tragedy*. His Dionysian faith is a faith that everything is redeemed and affirmed. (Pfeffer, 265, 250)

For him, Christianity killed the creative force in humankind by crushing passion. Nietzsche intends to restore us to passion, to return sensuality, feeling, and will to their pristine unity. His faith is a faith in fate (*amor fati* = a love of fate). (Pfeffer, 250) There is an inner necessity about things, about one's life, even its most painful and humiliating aspects. To act in accordance with the fate of things, to accept their determination can be an act of freedom, and indeed the only act that one can make when one is in the face of a compulsion in full spate. Things are one and eternal. He believed in this. To will the whole meant that one had to will and believe in each of its parts. Nietzsche did not distinguish between the goodness or wickedness of the parts in order to deal with his own debilitating and devastating sense of Teutonic guilt. His faith was a pastoral back door of mercy past the crushing burden of a corrupted and, for him, "Jewish morality." God, Nature, and humankind are one, and so are all the events of history. Will all and one deals with the tragedies of Nature's inexorable laws of death; will all and Nature shall return one to existence from the graves of its tragedies. Inner necessity is the essence of both things and humankind. Spinoza's *Ethics* (Part I, Def. VII) says, "That thing is said to be free which exists by mere necessity of its own nature and is determined in its actions by itself alone." Nietzsche accepts this and adds that one must not only accept fate, but also love both it and necessity. (Pfeffer, 253–58 passim)

Nietzsche's religion reveals the experience of postmodern men and women. He and they do not believe in a transcendent and anthropomorphic God anymore, but they still have religious faith. It is atheism, but religious atheism; or put another way, it is humanistic, not theistic, faith. Nietzsche was not so anti-Christian as his outrageous assertions would lead the unwary or sensitive to believe. Both Nietzsche and Goethe believed in the reconciliation of opposites, where good and evil, the ugly and the beautiful, the limited and unlimited are redeemed in the "fatality of the whole." Goethe and Spinoza believe on a macroscopic scale in the goodness of all things, that they are good because united. (Pfeffer, 260f.)

He is Dionysiac because he wishes to return us to a unity, not because he would open us to license; the passions were repressed or scotched out by Christian and Jewish morality and asceticism. He wishes to return us to a classic morality, based on the gods and heroes sharing our triumphs and tragedies to affirm them in the sharing of them. It is the Incarnation without the cross, made by negating time and place. His faith is a *cri de coeur* searching out its deepest truth past the encrustations of centuries of religious morality, which has tended to crush as many as it helped.

Like Rimbaud the poet, Nietzsche, the poet-philosopher, saw Nature Mysticism as religious aestheticism. Both poets went beyond good and evil to achieve a unity with the all; both went through hell to achieve heaven; both achieved a unity with the ego, not with God. Rimbaud's poetics opened him up to the unconscious forces of creativity, which allowed him to become a seer. He saw (intuited) his unity with matter in an undifferentiated and unitive state. Nietzsche said, "Religion is love above yourself—a work of art is the image of such a love." (Pfeffer, 252f.) One enters the unity with oneself and with all things through art. In *Birth of Tragedy* Nietzsche said that nature speaks through art and its tragic symbolism. Both nature and art are innocent of morality; they follow their own laws without purposes and ends. It is through the creative person that the unconscious aspects of nature break out into consciousness. Art shows the interconnectedness of all things. This is his faith and reverence. "Reverence for God is reverence for the interconnectedness of all things." (Pfeffer, 263, from Nietzsche's *Unpublished Notes*, XII, 327)

His faith, then, is a humanism, an anthropology. His method is dialectical, in which both good and evil, in which *all* opposites, clash to become united by going beyond themselves to a higher, unitive perfection. His theism is not *a*theism, but *pan*theism. His style is poetic and hyperbolic in order to clear away the pious airs surrounding theological thought to discover people first, last, and foremost. God is just too much to ask when the task is so overwhelming. Like Freud and Marx, he rediscovered us and a method—existential—to use in order to get at one's truth. His hope

187

is in the goodness of all things. His love is not so much universal—and whose is, really?—but one reserved for the talented whom narrow-minded Protestantism and Catholicism had crushed. The one he learned from his good father; the other he experienced wherever he went in Europe.

CHAPTER 8

Conclusion

What have we here with Marx, Freud, and Nietzsche? I think it is two Jews (one forcibly baptized in order to be assimilated) and one Protestant Christian struggling with modernity. Marx wanted a proletarian future without any religion, Jewish or goy. This would allow secular, humanistic reality to appear and history to seek its destined level. Freud wanted nothing better than to do away with the rites of his fathers, which embarrassed him before the secularized gentiles, and then to turn and rid himself of his own persecutors—the Christians he lived with—so that he could become assimilated, but to a non-Christian, totally secularized, elite culture in which one could be grown up facing into one's darkness, without the necessity of illusory idols. Nietzsche, the pastor's son, wanted to rid himself of the categories of his pain—a supernaturalistic theology that insinuated God into one's life so forcefully that there was no room left to be human. He, too, struggled with modernity; he hated it. He wanted an aristocracy of talent against the mediocrity of Christianity and democracy. But in forming our minds around an existential, rather than essential, core, he sculpted the contemporary mind-set no less than the other two. These, then, are the secular magi. Much of what we think of ourselves, of the good and the wicked, of politics and economics, of health and morbidity, even of God and where God is to be found in our lives derives positively and negatively from their thought.

I base my contention on my slowly formed but firm conviction that the transcendent—the One, the Good, and the True—is a prejudice in the medieval sense: a formative process of teaching one about God, parents, right and wrong, country. It is, therefore, the prejudged (prejudiced) ambience in which we emote, think (and the one is umbilically connected

189

to the other), and live out the rest of our lives. We think through and with our prejudices; they are the organs of our perceptions and distortions. They are the locus of the transcendent. But transcendence is not only a formation process; it is also a dynamic, shaping presence—more or less articulated—allowing one to live and judge between the obvious and the self-evident. The one feeds into easy solutions for tough questions; the other is not obvious, but is there to see when the debris of infantile illusions are cleared away through education and life decisions, revealing what is unifying or disintegrating, good or evil, true or false. Marx, Freud, and Nietzsche shifted us from the sovereign but hidden set of assumptions (paradigms) that we call modern to those some call postmodern. The former are easier to define than the latter, contemporary ones for obvious reasons: the past reveals itself more readily than the present. The way we perceive the transcendent depends, in large part, on the efforts of these three great men to live honestly in their world.

Huston Smith says that the assumptions of the Judeo-Christian mind—against which these three raged, out of which they grew, and on which they stood—are, first, reality focuses on a person, God or man and woman. Second, the world's mechanics are beyond our ken. Third, salvation consists in following the commandments, not in conquering the world. Moderns, beginning with the Reformation, assume, first, that reality *may be* personal, but the order of reality is more important than person. Second, reason can discern that order. Third, human fulfillment consists in the discovery, use of, and following of these laws of nature. The postmodern mind assumes, first, that the world may not be ordered, or if so, it may be beyond our comprehension. Second, reality is not personal.[1] But if the modern mind mistrusts categories such as God, soul, good, nobility, and even person—in a word, transcendence— postmoderns, with their predilection for objectivity, prediction, control, and number, infuse the souls of their devotees with sadness, since their thin but brilliant certitudes are insufficient to live off happily. (H. Smith, 96) Our contemporaries have created a human and therefore philosophical chain, since all humanity is in answer to the great questions of the philosopher. If the nub of the modern heart is Promethean in its desire to control things through knowledge, then its epistemology is empiricist and mechanist in imposing an impersonal hermeneutics on the world. Its ontology is naturalistic; the supernatural does not exist, since what is real is matter. (H. Smith, 77) Postmoderns have turned it one notch further; truth is what we want and takes us where we want to go. If one can know, then one can say what the real is—epistemologies create ontologies; and these ontologies say that only matter (Nature) is real. And ontologies create anthropologies; man and woman are part of Nature; and Nature, not God or transcendence, makes one meaningful. An epistemology so relentless in its desire to control can't help but rule out the possibility of transcendence in principle. (H. Smith, 134) The scientific mind is self-contained, asking and answering its questions on the basis of its self-chosen assumptions. It verifies its data with hypotheses, not facts. Its findings must, therefore, be interpreted; they need a hermeneutics. Theisms take their assumptions (paradigms) from both outside revelations and culture-specific sources. Both moderns and postmoderns gagged at the authoritarian and parochial mind-sets that religious people had adopted. Marx, Freud, and Nietzsche challenged the church for the same reasons and freed many from the obscurantisms of the day. Now the church must do the same for postmodernity; it has listened to these three and changed; and looking at its muscular secular brothers, it challenges them for their circular reasoning, which disallows them from knowing that their paradigms and prejudices are good for what they do, but they don't do enough; pushed too far, they become not organs of perception, but organs of distortion. The three men we have studied wished to place us in the world again; faith had put us there but slowly moved us away from what was truly human and decent and lodged us in an eschatological shelf far away from reality, not only secular, but religious as well. What is real is what is here; God is not the here and now but is the pith of it; and where we are, there God is. Marx, Freud, and Nietzsche helped us to find this "here and now" amid the vapid eschatologies of their youth, which hid it by making illusions of those eschatologies. This cut us off from our truest feelings and thoughts by placing a scrim, benign but immovable, between a changed world and those touchstones of the Self and God.

I have outlined the great good they did for us in "reinventing" humankind; and the careful reader knows why they had to do it without God and the transcendent. They had the intestinal fortitude to do in the religious field just what secular society thought but had neither the inclination nor the courage to do: they did a bypass on God in a systematic way, footnoting for all to see just where they really lived, anyway. Religious people lived in a secularized society but thought in a schizoid way about the real and about God; they lived as if God were not real. Our trinity of critics brought into the drawing room what actually was felt in the university and the boardroom. In doing so, Marx and Freud paid their dues as intellectuals but refused to accept assimilation as Jews. Nietzsche is another case.

John Murray Cuddihy, in *The Ordeal of Civility: Freud, Marx, Levi-Strauss, and the Jewish Struggle with Modernity,* demonstrates what I had thought only probable. He goes much further than I could have, without having done his extensive research. His bold hypothesis is that Marx and Freud refused to pay the price of assimilation to gentile, Christian, society and instead totally secularized the goyim, making it possible for both secular Jew and secular gentile to meet on neutral territory.[2]

Cuddihy says that the emancipation offered the Jew after the French Revolution held out utopia but destroyed ethnocentrism and the strong family orientations of those who accepted it. Now the Jew lives among goy strangers and Jewish strangers. Emancipation happens when people can exchange gifts in face-to-face encounters in what Cuddihy calls "civility." This never happened. The Jew was still a stranger to the gentile; but worse, now he was a stranger to the Jew. Emancipation really destroyed Jewish brotherhood. The Jews were to be no more; yet they perdured. The shock of their presence among liberal Europeans became the so-called Jewish Question of the past century. The cultural and societal identity of the Jew, which they called *Yiddishkeit,* clashed with elite Protestant etiquette. (Cuddihy, 3f.) It was the Jewish failure with modernity that galled Christian and secular intellectuals alike. Leo Strauss said: "Or is it obvious to everyone what the Jews have learned from Christianity since it is obvious what the Jews have learned from modernity and it is obvious that modernity is secularized Christianity? But is modernity in fact secularized Christianity?" (Cuddihy, ix)

The Jews, as do any formerly colonized people, realized that they were hopelessly behind the times and sought to analyze the problem and not only find its solution, but also its cause. Norman Mailer said, "No anti-Semite can begin to comprehend the malicious analysis of his soul which every Jew indulges every day." (Ibid.) The Jews, especially those from Germany, were consummately embarrassed by the bad manners of those who came from "beyond the pale"—which was their term for Eastern, especially Russian and Polish, Jews. About this Jerome Weidman said, "I had to laugh at these *goyim* and their politeness. They aren't born smart, like Jews. . . . They're polite all the time, so they can be sure one won't screw the other." (Cuddihy, x) The Jews, analyzing themselves, were constantly brought up short by the split between the nobility of Jewish thought and the vulgarity and chaos of Jewish life." (Norma Rosen, in

Cuddihy, x) And Albert Goldman said, "The Jews have always been students, and their greatest study is themselves." (Ibid.) The urbane Michael Polanyi said of his people: "Many of our ancestors, recognizing themselves as disgracefully backward, were overwhelmed by the contact with a superior civilization." (Cuddihy, xi) Writing on Jewish rudeness, Leon Poliakov said, " 'Are Jews *congenitally* unsociable and rude, or are they this way as a result of having been segregated into ghettos?' Such was the form of the question over which argument raged in the Eighteenth Century, on the eve of the Emancipation." (Cuddihy, ix) Talcott Parsons, refuting Salo Baron, said that the latter had not, himself, refuted Max Weber's hypothesis that Jews had ritually self-excluded themselves from the gentiles and not vice versa. The implication being that Jews felt inferior. (Cuddihy, xi) These assertions, almost exclusively made by Jewish writers, may seem outrageous to "liberal" outsiders, but to anyone who grew up in a minority group they are apposite, if painful, reminding them of their lifetime struggle to assimilate without losing their souls.

Therefore, Cuddihy concludes that emancipation, assimilation, and modernization are a single phenomenon. The secularizing Jewish elite suffered the shock of decolonization and the shame of seeing vulgar and backward Eastern Jews setting their cause of assimilation back. For Cuddihy, this makes Freud's and Marx's ideologies an apologia to the goyim of good will. Theirs was the high-level exercise in antidefamation to reinterpret and explain the odd look of Eastern Jews, and even secular ones. Both Freud and Marx offered not only a hermeneutic, however; they presented a praxis that would be an agent of change, impelling both Jew and gentile into a homogenized neutrality, without the Jew losing personal identity. (Cuddihy, 4) This may seem contradictory. Arthur Herzberg offers us help out of the seeming muddle. His thesis is that modern republican democracy was the seedbed of totalitarianism as far as Jews were concerned. The Jews, in order to accept emancipation, had to denature themselves and disappear as Jews. The person who linked classic anti-Semitism with its contemporary successor was Voltaire, the father of all liberation movements in the West and an unregenerate anti-Semite. So, the cards were stacked against the Jews long before the Germans sent them to the gas chambers. Their hand was dealt when modernity's freedoms were fashioned.[3] There was only one avenue open for the assimilated Jew: disappear as person.

Socialism from Marx to Walter Lippmann is rooted in the Jewish Question, which, again, is another way of dealing with the problem of the public misbehavior of Eastern Jews before their German Jewish and Christian "betters." Marx indicted Jewish crudeness and gentile avarice. His theory said, "Be moderate in consumption" to both Jew and gentile. The thrust of his two essays on the Jewish Question was to tell the Jews to be neither exploitative nor the victims of conspicuous consumption, but he projected it onto the gentiles. But Marxism, whether consciously or unconsciously, was first and foremost for German Jews and only secondarily for Christian reform. (Cuddihy, 5)

Jewish intellectuals thought that they could move freely among people without being destroyed if there were a value-free society based on science. Thus, Freud and Marx based their ideas of politics, economics, humanism, and healing, respectively, on science. This allowed Judaism to become secularized and transmogrified into what we know as "Jewishness." The radical secularism of both Freud and Marx extends beyond socialism and psychoanalysis to liberalism and Zionism; I think the last is stretching it too far. (Cuddihy, 6) What Freud's and Marx's theories did, however, was to supply transformation formulas to Jews by which they could disappear as Jews and reappear in acceptable bland secular liberal attire; and to gentiles to disappear as Christians and reappear as secularized as Jews. Marx and Freud made an affective problem (Jewishness) a cognitive one, thus covering over the crudeness of those from beyond the pale. As such, therefore, they are analogues to the early Christian apologists, who had to argue their coreligionists into the more advanced Greco-Roman civilization. They did this by using the conventional wisdom of their tormentors: philosophy. Marx and Freud argued on secularity's ground by using its language, science. It conferred on them and their Jewish followers the respectability they so earnestly sought. Thus, scientific socialism and psychoanalysis made the despised capitalist Jew disappear, leaving instead a socialist, liberal, totally secularized postmodern person. Jews were feared and despised for their talent, drive, and cutting wit; the gentile had emotional problems with the Jew. The secularizing Jewish intellectuals turned this emotive problem into an intellectual one in order to defuse it. With Freud's science, Jewish offenses (crudity) became defenses (defense mechanisms caused by gentile anti-Semitism). Bad behavior became mental illness. (Cuddihy, 6–7 passim). Freemasonry became a haven for bad Christians and modernized Jews, in which men of leadership caliber could meet on equal ground.

Thus, the affectively charged atmosphere of Germany had been neutralized by Marx and Freud and other Jewish secularizers. They took the

Jew from particularism to universalism. As Hegel secularized Lutheranism, the modernism of Feuerbach, Marx, and Freud secularized Protestant Christianity. Thus, modernity, the child of Protestant Christianity, returned the compliment, and by the chiasmus peculiar not only to Marx, but to all postmodernity, turned things upside down and secularized religion. Catholic secularity (modernization) was to come at the time of Vatican Council II, generations later. The essence of modernization's dynamics is differentiation. Tradition joined disparate groups into brotherhoods and sisterhoods. Modernization split that wholeness: church from state (the Catholic trauma) and ethnicity from religion (the Jewish trauma); all this became a separated, limited, state in a differentiated—fragmented, free, and lonely—society. This differentiation leaves what Cuddihy calls a "wholeness hunger," divorcing ends from means, the nuclear from the extended families. Modern revolutions have interiorized this differentiation in a "civic culture" and call any resisters to it ideologues; any attempt at suppressing differentiation is viewed as ideology. (Cuddihy, 8–10) Civic society forces the individual to be free. As Herzberg says, society doesn't care anymore what one believes, but it does care what one's politics are; this is the reverse of the medieval ethos. Modernization calls for refinement. To be modern is to go along with civilization. Thus, moderns must have a private-public differentiation. The process runs thus: modernization becomes a civilizing force leading to assimilation of all into one homogeneous mass. (Cuddihy, 12) This is the price of admission to modern bourgeois civil society in the West. Jews groaned under its burden and both Marx and Freud heard. Maurice Asmuel says, "The Jews are probably the only people in the world to whom it has ever been proposed that their historic destiny is—to be nice." (Cuddihy, 14) But as Irving Howe said, catching "the *Gemeinschaft*-affect of Eastern Europe *shtetl Yiddishkeit's* 'life is with people': 'Having love, they had no need for politeness.'" (Ibid.)

Of this politeness Freud said, "The politeness which I practise every day, is to a large extent dissimulation . . . and when I interpret my dreams for my readers I am obliged to adopt similar distortions." (Cuddihy, 17) Cuddihy says that the importunate "Yid" is the model of Freud's "importunate id."

Both are saddled with the problem of "passing" from a latent existence "beyond the pale" of Western respectability into an open and manifest relation to Gentile society *within* Gentile society, from a state of unconsciousness to a state of consciousness. Freud's internal censor represents bourgeois-Christian nineteenth-century culture. (Cuddihy, 18f.)

Freud loved nothing better than pulling the masks off gentile civility to show the powerfully vulgar gentile id beneath. The norm for Jewish intellectuals was to cloak their true thoughts about gentile civility with gentle irony. Marx thought that this was a "sellout" of the truth: he would call the hypocrite exploiters by their true name and deal with his rage in a more honest way. Cuddihy theorizes that the classic Jewish joke, Freud's theory of dreams, and the nineteenth-century Jewish Question all have the same structure. All three have a latent "dark" id or "Yid" elbowing his or its way toward conscious recognition and acceptance by civil society. Next, the censor is the social-moral authority of gentile culture demanding that the coarse id-Yid "first disguise itself (assimilate) or refine itself (sublimate)—in a word, civilize itself, at whatever price in discontent." Finally, in the process of passing into gentile society, the Jew's ego has to closely monitor Jewish behavior lest the Yid poke through its newfound civility. Thus, the process of modernization in which the Jew passed from the medieval world into the modern one was really a civilizing process in which enfranchisement meant becoming bourgeois. (Cuddihy, 20f.) The tool for the Jew's entrance into the German middle class was the same one that Germans demanded of gentile burghers desiring to enter the noble classes: education. Thus, the Jews crowded into the universities, seeking a professional education habilitating them to take the place nature demanded that they have and society forbid them to have unless it follow society's rites of passage. (Cuddihy, 27) When Germans have a problem in philosophy, they almost invariably make it into an epistemological problem. When they face difficulties in domesticating the hustling lower classes, they make it a knowledge problem.

In studying Christian sexual mores, Freud thought that beneath the niceties of courtly love there was—always—the fact of the erectile penis; and he meant to confront gentile society with this fact. (Cuddihy, 23) If they meant to make him nice, he meant to make psychoanalysis a process of going at it with the gloves off, showing that their id was the same as his; no better, no worse. He maintained that "an analysis is not a place for polite exchanges." (Cuddihy, 35) He delighted, furthermore, in calling a spade a spade, especially when prudish Christians were covering up something sexual with euphemisms. Repression breeds expression— indeed, it demands it. Whereas Christians had drawn out their sexual mores into the filaments of moral theology, regulating every thought and deed, demanding that what was so coarse and natural be supernaturalized, Jews were, above all, quite natural and relaxed about things sexual. If Christians were shocked at Jewish coarseness, so were Jews shocked by Christian sexual "backwardness." Freud wanted to naturalize sexuality in the mainstream society. Marx wanted economic naturalism in place of the greed dressed up in fancy clothes; Freud wanted the same thing in sexual matters. (Cuddihy, 65) Freud would not accept a superego as replacement for an ego that had integrated its id: "Where Id was, there shall Ego be." (Cuddihy, 65) Hence, neither Freud nor Marx would accept assimilation to Christian society on its terms; supernaturalism had destroyed something good and relaxed, if a bit crude and roistering, in both the bedroom and the marketplace. Cuddihy says, "Bourgeois-Protestant love may have eliminated haggling from courtship, as bourgeois-Protestant capitalism eliminates haggling from economic exchange, but sexuality and avarice endure unchanged." (Cuddihy, 68)

Freud's Oedipus complex perhaps derives from his own father's humiliation, when, as a boy, he had his hat knocked into the mud by a Christian hooligan, who demanded that Freud's father get off the sidewalk and into the mud so he could pass. The ancient cry of the gentile, *"Mach mores Jud!"* (mind your manners, Jew) was well known to all Jews in those days. The elder Freud told Sigmund this story when the lad was between ten and twelve years of age, and Freud never restored his father to the esteem that he had held before he heard it. In the play *Oedipus Rex,* the young Oedipus is confronted by the king's carriage and knocked out of the way. But instead of taking it passively, as had Freud's father, the hero struck back and slew everyone within reach of his staff. Freud was deeply affected by, almost hung up on, this story. It turned not only on the heroism of the young Greek, but also on Freud's own experiences with Moravian Catholic youths as a schoolboy, as well as the vicarious humiliation he took from his father's story. (Cuddihy, 48–52) Hannah Arendt says that had Freud not lived in a German milieu, we might never have heard of Oedipus. But it was not so; and Freud was his own first patient, courageously bearding his darkness with the probe of his fledgling analysis. (Cuddihy, 57)

Thus, Freud said that the price of admission to gentile society was civility, niceness. Howard Morley Sacher said that the "unconscious desire to Jews, as social pariahs, [was] to unmask the respectability of the European society which closed them out . . . [and the best way of doing this was] by dredging up from the human psyche the sordid and infantile sexual aberrations that were frequently the sources of human behavior, or misbehavior." The Jews were associated with vulgarity and lack of refinement, but they were free of the neuroses of frustrated modern ambition. Freud found that strangled emotion, especially fear, anger, and sexual feelings, held in by gentile niceness, caused much neurosis in the emergent Jewish middle class. (Cuddihy, 38f.)

Little by little, Freud came to see the etiology of neurosis in sexual distress. He was shocked to find that others before him knew this but either would not mention it—except euphemistically and obliquely—or could not mention it. For a woman whose husband was impotent, a colleague wryly remarked that his prescription for her was *Rx: penis normalis; dosim repetatur* (repeated doses of a normal penis). Again, he was constantly reminded that the genitals were *inter urinas et faeces* (between urine and feces). (Cuddihy, 91). His gorge rose when he saw how Roman Catholics, especially, had raised the coarseness of sex to a high spirituality, a spirituality that Protestantism had also accepted, except for its married clergy and lack of nuns. His strategy for his Jewish patients— saddled as they were by a bourgeois ethos alien to them—was to invert and convert, just as I said Marx had done. He inverted all that was supernatural by showing just how terribly natural it all was, how material, how fraught it was with the "throes of matter" and its longings to return from its states of excitement to one of rest. After naturalizing the goyim, he converted them to a Jewish way of looking at things: since there was no supernatural involved in sex, one could convert to naturalism. Thus, the tactic was inversion; the strategy was the disappearance of the gentile in a conversion to a secular (read Jewish) way of looking at things. Hence, much of what passes for secularism was not born of Protestantism, but of Judaism and Freud's Jewish naturalism. The id of the Christian was no different from that of the Jew, and he demonstrated it time and again both in his writings and with his patients. His was a liberation ethos; his patients were freed of the constraints of a badly interiorized moral code and now were free to discover, first, just who they were and how they were to comport themselves lovingly in the world. (Cuddihy, 97)

Naturalism is the word for Marx as well. His strategy was the hominization of an inhuman world by inversion and conversion. Chiasmus fills his works; he turns things upside down and inside out. God goes, to be replaced by man and woman; heaven gives way to earth, and theology, to economics and politics. Civility and its sequelae, liberalism and roman-

198

ticism, fall away before the incivility—tough love—necessary to be decent to one another, shorn of all the Calvinistic pleasantries and hypocrisies that covered Christian avarice. Marx was never so sharp as he was in his two least scientific works, the reviews of Bruno Bauer's works on the Jewish Question. His Jewishness comes right to the fore. He blasts Jews for being as bad as the goyim and the goyim for emulating the worst of "Jewish Jesuitism"—by which he meant slyness. His vulgarities, slights, and anti-Semitic outrages are to be taken in the same way that I suggested one take Nietzsche's eruptions: with a grain of salt. He was no anti-Semite. He simply had no time for religion—any religion. He focused on the Jews because Germans and Europeans in general had done so and, I think, because he himself was a Jew. (He was so swarthy that his children called him "the Moor"; he was feisty, pushy, demanded answers to his tough questions, displayed bad manners in public—though to his family and intimates he was the soul of urbanity. No baptismal waters could cover up what Germans and he knew to be all too true: he was a Jew and could get no fair hearing, whether in Germany, France, or England. The infected spot of Germany—anti-Semitism—raged all over Europe.) He wished to naturalize man and woman and their relations, both affective and mercantile, with each other. Covering the dung heap of exploitation, conspicuous consumption, and outright theft from the poor with the snowy grace of Christian redemption, thus supernaturalizing all that was corrupt in the world of commerce, was called what it was. He excoriated the Jews for not knowing better; they were merely Christians, and they wanted to become part of the society in which they led the way with avarice and lust for money and possessions. And Christians were Jews, and they meant to bring innocent Eastern Jews into this? He cut both ways because he was both Jew and Christian. In so doing he liberated the vision of Protestant Europeans—he was writing especially for them, since they ran things in Germany and France at the time—so they could see the world for the first time. He, too, made the goyim disappear, leaving a secularized person. Thus, both Freud and Marx pulled off the best Jewish joke of all; they made their tormentors vanish and left persons secularized by Jews, no different from them, in their place: shorn of their gods, their rites, even their race. They could now get down to the business at hand: being equal in all things, they could be decent but not necessarily nice—one mustn't push the revolution too far.

Each of the three, Freud, Marx, and Nietzsche—I don't, now, mention them chronologically—gave the weak, the fragile, and the disenfranchised—both Jewish and gentile—strategies and tactics for survival, at worst, and health, at best. Nietzsche's contribution, in my view, is hoving us to our good, raw being, rather than the benignly derived categories by which we tailored our sanities and civilities. These categories were no longer working; man's and woman's innate goodness was covered over by an avalanche of a priorism. Goodness and talent were buried beneath the weight of system and its surrogate, mediocrity. Nietzsche hymned the necessary; when it became necessary, will it. Tragedy was our term, but the journey could now be made in joy. He found our divinity under the slag strewn before the Christian mines; and he battened on that divine kernel at the core of our beings: good, joyous, rollicking, uncivil, funny, outrageous humanity. He, too, was a naturalist in reaction against the supernaturalism of his good pastor father and the Protestantism of his day. He, Freud, and Marx went for evangelicals' throats, since they ran things; Catholics were powerful but irrelevant intellectually. Willing the necessary allowed one to listen to the rushes of one's insides to find what was the good and the bad and to find what was the best—the necessary—course to take with what one had. This is the nub of existential ethics, founded on the irrefragable faith in the goodness of men and women and things. All three of our subjects had this faith—an optimism founded, not on youthful expectations, but on a hope surviving severe suffering. That is his gift to us: hope as strategy and finding the necessary as a tactic for survival, at worst, and joy, at best.

Many see Freud, Marx, and Nietzsche as modernizers. But Nietzsche hated things modern and republican. He wanted an aristocracy of nature's elite. He railed against modernity even as he gave us the devices for living in it. Freud's genius was not usable by the common herd; for one, they had neither the time nor the money to bring to his analytic enterprise. For another, they were and are incapable of deciding the great issues by themselves. Anyone who has experience in teaching or counseling knows that the hardest thing of all is to lead people to think and decide for themselves. It can be done, but recidivism is rampant, and the healed client so frequently comes crawling back to demand: "What shall I think? What shall I do?" Second, Freud, too, is no modernizer. Cuddihy sees him as allowing the Jew to live in the modern world and makes a good case for it. Freud wanted to make both Jew and gentile capable of living in the real world, but he helped to destroy modernity, Protestantism's child, as he tried to dismantle both Protestantism and Catholicism, as well as Judaism, but never to get rid of Jewishness, which he loved. In pushing men and women past supernaturalism—the offspring of Catholic Scholasticism and Protestant modernity—he effectively caused them to live in a world naked of rite, rule, and God. Marx joins him in despising bourgeois modernity. He hated Enlightenment wisdoms, liberalism's do-gooderism, and Romanticism's flirtation with mysticism. He plugged men and women into reality without the resistors provided by code, creed, and cult. Modernity died with him, Freud, and Nietzsche. Postmodernity is a nonterm. I don't really know what to call our age, but it certainly is not modern, and to call it "post" anything simply tells us where we have been, certainly not where we are or where we are going. History seems to run in four-hundred-year cycles, the ages of which are born, peak, and fall apart with a bone-rattling revolution. The modern era was born with Luther and died in due time with our three subjects. Modernity had not made an end of God or religion; they lived "out there," beyond the workaday world; but they had a place, albeit a tangential one. These three men got rid of the human More—transcendence and its source, God—in order to live with the humanless and be decent and happy.

Religion has burgeoned again, Freudian healed, Marxist analyzed, and Nietzsche necessary. God took a back seat for two or three generations and now is found in the spiritual and physical longings of celibate as well as married, cleric as well as lay. The necessary tactics of Christians and Jews everywhere allow them to remain in the fold, at the periphery but— as Gregory Baum says—not peripheral. God's good Spirit is discerned, not so much in the atomized acts of our lives, but in our love over the long haul. Galatians 5 says that the works of the evil one are "fornication, gross indecency, and sexual irresponsibility; idolatry and sorcery; feuds and wrangling, jealousy, bad temper and quarrels; disagreements, factions, envy; drunkenness, orgies and similar things." The works of the Spirit are "love, joy, peace, patience, kindness, goodness, trustfulness, gentleness, and self-control. There can be no law against things like that, of course" (see Galatians 5:19–24). Using Paul's categories as discerners of the Holy Spirit has allowed the churches to "see" the divine Presence, whereas it was categorically impossible before. If faith is a vision, then whereas we had been functionally blind before, we can now see; in large part, Freud, Marx, and Nietzsche clarified our sight. The vision is God's, but the human eyes are theirs—and we see God with human eyes.

Base Ecclesial Communities in South American Catholic dioceses follow a somewhat Marxist bent in shaping their Christian praxis of love subsequent to a Marxist analysis of what is the just thing to do in their situation. North American Christian communities, both Protestant and Catholic, follow along lines more distinctly their own in using theological reflection to form their vision based on a justice-praxis (Marxist) axis.

Thus, Freud, Marx, and Nietzsche are in large part the fathers of the age. But it is not modernity that claims their paternity; what it is remains to be named. Whatever it is, they help us to live in it, in God.

But the chief figure of this book is not this troika as fathers, but as Magi, Wise Men from the West. It is as critics that they serve us in the churches. They are wisdom figures. It is not so much that they were atheists and, as such, unbelievers—I have reservations about Nietzsche's atheism, at least. Rather, it is that they had beliefs; each was a man driven by a vision that endowed him with faith. The faith of each was that things were radically good, that being was flawed with a variety of evil surds, but it was all right, at its base. It was that things, people, would be all right. In the words of Juliana of Norwich, it was that "all shall be well." This faith is isomorphic—different in genesis but convergent with ours—because our Christian faith, and the faith of all people, is rooted in this optimism about being. Faith is an ontological statement, although we don't like to think of it as philosophical. For us Christians, the basic question is "Is God good? Is God worth all the trouble God puts us to? Is God really good?" There is no other question than that in religion, our religion, anyway. All the rest is subsequent and subservient to that problem.

And what that question really means, putting it the other way, is "Are we good? Are we worth it? Are we really good?" since we are in God's image made. If the answer to either question is in the affirmative, then religion makes sense and is quite necessary for our ontological salvation.

These three men converge with us on the latter assertion, that men and women are good. They short-circuited the *theodicy* question for the *anthropodicy* one, since religion and its God had become odious for all the reasons given earlier. Odious and otiose, and *otiosa restringeudd sunt*. They converge with us, Jews, Christians, Muslims, Hindus, Buddhists, and Taoists, to name only the so-called classic religions, as well as with optimistic atheists and agnostics, in this faith in the goodness of things and people.

They followed their natural (secular) light to the cave of human invention and found a babe. As the Transfiguration narrative relates to us in much more telling ways than the charming infancy narratives do, after the transitory vision went, there was Jesus, just Jesus alone ("When they lifted up their eyes, they saw no one but Jesus only" [Matt. 17:8]). This man, this human, this samsara left after the nirvana left is all we have to go on, so "listen to him" [Matt. 17:5]. This is the root paradigm of Christianity. The nirvana of God is to be found in the samsara of men and women. Listen to our humanity. Listen to our intellects and hearts. Listen to the transfiguring effects of being human. Be yourselves, know yourselves. Be human; be humane.

These are the plaints of our Wise Men from the West. Their gifts were humanity, what we called secularity with Bonhoeffer and Harvey Cox. And what we call creatureliness once again, now that we are coming to the "second naivete" of a renewed faith. A creatureliness that implies a creator, and a faith that allows one to find that creator in the fully mundane details and entails of our world and lives. We are to find God in the muck and mire, the samsara and duhkha (wretchedness, Sanskrit); a lotus blossoming in the only place it can, in wet dirt, what we would call "filth" were it not for this faith in the radical goodness of things.

These Wise Men brought their gift of criticism to us, and like the Child's parents, we reeled from them. What good are gold, incense, and myrrh to a child? What good is atheistic humanism and a new economic order to us? Plenty and we know it now. What good is atheistic healing, especially when it overturns morality? Plenty when it allows one to become human again and, ultimately, find God because of one's love for the Self, a first time love for our vision and intimacy with our good and flawed selves. What good is the atheistic (or nontheistic) elitism of Nietzsche? Plenty when it allows one to find God and talent in a mixed-up person and the world that person inhabits. Plenty good.

These three critics recovered humanity for us in their various ways. The babe in the manger was new and pink and unnamed. We call him by new names because of these three Magi. Their epiphany was in criticism that led to the invention of a child in a manger. No one wanted it. No one wanted to go there. It was dirty and unkempt. Illegitimacy stalked its doors: virgin birth still rattles us. (Send the kid away to have the baby and get on with things.) But the virgin and her child won't go away. The mother is the womb of humanity, fertile and seemingly without any paternity to point to but voices heard in the pockets of the heart. The child is still aborning. So the child is without a fixed name. So is the age. We call it post-something-or-other, not knowing who we are or where we live or where we are going. But we have come to the conclusion in faith that eschatology really means that God is in rehearsal, but we are here and we are to find God in the best that's in us, since God put it there in very human, muddy, and begrimed ways.

Criticism is the gift of these latter day Magi. It is something we Christians have had to learn. Something we theologians have had to learn the hard way; and something we have had to teach pastors and they their flocks. There is a big difference between being a critic and a faithful hack. The hack does theology without really thinking, without really addressing himself or herself to the nuts and bolts of the gospel and the workaday situation of each of us. The muck and mire is too dirty for bishops' chanceries and national church boards. So the temptation is to hire as spokespersons for the faith people who have doctorates but who haven't the *habitus theologicus*, which is just the Latin term for the wherewithal and courage to use it. Degree doesn't mean talent; it just means that one has survived a program. It takes talent, brains, and courage to face up to the realities of God in one's life and age. It's messy, dirty business. It takes too much faith in God and in oneself and in one's church to find God in all things, which is not only the Jesuit's spirituality, but the mainline Christian's spirituality as well.

So the church likes to hear the courageous and beloved formulae from other ages. Likes to rehearse the smoothed over tales of saints and scholars finding God in their day. Likes to narrate those tales, telling us to memorize them. But doesn't like to get down to the details of really looking for God today in a way that is meaningful and telling for this age and that can be passed off as tales for another time (Tradition). This is where criticism goes out the window and hacks enter by the main entrance. Church leadership brings in its theological lap dogs, who give us the tried and true answers to questions that no one is asking anymore as replies to our pleas for help or mercy. Hacks can do no other. The shepherds had to be told what they were seeing by unbelieving Magi and angels. Shepherds are good with sheep, not with thought. The two are different charisms in church history. Classically, the bishop held down the Pastoral Chair and theologians, the Magisterial Chair. In both Catholic and Protestant churches these roles have fused and pastors have assumed the dual role, to the sadness of anybody who knows church history at all.

The theologian must have a bit of unfaith (criticism is a nicer way of putting it) in order to do his or her job. Criticism is to see things in a different way; to say, "Oh, yeah?" when everybody is saying "Amen"; to put unholy rocks in bishops' shoes to enable them to limp a bit and remember that they are just pilgrims, not the lords of the manor; to walk out on the teedy benders (unsafe New England ice that gave us such fun as kids and dunked most of us up to our knees, or worse) to see just how far one could go, not just to do it, but because people needed to find out God's parameters and someone with a Holy Spirit in him or her had to do it because he or she was the only one with the gift of guts and learning. This causes consternation in the churches at first. If it is of God, it will ultimately have a centripetal effect on the church and allow its leadership to fuse their flocks at the center, once again. It is an unfaith in the old formulae and in unsafe, bland-lead-the-bland leadership that impels the teacher to pioneer the Spirit. This is a faith in one's charism and takes courage and humility. The courage to do it and the humility to know that one must believe not only in God, but also in God's Holy Catholic Church, as the creed goes. The courage to do it in the face of opposition in the university, where colleagues are more fearsome than bishops, and the humility to take correction when wrong, both from colleagues and from the more mediocre in mind holding down the Pastoral Chair.

But the hack. Ah, the hack! Beloved of men, women, and church leadership. He or she repeats the past without having learned it. This is supposed to have a calming centripetal effect on the church members. It does, on those who need anodyne more than reality in religion. But its ultimate effect is centrifugal. Future generations flee the church, as did those of Freud, Marx, and Nietzsche. Hacks are the quacks of the theological vocation. They don't hold down the Magisterial Chair; they are too light authoritatively to do so. Only those who are really teaching the truth hold down that chair. It does not come by dint of ordination, but it can; nor does it come by appointment from on church high. It comes from being instinct with the Holy Spirit in the depths of one's humanity. This doesn't show up until well after a good theologian is dead; the Spirit must rise more slowly from the grave than did Christ (She must love the world and the earth She created). This means that one must try to understand which is really holding down the chair and which is merely warming it, sometimes causing mischief by spouting past authorities to cure new illnesses. This understanding doesn't come easily. It takes honesty, courage, and study, not just in the university, but in the parish and the home as well. Studying the Spirit takes the humility of courage, a humility to stick to seemingly dull and hard stuff, to fail—here's where humility comes in, it means "down in the dust"—and get up and go at it again. It means the humility of docility, not being a wimp type of docility, but the ability to be taught when one is either ignorant or, worse, wrong.

Criticism is the royal road to the Spirit, theologically. It is an unsavory and frightening road because one must go into unfaith to reach mature faith. We don't know whether the first Magi ever reached the faith. It's irrelevant. They followed the Spirit as they saw the Spirit. Whether Freud, Marx, and Nietzsche attained faith is not for us to say. What is for us to say is that it is through the faith of their unfaith (criticism) that they became Secular Magi, leading us on to the child with the clarified innocence of vision and love that we have now and don't really know what to do with. That is the stuff of a future creed. Living it is the stuff of faith.

Epilogue

The changed shape of religion that these three men helped to father demands a new humanity; and a new humanity demands a new God, since the one is defined in terms of the other. God, certainly is not defined in terms of us, theologically speaking; but psychologically speaking—and that's the way we experience and know things—if we change, so must God. In the deepest sense there is no such thing as religion: just God and us and our interrelations. Marx, Freud, and Nietzsche knew before Barth and W. C. Smith that religion had become, in so many ways, a mischievous distillate getting in the way of our ever finding God. And since those relations have changed, so have we. So has God.

What shapes does God take today? The past century killed God off in the full spate of its scientific and philosophic hubris. If the scriptures weren't what they were cracked up to be, then how could God be what God purported to be all these years? Where God had been, all that was left was a pervasive grief, a longing for God. Our eschatologies had been shattered and all we had were a few human joys held down by the grief of God's separation.

The first and best shape God took in our age was this longing for God. It was all we had, but coupled with a desire to live a decent life, it was the shibboleth that God hadn't left us. It was the one sign that the great mystics had to go on as they went into their dark night of the soul. And dark night it was for us all. A night of bright hubris shattered by the two world wars and the ultimate bestiality of atomic warfare launched by the side that had set out to protect us against other more obvious evils.

So, God had removed to another place, leaving beside the empty tomb a "closed for alteration" sign that no one dared question and everyone despaired at a bit. It was as if God had really died again and left us tremulous at the grave, with only memories and a handful of sayings to sustain us in the face of the sufferings that pressed us away from God. But again, this grief is a sign that God lives. It is how love feels in separation; and one cannot love so fiercely unless it come of the Holy Spirit. This hunger for a God made timid by our narcissisms and orchestrated disbeliefs is the best we have to go on even yet. Whatever new name God will emerge with, when the name of our age finally emerges, we do not know.

There are other shapes that God has taken of late. To the fundamentalists, God appears as Text and Certitude, endowing the Moral Majority with the knowledge that God is an ethic that may be held without an asterisk of doubt. To the Charismatics, God is Joy and spiritual gifts. To both there is an immediacy and accessibility to God. For both, though, God is not in the hurly-burly of life, but comes to where we live far away in our deepest, remotest self, far removed from the ego. This God is not a God of political movement involved with changing people's lives through changing the people and the processes by which they live to better their lot and bring about the eschatological community. To these people, God is not communitarian or here as we are here. Transcendence brings us beyond all that, as if it's not good enough for God or us. It's the world as evil and a God not desirous of being tarnished by it or allowing us to be so that they see.

And to the social gospelers, God is Justice. As such, God is one who lives in but, more, among us. This God roots the more easily among liberal Protestants and those Catholics who hew to lines drawn by papal teachings on social justice. This God brings anger before the peace of justice. This God demands community by paradoxically splitting the unjust social compacts of the past. This is a God of the poor and demands that we give them preference over the rich. This makes Protestants of the classic Calvinist and Lutheran stripe nervous. God is not choosing the middle class, but prefers the poor. Upper-class Catholics, steeped in the noblesse oblige school of medieval spirituality see no God here at all. They see only meddlesome popes and do-gooder bishops manipulated by Jesuits who are too eager to "mullaize" their religion. This brings dis-ease and promise of future peace and justice.

To Catholic mystics, God appears as the Consoler—sometimes gentle and at others quite disruptive—amid their discernment of spirits. To those Christians bruised by their attempts to meet the demands of postmodernity, God is a refuge found in conservative liturgies and strict constructionism of the Decalogue.

To all God's sectarian clients, God appears sovereign, but to a more casual observer God appears terribly fragmented, as if God hadn't yet decided which mask God wants, or is God telling us that all of them are wanted, that that's the point: that God loves each mask democratically?

Over all these Christian avatars there hovers a silence bespeaking an unquestionably benign Presence, possessed of the infinitely good breeding to change us only when we reject the amnesias of our darknesses and allow God to recall our truest names to us in the striations of our lives. Slowly, quietly, God is reappearing in us and our churches, gathering up the fragments of the epiphanies into the twelve baskets of our diverse apostleships.

God gives the divine self many names, but the most telling one is The One We Long For.

Notes

INTRODUCTION

1. Huston Smith, *Beyond the Post-Modern Mind* (New York: Crossroad, 1982), p. 7; hereafter, "H. Smith."
2. W. C. Smith, *Faith and Belief* (Princeton, NJ: Princeton University Press, 1979), pp. 144f.; hereafter, "Faith."

CHAPTER 1   RELIGION AS UNREALITY

1. Isaiah Berlin, *Karl Marx: His Life and Environment* (London: Oxford University Press, 1963), pp. 6–8 passim.
2. Karl Lowith, *From Hegel to Nietzsche, the Revolution in Nineteenth Century Thought*, trans. D. E. Green (Garden City, NY: Doubleday Anchor, 1967), p. 152.
3. Cf. Freud's *The Future of an Illusion*, trans. W. D. Robson-Scott; rev. and ed. James Strachey (Garden City, NY: Doubleday Anchor, 1961), pp. 81ff.
4. Roger Garaudy, *Karl Marx, The Evolution of His Thought* (New York: International Publishers, 1967), p. 25.
5. *Marx and Engels on Religion* (New York: Schocken Books, 1964), p. 69; hereafter, "Theses."
6. Karl Marx, *Karl Marx, Early Writings*, trans. and ed. T. B. Bottomore (New York: McGraw-Hill, 1963), p. 13.

CHAPTER 2   THE CELESTIAL REFUTATION

1. Karl Marx, *Karl Marx, Early Writings*, trans. and ed. T. B. Bottomore (New York: McGraw-Hill, 1963), p. 43; hereafter, "Contribution."
2. Karl Marx, "Critique of Hegel's Dialectic and General Philosophy," in *Early Writings*, p. 201; hereafter, "Dialectic."
3. Karl Marx, in *Early Writings*, the essay "On the Jewish Question, or Bruno Bauer *Die Judenfrage*," p. 12; hereafter, "The Question."
4. Cf. Thomas F. Kuhn's classic *The Structure of Scientific Revolutions* (Chicago: University of Chicago Press, 1962), pp. 2f.

5. *Marx and Engels: Basic Writings on Politics and Philosophy* (Garden City, NY: Doubleday Anchor, 1959), p. 70.
6. In *Marx and Engels on Religion* (New York: Schocken Books, 1964).
7. Robert Nisbet, *The Sociological Tradition* (New York: Basic Books, 1966), p. 226.
8. Isaiah Berlin, *Karl Marx: His Life and Environment* (London: Oxford University Press, 1963), pp. 99f.
9. Arthur McGovern, *Marxism, an American Christian Perspective* (Maryknoll, NY: Orbis Books, 1981), p. 246.
10. Karl Lowith, *From Hegel to Nietzsche* (Garden City, NY: Doubleday, 1967), p. 329.

CHAPTER 3   MARXISM'S MANTRAS FOR THE OPPRESSED

1. Friedrich Engels, *Ludwig Feuerbach*, in *Karl Marx and Friedrich Engels* (Moscow: Foreign Languages Publishing House, 1955), p. 373; hereafter cited as "Feuerbach."
2. *Marx and Engels on Religion* (New York: Schocken Books, 1964), pp. 62, 64.
3. Teilhard de Chardin, *Hymn of the Universe* (London: Collins, 1965), pp. 59–60.
4. Friedrich Engels, *Anti-Duhring* (Moscow: Foreign Languages Publishing House, 1954), p. 33.
5. Friedrich Engels, *The Dialectics of Nature* (Moscow: Foreign Languages Publishing House, 1954), p. 54; hereafter cited as "Nature."
6. Arthur McGovern, *Marxism, An American Christian Perspective* (Maryknoll, NY: Orbis Books, 1981), p. 259.
7. R. C. Zaehner, *Dialectical Christianity and Christian Materialism* (London: Oxford University Press, 1971), p. 51; hereafter cited as "Zaehner."
8. W. L. Newell, *The Triptych Heart: The Journey of 80–82*. Unpublished book of poems.
9. W. L. Newell. *Struggle and Submission: R. C. Zaehner on Mysticisms* (Washington, DC: University Press of America, 1981), pp. 133f.
10. Cf. Karl Lowith, *From Hegel to Nietzsche, the Revolution in Nineteenth Century Thought*, trans. D. E. Green (Garden City, NY: Doubleday Anchor, 1967), p. 329.
11. R. C. Zaehner, *Evolution in Religion, A Study of Sri Aurobindo and Teilhard de Chardin* (Oxford: Clarendon Press, 1971), pp. 21f.; from Teilhard's *Ecrits* . . . , pp. 30–32.

CHAPTER 4   RELIGION AS ILLUSION

1. Hans Kung, *Freud and the Problem of God*, The Terry Lectures, trans. E. Quinn (New Haven, CT: Yale University Press, 1979), pp. 9–11 passim; hereafter, "Kung."

2. Sigmund Freud, *Totem and Taboo, The Resemblances Between the Psychic Lives of Savages and Neurotics*, trans. A. A. Brill, M.D. (New York: Vintage Book, 1946), p. 27; hereafter, "Totem." Copyright 1918, renewed 1946 by Gioia B. Bernheim and Edmund Brill. Quotations are reprinted by permission.

3. Sigmund Freud, *The Future of an Illusion*, trans. and ed. W. D. Robson-Scott; newly ed. J. Strachey (Garden City, NY: Doubleday Anchor, 1964); hereafter, "Illusion."

CHAPTER 5   THE ONCE AND FUTURE ILLUSION

1. Friedrich Nietzsche, *Beyond Good and Evil: Prelude to a Philosophy of the Future*, trans. W. Kaufman (New York: Vintage Books, 1966), p. 14.

2. Jurgen Habermas, *Knowledge and Human Interests*, trans. Jeremy Shapiro (Boston: Beacon Press, 1971), p. 214; hereafter, "Habermas."

3. Paul Ricoeur, *Freud and Philosophy, An Essay on Interpretation*, trans. Denis Savage (New Haven, CT: Yale University Press, 1970), p. 26; hereafter, "Ricoeur."

4. Sigmund Freud, *Totem and Taboo, The Resemblances Between the Psychic Lives of Savages and Neurotics*, trans. A. A. Brill (New York: Vintage Books, 1946), p. 193.

5. Alfred L. Kroeber, "Totem and Taboo: An Ethnologic Psychoanalysis," in *American Anthropologist* 23 (1920): 48–55, taken from William A. Lessa and Evon Z. Vogt, *Reader in Comparative Religion, An Anthropological Approach*, 2d ed. (New York: Harper & Row, 1965), p. 49; hereafter, "Kroeber."

6. David C. McLelland, *The Roots of Consciousness* (Princeton, NJ: Van Nostrand, Insight Book, 1964), p. 120; hereafter, "McLelland."

7. David Bakan, *Sigmund Freud and the Jewish Mystical Tradition* (Princeton, NJ: Van Nostrand, 1958).

CHAPTER 6   THE WRONGDOING OF GOD

1. Friedrich Nietzsche, *Twilight of the Idols, or How to Philosophize with a Hammer*, trans. A. M. Ludovici (New York: Russel & Russel, 1964), vol. 16, p. 26; hereafter, "Idols."

2. Rose Pfeffer, *Discipline of Dionysus* (Lewisburg, PA: Bucknell University Press, 1972), p. 250; hereafter, "Pfeffer."

3. Walter Kaufmann, *Nietzsche, Philosopher, Psychologist, Anti-Christ* (Princeton, NJ: Princeton University Press, 1967); hereafter, "Kaufmann."

4. Friedrich Nietzsche, *Beyond Good and Evil, Prelude to a Philosophy of the Future*, trans. W. Kaufmann (New York: Vintage Books, 1966), Pt. I, "On the Prejudices of Philosophers," p. 10; hereafter, "Beyond."

5. Paul Ricoeur, *Freud and Philosophy, An Essay on Interpretation*, trans. Denis Savage (New Haven, CT: Yale University Press, 1970), pp. 27–30.

6. Friedrich Nietzsche, *Twilight of the Idols and the Anti-Christ*, trans. R. J.

Hollingdale (New York: Penguin Classics, 1968), p. 209; hereafter, "Anti-Christ." Copyright © R. J. Hollingdale, 1968. Quotations are reprinted by permission of Penguin Books Ltd.

7. W. L. Newell, *Struggle and Submission: R. C. Zaehner on Mysticisms* (Washington, DC: University Press of America, 1981), cf. especially ch. 3 on Nature Mysticism.

CHAPTER 7   NIETZSCHE'S RELIGION

1. Rose Pfeffer, *Disciple of Dionysus* (Lewisburg, PA: Bucknell University Press, 1972), p. 250; hereafter "Pfeffer."

2. I have dealt with this phenomenon extensively in my *Struggle and Submission: R. C. Zaehner on Mysticisms* (Washington, DC: University Press of America, 1981), chs. 2 and 4.

CHAPTER 8   CONCLUSION

1. Huston Smith, *Beyond the Post-Modern Mind* (New York: Crossroad, 1982), pp. 6f.; hereafter, "H. Smith."

2. John Murray Cuddihy, *The Ordeal of Civility: Freud, Marx, Levi-Strauss, and the Jewish Struggle with Modernity* (New York: Delta, 1974); hereafter, "Cuddihy."

3. Arthur Herzberg, *The French Enlightenment and the Jews, The Origins of Modern Anti-Semitism* (New York: Schocken Books, 1968).

Bibliography

SELECT BIBLIOGRAPHY

Barbour, Ian G. *Issues in Science and Religion*. New York: Harper & Row, 1966.
———. *Myths, Models and Paradigms*. New York: Harper & Row, 1974.
Fabro, Cornelia. *God in Exile, Modern Atheism*. Toronto: University of St. Michael's College, 1968.
Fromm, Erich. *The Sane Society*. New York: Reinhart & Co., 1955.
Kuhn, Thomas S. *The Structure of Scientific Revolutions*. Chicago: University of Chicago Press, 1970.
Lessa, William A., and Evon Z. Vogt. *Reader in Comparative Religion*. 2d ed. New York: Harper & Row, 1965.
Lowith, Karl. *Meaning in History*. Chicago: University of Chicago Press, 1949.
Siu, R. G. H. *The Tao of Science*. Cambridge, MA: Massachusetts Institute of Technology, 1957.
Smith, Huston. *Beyond the Post-Modern Mind*. New York: Crossroad, 1982.
Smith, Wilfred Cantwell. *Faith and Belief*. Princeton, NJ: Princeton University Press, 1979.
Van Buren, Paul M. *The Secular Meaning of the Gospel*. New York: Macmillan Co., 1966.

MARX AND ENGELS: PRIMARY SOURCES

Marx, Karl. *Karl Marx, Early Writings*. Edited by T. B. Bottomore. New York: McGraw-Hill, 1963.
———. *Karl Marx on Sociology and Social Philosophy, Selected Writings in Sociology and Social Philosophy*. Translated by Bottomore and Rubel. London: Penguin, 1963.
———. *Marx and Engels on Religion*. New York: Schocken Books, 1964.
———, and Friedrich Engels. *Selected Works in Two Volumes*. Moscow: Foreign Languages Publishing House, 1955.

Engels, Friedrich. *Anti-Duhring*. Moscow: Foreign Languages Publishing House, 1954.

————. *Dialectics of Nature*. Moscow: Foreign Languages Publishing House, 1954.

SECONDARY SOURCES

Allen, Edgar Leonard. *From Plato to Nietzsche: Ideas that Shape Our Lives*. New York: Association Press, 1971.

Anderson, David. *Simone Weil*. London: S.C.M. Press, 1971.

Berger, Peter L. *Invitation to Sociology: A Humanistic Perspective*. Garden City, NY: Doubleday, 1963.

————. *A Rumor of Angels*. Garden City, NY: Doubleday, 1970.

————. *The Sacred Canopy: Elements of a Sociological Theory of Religion*. Garden City, NY: Doubleday, 1970.

Berlin, Isaiah. *Karl Marx, His Life and Environment*. London: Oxford University Press, 1963.

Bologh, Roslyn Wallach. *Dialectical Phenomenology: Marx's Method*. Boston: Routledge & Kegan Paul, 1979.

Bonansea, Bernardino M. *God and Atheism*. Washington, DC: Catholic University Press, 1979.

Cameron, Kenneth Neill. *Marx and Engels Today: A Modern Dialogue on Philosophy and History*. Hicksville, NY: Exposition Press, 1976.

Copleston, Frederick. *A History of Philosophy*. Volume 7, *Fichte to Nietzsche*. Westminster, MD : Newman Press, 1963.

Dupre, Louis. *The Philosophical Foundations of Marxism*. New York: Brace & World, 1966.

Feuerbach, Ludwig. *The Essence of Christianity*. New York: Harper & Bros., 1957.

Fromm, Erich. *Marx's Concept of Man*. New York: Frederick Unger Publishing Co., 1961.

Garaudy, Roger. *Karl Marx: The Evolution of His Thought*. New York: International Publishers, 1967.

————, and J. Quentin Lauer. *A Christian Communist Dialogue*. Garden City, NY: Doubleday, 1968.

Greene, Norman N. *Jean-Paul Sartre: The Existentialist Ethic*. Ann Arbor: University of Michigan Press, 1960.

Gutkind, Eric. *The Body of God: First Steps Toward an Anti-Theology*. New York: Horizon Press, 1960.

Habermas, Jurgen. *Theory and Practice*. Boston: Beacon Press, 1973.

Harrington, Michael. *The Twilight of Capitalism*. New York: Simon & Schuster, 1976.

Herzberg, Arthur. *The French Enlightenment and the Jews: The Origins of Modern Anti-Semitism*. New York: Schocken Books, 1970.

216

Hook, Sidney. *From Hegel to Marx*. New York: Humanities Press, 1950.

Kalin, Martin G. *The Utopian Flight from Unhappiness*. Chicago: Nelson Hall, 1974.

Lowith, Karl. *Nature, History and Existentialism*. Evanston, IL: Northwestern University Press, 1966.

McGann, Thomas F. *A History of Philosophy in the West: A Synopsis from Descartes to Nietzsche*. Washington, DC: University Press of America, 1979.

McGovern, Arthur F. *Marxism: An American Perspective*. Maryknoll, NY: Orbis Books, 1981.

MacIntyre, Alisdair. *Marxism and Christianity*. New York: Schocken Books, 1968.

McLellan, David. *Karl Marx: His Life and Thought*. New York: Harper & Row, 1973.

Mannheim, Karl. *Ideology and Utopia*. New York: Harcourt, Brace & World, 1936.

Mayer, Gustav. *Friedrich Engels, A Biography*. New York: Howard Fertig, 1969.

Mayo, Henry B. *Introduction to Marxist Theory*. New York: Oxford University Press, 1960.

Newell, William Lloyd. *Struggle and Submission: R. C. Zaehner on Mysticisms*. Washington, DC: University Press of America, 1981.

Nisbet, Robert. *The Sociological Tradition*. New York: Basic Books, 1966.

————. *The Social Philosophers: Community and Conflict in Western Thought*. New York: Thomas Y. Crowell Co., 1973.

Passmore, John Arthur. *The Perfectibility of Man*. London: Duckworth, 1970.

Raines, John C., and Thomas Dean. *Marxism and Radical Religion*. Philadelphia: Temple University Press, 1970.

Ruether, Rosemary. *The Radical Kingdom, The Western Experience of Messianic Hope*. New York: Harper & Row, 1970.

Russell, Bertrand. *Fact and Fiction*. New York: Simon & Schuster, 1962.

Schmidt, Alfred. *The Concept of Nature in Marx*. London: NLB, 1971.

Spinka, Matthew. *Nicolas Berdyaev, Captive of Freedom*. Philadelphia: Westminster Press, 1950.

Vallon, M. A. *An Apostle of Freedom: Life and Teaching of Nicolas Berdyaev*. New York: Philosophical Library, 1960.

Veldhuis, Ruurd. *Realism Versus Utopianism: Reinhold Niebuhr's Christian Realism and the Relevance of Utopian Thought for Social Ethics*. Assen: Van Gorcum, 1975.

Weber, Max. *The Protestant Ethic and the Spirit of Capitalism*. New York: Charles Scribner's Sons, 1958.

Zaehner, R. C. *The Convergent Spirit, Towards a Dialectics of Religion*. London: Routledge & Kegan Paul, 1963.

————. *Concordant Discord, The Interdependence of Faiths*. Oxford: Oxford University Press, 1970.

————. *Dialectical Christianity and Christian Materialism*. London: Oxford University Press, 1971.

FREUD: PRIMARY SOURCES

Freud, Sigmund. *Totem and Taboo. Resemblances Between the Psychic Lives of Savages and Neurotics*. Translated by A. A. Brill. New York: Vintage Books, 1946.

————. *The Future of an Illusion*. New York: W. W. Norton & Co., 1961.

————. *Moses and Monotheism*. Vol. 23, *The Standard Edition of the Complete Psychological Works of Sigmund Freud*. New York: Hogarth Press, 1964.

————. *Introductory Lectures on Psychoanalysis*. New York: W. W. Norton & Co., 1966.

SECONDARY SOURCES

Becker, Ernest. *The Structure of Evil*. New York: The Free Press, 1968.

————. *The Denial of Death*. New York: The Free Press, 1973.

————. *Revolution in Psychiatry*. New York: The Free Press, 1974.

————. *Escape from Evil*. New York: The Free Press, 1976.

Brown, N. O. *Life Against Death, The Psychoanalytic Meaning of History*. Middletown, CT: Wesleyan University Press, 1970.

Cole, J. Preston. *The Problematic Self in Kierkegaard and Freud*. New Haven, CT: Yale University Press, 1971.

Gross, Leonard. *God and Freud*. New York: McKay, 1959.

Jones, Ernest. *The Life and Work of Sigmund Freud*. 3 volumes. New York: Basic Books, 1955.

Kung, Hans. *Freud and the Problem of God*. New Haven, CT: Yale University Press, 1979.

MacIsaac, Sharon. *Freud and Original Sin*. New York: Paulist Press, 1974.

McLelland, David C. *The Roots of Consciousness*. New York: Van Nostrand, 1964.

Maslow, Abraham H. *Toward a Psychology of Being*. New York: D. Van Nostrand, 1968.

Philip, Howard Littleton. *Freud and Religious Belief*. London: Rockliffe, 1956.

Puner, Helen Walker. *Freud: His Life and His Mind*. Howell Soskin Publishers, 1947.

Ricoeur, Paul. *Freud and Philosophy*. New Haven, CT: Yale University Press, 1970.

————. *The Conflict of Interpretations*. Evanston, IL: Northwestern University Press, 1974.

NIETZSCHE: PRIMARY SOURCES

Levy, Oscar. *The Complete Works of Friedrich Nietzsche*. New York: Macmillan, 1911.

Nietzsche, Friedrich. *The Birth of Tragedy and the Genealogy of Morals*. New York: Doubleday, 1956.

————. *Beyond Good and Evil*. New York: Random House, 1966.

————. *The Will to Power*. New York: Random House, 1967.

————. *The Twilight of the Idols and the Anti-Christ*. Translated by R. J. Hollingdale. London: Penguin, 1968.

————. *Thus Spoke Zarathustra*. Translated by R. J. Hollingdale. London: Penguin, 1969.

SECONDARY SOURCES

Bonifazi, Conrad. *Christendom Attacked: A Comparison of Kierkegaard and Nietzsche*. London: Rockliffe, 1953.

Copleston, Frederick. *Friedrich Nietzsche, Philosopher of Culture*. London: Search Press, 1942.

————. *A History of Philosophy*. Vol. 7, *Fichte to Nietzsche*. Westminster, MD: Newman Press, 1963.

Frenzel, Ivo. *Friedrich Nietzsche*. New York: Western Publishing Co., 1967.

Gilman, Sander L. *Nietzschean Parody: An Introduction to Reading Nietzsche*. Bonn: Bouvier, 1967.

Harper, Ralph, *The Seventh Solitude: Man's Isolation in Kierkegaard, Dostoevsky and Nietzsche*. Baltimore: The Johns Hopkins Press, 1965.

Hayman, Ronald. *Nietzsche, A Critical Life*. New York: Oxford University Press, 1980.

Heller, Peter. *Dialectics and Nihilism: Essays on Lessing, Nietzsche, Mann and Kafka*. Amherst: University of Massachusetts Press, 1966.

Hollingdale, R. J. *Nietzsche, The Man and His Philosophy*. London: Routledge & Kegan Paul, 1965.

Jette, Celine Rita. *The Philosophy of Nietzsche in the Light of Thomistic Principles*. New York: Pageant Press, 1967.

Kaufmann, Walter. *The Portable Nietzsche*. New York: Viking Press, 1954.

————. *Nietzsche: Philosopher, Psychologist, Anti-Christ*. Princeton, NJ: Princeton University Press, 1967.

Lowith, Karl. *From Hegel to Nietzsche*. Garden City, NY: Doubleday, 1967.

Marty, Martin E. *Varieties of Unbelief*. New York: Holt Rinehart & Winston, 1964.

Pfeffer, Rose. *Nietzsche: Disciple of Dionysus*. Lewisburg, PA: Bucknell University Press, 1972.

Radhakrishnan Sarvepalli. *Recovery of Faith*. New York: Harper Press, 1955.

Rayburn, H. A. *Nietzsche, The Story of a Human Philosopher*. London: Macmillan, 1948.

Solomon, Robert C. *Nietzsche: A Collection of Critical Essays*. Notre Dame, IN: University of Notre Dame Press, 1980.